Proficiency Masterclass

Teacher's Book

Kathy Gude
Michael Duckworth

OXFORD UNIVERSITY PRESS

INTRODUCTION

Proficiency Masterclass gives students comprehensive preparation and training for the Cambridge Proficiency in English examination. The course covers a variety of stimulating topic areas and a wide range of skills, with particular emphasis on the topics and skills students will meet in the exam. As the first Proficiency course book to appear in full colour, *Proficiency Masterclass* not only provides students and teachers with more visually stimulating material to work with, but also gives realistic practice for Paper 5. In addition, special attention has been given to specific areas where exam candidates persistently underperform. Summary and Composition are typical Proficiency weak spots which *Proficiency Masterclass* tackles by breaking down each task type and giving students plenty of guided practice.

The main emphasis in *Proficiency Masterclass* is on training students. Exercises are pitched at the level of the exam right from the start, and it is guidance that is graded rather than the tasks themselves. This training coupled with *exam tips*, which advise students on how to approach individual question types, will help to maximize students' performance on the day of the exam.

What's in Proficiency Masterclass?

The Student's Book

The course consists of 15 units, each of which is divided into five sections followed by an overview which revises and tests what has been covered. The Student's Book Contents page gives a clear and concise plan of the units, providing teachers with an easy reference point, and enabling them to map out individual course syllabuses.

The units are based on a central theme which is explored from a different angle in every section. Each unit has an overall title, eg *Unit 1 In Sickness and in Health*, and the first five sections in each unit have a heading, often an idiom or proverb, which introduces a fresh angle, eg *One Man's Meat is another Man's Poison*. These headings often provide material for discussion in themselves. Unit 1 has the following sections:

Unit 1 In Sickness and In Health

Reading	The lead text takes a light-hearted look at the current mania for exercise and leads on to work on vocabulary, reading skills and idioms.
Structure	The cloze test looks at the role of music in sport and leads to a grammar section on relative pronouns, followed by a re-writing exercise.
Summary Skills	The summary is based around a text that examines the life of a junior hospital doctor, and provides an introduction to summary writing and answering comprehension questions.
Listening and Speaking	This section includes a number of exam-type speaking and listening activities about hypnosis, acupuncture and massage.
Writing	This starts with a model argument composition and is followed by a series of discussion and composition planning activities, and a guided writing task on alternative medicine.

The overview contains multiple-choice vocabulary questions, transformations, blank-filling and rewriting exercises which recycle vocabulary and structures that have come up in the unit.

The Teacher's Book

As well as containing a key to the exercises and transcripts of all recorded material, the Teacher's Book also provides valuable pedagogical input in the form of detailed procedural notes, optional activities, and thorough grammatical explanations.

The Teacher's Book contains the following:

- comprehensive procedural notes, indicating how teachers might use the material in class, including suggestions for exploiting artwork.
- additional and alternative exercises, which include extra summary tasks and composition titles.
- supportive grammar sections with additional notes and extra exercises.
- points for students to include in their compositions and summaries, providing a framework for the teacher when marking students' work.
- models for summary writing.
- detailed background notes to the reading and listening material, including explanations of potentially difficult or culture-bound vocabulary.
- keys to all the exercises in the Student's Book.
- a full transcript of all the recorded material.
- extra exam practice material in the form of photocopiable Unit Tests and Progress Tests.

How long will lessons take?

Each section lasts on average between one and a half to two hours. The Overview could be set as homework, or alternatively could be done in class taking approximately half an hour. In total the course provides 120–150 hours of classroom teaching, although the exact amount of time will depend on the nature of the group, their language level, and the balance between class work and homework.

How are the units structured?

The five sections in each unit focus on one particular skill. However, there is flexibility within this framework, additional skills being integrated in each section, making the material more varied. For example, there could be a listening in the Writing section, or a discussion in the Structure section. *Talking points* usually precede the skills focus in each section introducing a new angle to the unit theme, stimulating student interest, and giving them an opportunity to practise their speaking skills.

The paragraphs below look at these unit sections in more detail.

Section 1 Reading

A wide variety of sources have been used for the reading texts, including extracts from books, magazines and newspapers. Texts have been specially selected to reflect the complexity of language and ideas that students will meet in the exam.

In the reading sections students are sensitized to the writer's attitude and style, and actively trained in text interpretation and recognizing nuance.They are also taught to interpret multiple-choice stems, and given plenty of practice in deducing meaning from context. In addition to this, there are exercises designed to develop general reading skills such as skimming, scanning and prediction.

The Student's Book provides, wherever possible, the original photograph used to accompany a specific article. The use of such photographs adds authenticity to the texts, but is also intended to provide a stimulus in the same way as in Paper 5, Part 1, where students have to describe a photograph and speculate on the subject matter, before going on to discuss the wider issues the photograph raises.

Often the reading text is followed by intensive vocabulary work. These exercises can focus on related sets of phrasal verbs, idioms or other expressions, or look at the shades of meaning in groups of similar words.

Section 2 Structure

This section contains the majority of the grammatical work, and includes the kinds of structural item that are commonly tested in the exam. In addition, the grammatical work is essential in raising students' level of accuracy so that they can perform well in the composition paper and the interview.

At the beginning of each section is a *cloze development* which contains a modified cloze designed to encourage students to think around the task. For example, students could be asked to proof-read a text, insert missing words in a line, or identify what kind of word is missing. All these activities train students to refer to the wider context of the passage, and are often reinforced by initial skimming questions.

The variations in the *cloze development* provide a motivating alternative to the standard type of cloze test, but the items that are tested reflect those tested in the exam, such as phrasal verbs, relative pronouns, dependent prepositions, idioms and lexis. There are also a number of standard cloze tests so that students are familiar with the exam format.

The grammar point is extracted from the cloze passage and taught inductively. Students may be asked to compare and contrast structures, match halves of sentences, identify functions, or provide new contexts for structures taught. The emphasis in these sections is on students working out grammatical rules for themselves.

Vocabulary exploitation is another feature of the structure section, the cloze passage often containing idioms or expressions suitable for further vocabulary work.

Blank-filling, transformation or rewriting exercises follow up and practise grammar points explored in the unit. Training on how to approach these questions is given in the form of clues in the rewriting exercises, and reworking a sentence in two or three ways in the transformation exercises. There may also be a guided discussion activity giving students fluency practice of the grammar points presented.

Additional information about grammar is included in the Teacher's Book, the notes containing ideas on how to present the material, what to write on the board, and what further examples to give.

Section 3 Summary Skills

The comprehension and summary section in Paper 3 of the Proficiency exam is an area where students persistently underachieve. As a result, *Proficiency Masterclass* contains a considerable amount of training in answering comprehension questions and writing summaries. Extensive work is necessary as this is one area where Proficiency differs radically from First Certificate, and many students will be attempting these tasks for the first time.

Proficiency Masterclass adopts a guided approach to answering comprehension questions. Practice is given in referencing, paraphrasing, deducing meaning from context, working out what a text implies, and interpreting attitude. The guidance is graded, as students are initially given clues which help them interpret the meaning of words and phrases. As they progress through the book, support is reduced, and they are even asked to identify words and phrases which they think would be tested in an exam.

The approach to writing summaries is thorough and systematic, training students to decipher the text at global, paragraph and sentence level, and to analyse the way ideas are structured and expressed. Students are provided with valuable practice on how to extract and organize complex arguments and paraphrase the main points in a text, before connecting the paraphrased sections to form a cohesive summary.

Points to be included in summaries appear in the Teacher's Book.

Section 4 Listening and Speaking

Each unit has one or two listening passages which reflect those that students can expect to meet in the exam. The material includes passages that come from authentic sources such as radio broadcasts and taped conversations, which are recorded at normal speaking speed and in a variety of accents. The questions are designed to prepare students for the exam, and students are exposed to question formats such as blank-filling, labelling, true / false questions, multiple-choice, and note-taking. Exercises practise not only comprehension but also areas such as stress and intonation.

The Teacher's Book contains transcripts of all the passages, with parts of the tapescripts that help provide the correct answers underlined.

This section also contains preparation and training for Paper 5. There are opportunities to speak individually, in pairs or in groups in a wide range of activities which enable students to discuss issues raised in the unit, or assume roles. For example, there are picture discussions, short passages for comment, rank-ordering exercises, discussions, simulation and problem solving activities. Most of the photographs for the picture discussions are in colour, reflecting recent changes in the exam.

Because of the way that the units have been structured, students have the chance to do oral work after the input in Sections 1, 2 and 3. This creates an opportunity for informed discussion and the development of ideas. However, speaking skills are not restricted to Section 4. Most of the sections throughout the book begin with a *talking points* activity, and many of the grammar sections have a guided speaking activity to practise a particular grammatical point. In this there is exposure to a great deal of oral work, developing students' confidence in their ability to express complex ideas, and making the course highly effective in terms of classroom dynamics.

Section 5 Writing

The composition is a problem area for many Proficiency students, so in response to this an extensive amount of work on compositions has been built into the course. Section 5 of each unit deals with writing compositions, and the subjects covered are linked to the main theme of the unit. In the exam, there are four main types of composition: the argument, the descriptive, the narrative and the task-based composition. These four composition types recur regularly throughout the Student's Book, so that by the end of the course students will have practised each type of composition four times – the final unit asks for two shorter task-based compositions.

As the students practise each kind of composition, they are exposed to variations within that category. For example, the four descriptive compositions are: describing a person (Unit 2), describing a journey (Unit 5), describing an ideal (Unit 9), and a blended description looking at national character and entertainment (Unit 13). This approach helps students to become familiar with the composition types and to concentrate on specific areas of language and style.

Throughout the book, there is a five-stage approach to composition writing. The five stages are as follows:

Stage 1 **Question interpretation** – ie looking carefully at the question and deciding how best to produce a relevant answer.

Stage 2 **Brainstorming** – ie thinking of ideas, examples, arguments etc. that may be useful.

Stage 3 **Paragraph planning** – ie selection and organization of the ideas that have been generated.

Stage 4 **Writing.**

Stage 5 **Checking.**

After the introductory unit (Unit 1), each composition section falls into two main parts.

The first and longest part presents students with a sample composition and a number of exercises that raise important points of language or organization through a guided analysis of the sample. The second part is the writing task itself, which consists of the question and the five-point plan giving hints on organization and content.

The first part of each writing section makes up most of the teaching material, and is directed at training students to think creatively and to organize their thoughts clearly. While some of this may be done at home, there should be some time in class spent analysing the sample composition. In most units this is a high level composition, which presents students with a clear organizational model that they can follow. These compositions are of the correct length, and their language level represents an A grade in the exam. In a few units, students are given weaker compositions and asked what the main failings are. Hints are then given as to how these compositions could be improved. Follow-up training on style, register, vocabulary and accuracy help build up the range of skills necessary for students to perform well in the exam.

In addition to the work on creative thinking and planning, there are exercises on style, register, vocabulary and accuracy so that students have a chance to build up a range of skills.

The second part of the writing section consists of the writing task. Guidance is given on the stages of planning and writing, and the questions have been chosen so that the students can follow the organizational pattern of the model.

It is useful to establish a marking scheme at the beginning of the course that can be maintained consistently. It may be helpful to award a set of three different marks for each composition as follows, although many teachers will have their own approach:

1 marks for grammatical accuracy and range of structures. The standard of accuracy required for Proficiency is substantially higher than at First Certificate level. This must be made clear to the students, and remedial steps should be taken if necessary.
2 marks for the general content and organization, the degree to which the task has been fulfilled, the clarity or originality of thought and relevance to the question.
3 marks for language content, ie style and register, naturalness, avoidance of direct translation from the mother tongue, range and appropriacy of vocabulary. Students should be made aware that while complex vocabulary is welcomed, it must be appropriate, and over-reliance on a dictionary should be discouraged.

Students should be encouraged to keep all their work.

Vocabulary

Vocabulary is tested throughout the exam. In Paper 1 the multiple-choice questions test knowledge of areas such as semantic sets, collocations, semantic precision, connectives, structure and idioms.

Extensive vocabulary teaching occurs throughout *Proficiency Masterclass* and includes work on collocations, easily confused words, shades of meaning and lexical sets. The input and testing of phrasal verbs and idioms appear under the heading *expressions*, which look at words and phrases students may know, together with others which may be frequently used in English but are not yet familiar to students. For example, *expressions with come* presents and practises phrasal verbs such as *come round*, as well as common idiomatic expressions such as *come to light*. Cartoons are included next to vocabulary exercises, often as a humorous illustration of an idiom, and are intended to help both teacher and student with the vocabulary point in question.

It is important to encourage students to read extensively out of class, especially books that are of interest to them. These may be detective stories, romances, thrillers, newspapers or magazines. It is worth noting that the literary quality of the texts a student reads is of secondary importance; what matters most is that he or she should read extensively.

exam tips

As well as having graded guidance and exam training throughout each unit, students also have *exam tips*. These give practical advice on how to tackle exam questions, highlight typical mistakes, and give advice on what to do on the day of the exam.

Using the revision and recycling material

Vocabulary and grammar is recycled in a number of different ways in the Student's Book and the Teacher's Book. There is also a comprehensive *Index* on pages 216–17 of the Student's Book which lists all the structure and vocabulary taught in the units, providing a useful reference list for revision purposes.

Overviews

There is a two-page *Overview* at the end of each unit. They consist of a multiple-choice vocabulary exercise followed by transformation, rewriting, or blank-filling exercises. These test and revise vocabulary items and grammatical points that have come up in the unit, and can be done in class or as homework.

Unit Tests

These photocopiable tests appear only in the Teacher's Book, so students will not have seen the questions beforehand. They contain vocabulary, multiple-choice exercises, and mini-cloze tests, as well as blank-filling, rewriting or transformation exercises.

Ideally these tests should be done under exam conditions in class, and immediately after each unit. However, they may be set for homework, provided that students realize the usefulness of doing the test under 'exam conditions' at home. Students should be allowed no more than half an hour per test.

Progress Tests

These photocopiable tests also appear only in the Teacher's Book. They come at the end of Units 5, 10 and 15, and each one tests the skills developed in the preceding five units. The tests are designed to give students practice in doing the different papers under exam conditions, and although each one is shorter than a complete exam, over the course of the three tests, students will have the opportunity to practise questions from Papers 1, 2, 3 and 5 of the exam. Pictures for the interview sections appear on pages 212–14 of the Student's Book and are not photocopiable.

Progress Tests will take one and a half to three hours to complete. The timing for each Test is given on the first page, and does not include the interview section.

Marking

Total marks for the Unit Tests will be either 35 or 40 marks. Marks could be shown as a percentage to enable students to gauge their progress. Total marks for the Progress Tests vary according to the questions tested.

The following scheme may be used when marking the Unit Tests and Progress Tests:

Paper 1

Multiple-choice vocabulary items: 1 mark each
Reading comprehension questions: 2 marks each

Paper 2

Compositions: 20 marks each

The criteria for marks awarded are as follows:

16–20	High quality language used with only occasional native-speaker-type lapses; ambitious in concept and approach.
11–15	Natural and appropriate style with only occasional errors and some sophisticated language; task well developed.
8–10	Structure and usage acceptable but limited; task attempted but not entirely successfully.
5–7	Lack of language control shown by numerous errors; topic area neither extended nor explored.
0–4	Errors and narrowness of vocabulary prevent communication; content irrelevant or too little for assessment.

Paper 3

Cloze items: 1 mark each
Transformations: 2 marks each
Rewriting: 2 marks each
Blank-filling: 1 mark each
Comprehension questions: 2 marks each
Summary passage: 10 marks
5 marks awarded for mentioning points relevant to the summary
5 marks awarded for demonstrating good summarizing skills and proper expression

Paper 5

Interview: Award marks on a scale of 0 (bottom of the range) to 5 (top of the range) for each of the following categories:

FLUENCY	Speed and rhythm, choice of structures, general naturalness and clarity.
ACCURACY	Control of structures including tenses, prepositions, etc. to an effective level of communication.
PRONUNCIATION (Individual sounds)	Correct use of consonants and vowels in stressed and unstressed position for ease of understanding.
PRONUNCIATION (Sentences)	Stress timing, rhythm and intonation patterns, linking of phrases.
INTERACTIVE COMMUNICATION	Flexibility and linguistic resource in exchange of information and social interaction.
VOCABULARY	Variety and correctness of vocabulary in the communicative context.

Students should be aiming for marks in the 3–4 range to perform adequately.

In the exam the balance of the papers is as follows:

Paper 1 40 marks*
Paper 2 40 marks
Paper 3 40 marks*
Paper 4 20 marks
Paper 5 40 marks*

* The maximum possible 'raw' scores are 55 for Paper 1 and about 80 for Paper 3. These scores are scaled down to a mark out of 40 for each paper. The maximum possible 'raw' score for Paper 5 is 30. Scores are scaled up and expressed as a mark out of 40.

The pass mark fluctuates between 110 and 115 marks out of a possible 180.

UNIT 1

IN SICKNESS AND IN HEALTH

READING

One Man's Meat is another Man's Poison

Ask students to explain the meaning of *One man's meat is another man's poison*, and say how it might relate to the theme of the unit. Ask them to decide whether they agree with it or not. If necessary, explain that *meat* means food and the phrase itself means that what is considered beneficial and nutritious for some people, may be completely undesirable for others. The phrase is mainly used to describe differences in taste generally, ie in interests and activities, as it is here.

● *talking points p1*

A GROUP WORK Ask students to rank items in order of importance, then compare their list with that of another group. They should make suggestions of their own for the most / least effective ways of ensuring physical fitness. Stress that there are no right or wrong answers, just those that students have decided on themselves.

B Put the following words and phrases on the board: *take-aways, trainers, subdued lighting, remote control, stack of video cassettes, rubbish tip, glued to the box.*
Ask students to describe the main picture on page 1 (incorporating the words on the board) and what it is portraying, then get them to explain what *couch potato* means. ANSWER someone who likes lazing at home. Ask students to comment on whether the picture successfully conveys the meaning of the term *couch potato*.

● *reading p2*

PE (line 42) = Physical Education.

A Ask students to comment on the advice and to explain why it seems contradictory for those trying to realize their physical fitness potential. Note the use of the simple past form *hung* in *It's high time you hung up …* . If students comment, paraphrase the sentence as *I think it would be better if you hung up …*

Optional activity
Divide the class into five groups. Give one group the first three paragraphs and the other four groups two paragraphs each. Tell them to skim read their section only, then tell the rest of the class what their paragraphs are about.

B PAIR WORK Ask students to scan the passage quickly for answers to the true / false questions. Tell them to compare their answers with a partner and correct the statements which are false.

Follow this by asking students to express their own opinions about the writer's point of view, and to assess the effect the article might have on a fitness fanatic.

K **1** T **2** F **3** T **4** F **5** T **6** T **7** F **8** T **9** T **10** T

C **Style.** Ask students to work in groups of two or three and find examples to illustrate the points of style mentioned. The author uses all the devices to achieve an informal style. If time in class is short, this exercise could be set for homework.

K Suggested answers

Rhetorical questions
Where's the virtue in …? (line 1)
Watching television, perhaps, …? (line 7)
How about eating …? (line 8)
What do they all have …? (line 10)
Why then this present mania …? (line 14)
Wouldn't they rather …? (line 55)

Abbreviations
Where's / It's / Let's / Don't / PE / wouldn't

Imperatives
Think about … (line 6)
Don't let … (line 48)
Take heart … (line 91)

Repetition
Same idea recurring
I abhor the smugness and self-righteousness … (line 17)
They are full of their own importance and rightness. (line 69)

Slang
mates (line 57), *flab* (line 85), *a real drag* (line 63), *snazzy* (line 50), *high tech* (line 51)

Direct address
to reader – *you* (hurry up, etc.) (line 51), *Welcome* (line 94)

Others
Made up words: Tell students that words are sometimes 'made up' by adding a prefix or a suffix. Answer: *oldsters* (line 49)
Mixed metaphor: Ask students if they noted any descriptive phrases that are imaginatively, but not literally, applicable.
ANSWER: *inflate their insoles and their egos* (line 52–3)

● *vocabulary p3*

A Words of disapproval.

K Suggested explanations

1 think of with hatred and disgust
2 expression of an intense self-satisfaction
3 a belief that one's own goodness is better than that of others
4 weaknesses or faults of character
5 cruelty or savagery
6 false or mistaken beliefs
7 a feeling of shame
8 an abnormal person
9 a fashion unlikely to last long
10 something that bores you rigid
11 people with no religious beliefs
12 a fixed or persistent idea

Ask students to try and use the words in a sentence of their own.

B Expressions 1. Stress the importance of using the correct form of the verb *come*.

K
1 come to terms with
2 comes down heavily on
3 comes out with
4 come to the point
5 came up with
6 came down with
7 came round
8 come in for

C Expressions 2. This section provides a range of idioms connected with different (stereo)types of people. Ask students to look at the illustration and match it with an idiom.

K **1** g **2** h **3** c **4** f **5** a **6** e **7** d **8** b
(The full expression is *a rolling stone gathers no moss*.)

Students could do both of the suggested tasks if time permits, or they could do the illustration and prepare their dialogue for homework.

STRUCTURE

The Sporting Life

● *talking points p4*

This exercise leads into vocabulary, some of which appears in the cloze passage, and encourages students to identify objects whose names they might not know. Ask students to work in pairs or groups and to 'think aloud'.

A Objects in the picture on page 4 and corresponding sporting activities:

K **1** skittles (10-pin bowling), **2** javelin (athletics), **3** bat (cricket), **4** club (golf), **5** skates (ice-skating), **6** racket (tennis), **7** paddle (canoeing), **8** dumb-bells (weightlifting)

B Association of objects and places:

K
1 skittles / alley
2 javelin / field
3 bat / pitch
4 club / course
5 skates / rink
6 net / court
7 paddle / rapids
8 dumb-bells / gym

> **Optional activity**
> Ask students to think of other words in each group, or of other groups. Point out that compiling word fields is a useful method of acquiring and storing vocabulary.

● *cloze development p4*

This exercise aims to build up students' confidence in tackling the cloze by encouraging them to think of the types of word which may be missing from the gaps. Before doing the exercise, ask students to make a list of the type of words they think are usually omitted from cloze tests, then refer them to the list in their books. Tell students to read the text through quickly once, then go back and try to supply a suitable word of the type given. Point out that there may be more than one possible answer in some cases.

K
1 play / (have)
2 considered / regarded / treated
3 well (possibly 'much')
4 idea / notion / concept
5 receiving / having
6 on
7 widely
8 performed
9 forms
10 pleasing
11 which
12 greater / more
13 demand
14 up
15 their
16 part
17 competitors / participants
18 makes / (keeps)
19 in
20 a

● *relative clauses p5*

In the Proficiency examination students will need to show that they are capable of writing complex sentences containing relative and other dependent clauses.

A Defining and non-defining relative clauses.

K
1 *that are also pleasing to the eye* (line 17). Defining.
2 *both of which demand high standards of balance, co-ordination and suppleness* (line 19). Non-defining.
3 *which seem to demand muscular strength more than any other physical requirement* (line 24). Defining.
4 *who take part in weightlifting* (line 30). Defining.
5 *which demands enormous physical strength* (line 31). Non-defining.

B Check that students understand the terms 'defining' and 'non-defining' by putting an example of each on the board, eg

The former grand prix racing driver, who was known to millions, died peacefully, aged 75, at his home in the south of France yesterday.
The racing driver who was injured while training on the circuit yesterday will not be competing in today's grand prix.

Ask students to identify the types of relative clause and explain the difference in meaning between them.

Suggested explanations
In the first, we are talking about one specific racing driver – no others are mentioned. The relative clause simply gives extra information, and can be omitted. This is an example of a non-defining relative clause. In the second, there may have been other drivers

practising on the circuit but only one was injured. The relative clause identifies which driver, and cannot be omitted. This is an example of a defining relative clause.
Remind students that non-defining relative clauses are not usually used in conversational English, and are always separated from the rest of the sentence by commas.

K 1 In the first sentence only the footballers who attended the dinner had won the championships (Defining).
In the second sentence all the footballers attended the dinner and they had all won the championships (Non-defining).

2 The relative pronoun can only be omitted when it is the object of the verb in a defining relative clause (ie the second sentence), and not when it is the subject. It can never be omitted from non-defining relative clauses.

3 *That* cannot be used in non-defining relative clauses, ie in the second sentence. *Which* or *who* can be used in both defining and non-defining relative clauses.
Tell students that *in/at which* can be used to replace *where*. Write these sentences on the board.
1 *The stadium where the games were taking place was enormous.*
2 *The stadium in which the games were taking place was enormous.*
Ask students whether the relative pronoun or adverb can be omitted in these sentences. ANSWER They cannot. In the first sentence *where* has the same meaning as *in which*, and the relative pronoun cannot be omitted after a preposition.
Now write this sentence on the board.
The stadium that the games were taking place in was enormous.
Ask students whether the relative pronoun can be omitted in this sentence. ANSWER Yes, because the word *in* appears later in the sentence.

4 *Which* or *whom* must be used after prepositions.

5 *Whose* is used to mean 'belonging to, of whom, of which' in defining and non defining relative clauses.

6 *Which* can be used to refer back to or elaborate on information in a whole clause as opposed to a noun phrase.

C This exercise introduces students to the sentence transformations they will meet in Paper 3, but is based exclusively on the points taught in the grammar section in this unit.

K 1 The American journalist who / that interviewed the tennis champion reminded me of my brother.

2 The liver, which is about 30 centimetres long, helps in the digestion of food.

3 We decided to engage the two young dancers whom / who / that we had seen perform on television.

4 The new concert hall, which holds two thousand people, was opened yesterday.

5 The pop group ICE, whose manager has just resigned, is currently touring the USA.

6 He had never had any formal education, which amazed me.
Ask students whether the sentences they have made are defining or non-defining. Then ask them which sentences could be written as either defining or non-defining clauses, and what the difference in structure and meaning would be.

1 (alternative) The American journalist, who (no other possibilities) interviewed that famous tennis star, reminded me of my brother.
There is only one American journalist, there may have been other journalists, but they were not American, whereas in the defining clause there were other American journalists but they did not interview the tennis star.

3 (alternative) We decided to engage the two young dancers, who(m) we had seen perform on television. We only considered these two, whereas in the defining clause we had seen other dancers perform elsewhere. NB The correct grammatical answer is *whom* as it is the object of *had seen*, but the less grammatical *who* is sometimes heard.

K D The relative pronoun could be omitted in number **3** if written as a defining clause.

● *rewriting p5*

In this exercise clues are given to help students, and make them aware that often it is necessary to make two or three (unexpected) changes to the original sentence. Remind students that **the given word must not be changed in any way**.

A The example shows students how they have to change the grammar and structure of the original sentence.

B

K 1 He has taken up swimming as a (new) hobby.
In this sentence students may be aware that *take up* is needed but they may not realize that they need to make other changes as well.
As *taken up* means 'to start', *new* is virtually redundant in the meaning of the sentence.

2 Exercise not only improves our health but also enhances our appearance.
or Not only does exercise improve our health but it also enhances our appearance.

3 Nobody offered to take part in the school concert.

4 The leisure industry has greatly benefited / benefited greatly from the global interest in physical exercise.

5 Serious injuries can be prevented by wearing seat-belts in cars.

6 Seeing Jim suddenly brought it home to me how much he must have suffered.

7 Playing tennis professionally demands great powers of concentration.

8 There are two different models of this car, both of which have an automatic gear box.

Optional activity
Read out sentences **1–8** with the prompt words below each sentence, but do not read the clues. After reading each sentence and prompt, ask students to reproduce their original rewritten version orally.

SUMMARY SKILLS

Carers and Curers

Ask students what they understand by the terms 'carer' and 'curer', and whether their definitions overlap. Ask them who the 'carers' and 'curers' are in their society. **NB** In the summary passage 'curers' are not seen as 'carers'.

● *talking points p6*

Suggested introduction

Ask students to look at the illustration on page 6 and to try and identify the problem. ANSWER tennis elbow.

Spend about five to ten minutes brainstorming as many illnesses and diseases as students can think of and put them on the board. Group them according to whether they are serious or not, then ask students to decide who might look after people suffering from these illnesses, and where these people might be looked after. Now ask them in small groups to arrange the complaints in their books correctly and explain what they are.

NB If students don't know the name of an illness in English, they can explain or mime the symptoms. The teacher can then provide the word.

K *writer's cramp* – a painful tightening of the finger muscles
sprained ankle – a violent twist which causes pain and swelling to the ankle
tennis elbow – a sprain caused by playing tennis
a torn ligament – damage to the tough flexible tissue linking bones together
eye strain – injury caused by overuse of or excessive demands on the eyes
a slipped disc – a layer of cartilage between the vertebrae which has become displaced and causes pain

If students have not suffered from any of the complaints themselves, they could talk about friends or relatives who have.

● *introduction to summary writing p6*

A Tell students to skim read the passage and decide who might have written it. Encourage them to give reasons for their opinion, and discuss why they could have been distracted by some other plausible but incorrect alternatives. If necessary, explain the difference between a *doctor* and a *consultant* (a senior specialist in a branch of medicine responsible for patients in a hospital).

K ANSWER 2

Explain to students that although a book is referred to in the article, the article itself was written by a male doctor and appeared in *The Observer Magazine* (a quality paper).
Refer students to the exam tip next to the comprehension questions before asking them to do the questions.

B **Answering comprehension questions.** At this stage guidance is given to help students 'think through' a word or phrase they might not understand initially.

K Suggested answers

1 The bleeper or warning buzzer is intended to ensure that the doctor can be contacted as quickly as possible in case of emergency. However, the writer sees it as a permanent intrusion into what he is currently doing when it goes off, so rather than being a help, it is a hindrance in his work since he feels compelled to obey its call.

2 The writer is comparing the hospital to a battlefield, where the patients are hostile and the nurses are a buffer used to cushion the effect of the patients' attacks on the doctors. It is a paradoxical comparison because hospital patients are usually seen as victims in need of care and attention, and a hospital as a benevolent, caring institution. Patients, nurses and doctors are normally regarded as united in the same purpose, rather than engaging in a fight against one another.

3 In order to explain the words, you need to know that an armada is a great fleet of warships (like the Armada sent by King Philip of Spain against England in 1588). Here the writer picks up the idea of a scene of war, and the armada is the consultant's entourage or band of followers, possibly medical students and nurses. The metaphor reinforces the idea that the patient sees the doctors, etc. as the enemy, in the same way that the doctors see the patients as their enemies, thus a feeling of hostility is created.
Blithely is a poetic word meaning 'happy and joyous' and it conveys the impression that the medical staff had no real interest in or commitment to the patients or their welfare, for they had ignored him completely.
The writer stammered or stuttered because he was unable to say what he wanted to say. The words refused to come out properly because he felt intimidated by the attitude of the doctors towards him.

Point out that although there are no 'correct' answers, the best answers will capture the meaning and implications of what the writer says without repeating word for word what he has written.

C **Summary.** This guided summary focuses on the feelings of both doctor and patient and gives help in writing a short summary.

K 1 C 2 D

Suggested summary
The writer ironically states that a junior surgeon feels that the patients are an intrusion into the efficient running of the hospital, while the patients feel they are quite simply an insignificant cog in a much larger and more important wheel. (41 words)

Optional summary
Ask students to write a short summary (40 words) of how junior surgeons perceive their role in the hospital environment and how patients feel about the treatment they are receiving.

LISTENING AND SPEAKING

Your Body at Risk

● *talking points p8*

Ask students if they know of any forms of alternative medicine, and, if so, what they are and how they are used to cure people or relieve pain, etc.

A If necessary, explain the forms of alternative medicine or ask students to check them in a dictionary.

K *hypnotherapy* – a treatment inducing deep sleep where consciousness and will are suspended but other functions, such as hearing, are not affected
acupuncture – the insertion of metal needles into the body at points determined by a (Chinese) system, which requires ten years of study
acupressure – the application of finger and thumb pressure and movement to certain points of the body
herbalism – the use of medicinal herbs to cure and treat patients

B Ask students to suggest which treatments might be suitable for the complaints, and what other complaints these forms of medicine might cure.

● *listening p8*

Explain that the tape consists of eight snippets of conversation. Tell students that reading through the questions before they listen to the tape will give them an idea of what the tape will contain and what they will be expected to listen for. Remind students that in the exam they will hear the tape twice, but encourage them to try and choose the correct answer by listening only once. Ask students what they think they will hear on the tape before they listen to it, then ask them for their answers before the second listening.

K 1 D 2 A 3 C 4 D 5 D 6 A 7 C 8 B

Play the tape twice. Ask students which of the speakers they themselves identify with and how they think they would react to such treatment.

Tapescript:
(**P** = Presenter)

P Good evening and welcome to our regular slot on *You and Your Body*. Tonight we are looking at hypnotherapy. We talked to eight people from different walks of life. This is what they had to say about their reactions to hypnotherapy treatment. First, author Robert Croft.

Robert I'd done a great deal of research into hypnosis and, um, although there's no doubt that it can be incredibly effective, I was very apprehensive, I can tell you. But after the first session I had the best night's sleep I'd had in twenty years.

P Next, TV presenter Lynn Ronson.

Lynn I was having trouble sleeping and had been prescribed … well, given some mild sleeping pills. I went to see a hypnotherapist because I honestly felt I was becoming addicted. Although I never felt I went under, the insomnia sort of cleared up, so perhaps I, well, learned something subconsciously.

P We then talked to boxer Frank Temple.

Frank After the first session my mind seemed razor-sharp and I had this feeling of great power. It only took a minute or so to put me to sleep. Then, when I woke up I felt I could fight King Kong!

P Then artist Andrew Stein.

Andrew I've been hypnotized twice to try to give up smoking and the first time I didn't feel like having a cigarette for twenty-four hours but the urge slowly came back. And I think, well, I knew it would fail the second time. I'd given up faith. However I'm not cynical about it – the timing just wasn't right.

P And then tennis champion Annabel Wood.

Annabel I had hypnosis for about two years. It helped me concentrate on my game and block out the crowd. I'm fascinated by the fact that apparently we only use ten per cent of our brains. It seems that the creative possibilities in the subconscious are enormous.

P Psychic Uri Stahl.

Uri A scientist put me under hypnosis to try to see … to establish whether my powers were genuine. I am now able to talk myself into a semi-hypnotic state when under stress, um, for instance when I'm flying. I'm not scared – it just helps me to relax.

P Columnist Jon Rayner.

Jon Yeah, I've been hypnotized – once – to give up smoking, and, yeah, it did work – up till lunchtime! I was given a word – freedom – and told to think of it every time I had a craving. But by the time I think of the word, I've lit up. I don't think I want to give up enough.

P And finally actress Sheila Young.

Sheila I was suffering from stage fright when I went to a hypnotherapist. He suggested that I should, er, think about how I was looking forward to playing the character, and while on stage, I should simply *be* her. Well, it was a miracle. All the first night fears were dissolved!

P Well, now we're going to ask you, the listeners, for some of your views …

• *speaking p8*

A Describing actions. This part focuses on the use of the present tenses for description and the imperative for instructions. Refer students to the exam tip next to 'Describing actions' and stress the importance of using the present progressive form for descriptions, pointing out those verbs in **2** which are rarely or never used in the progressive form.

For further information on which verbs are rarely or never used in the progressive tenses, see Unit 2, Structure.

K Suggested answers to Question **3**

1 He's clasping the sides of his head with each hand, with his thumbs at the edge of the skull.
2 He's holding one hand on his forehead and the other at the back of his head with his thumb placed in the hollow at the base of the skull. He's rotating his thumb.
3 He's clasping his shoulder.
4 He's using a towel to massage his neck.
5 Another person is clasping his shoulder and touching his other shoulder with his index finger.
6 He's pressing the side of his arm hard at the elbow.
7 With a loosely clenched fist he's drumming hard down the back of the neck.

B Giving instructions.

K **a** 3 **b** 1 **c** 5 **d** 7 **e** 6 **f** 2 **g** 4

C Check that students remember the meaning of *insomnia* (a word which appeared on the tape). Ask students to suggest ways of coping with insomnia before referring them to the self-help techniques shown.

K Suggested descriptions (students need not describe the pictures or give instructions in so much detail!)

1 He's pressing firmly on a point just below the knee.
2 He's pressing evenly between the eyebrows.
3 He's clenching his fingers loosely and massaging them gently over his forehead.
4 He's clenching his fists with the second knuckle over his eyebrows and he's making a circular movement just above his eyes.
5 With his thumb, he's gripping his arm tightly and applying pressure with his fingers at the back of his arm.
6 He's placing his thumb firmly in the small hollow at the side of his wrist and massaging with a circular movement.

Suggested instructions

1 Press firmly just below the knee.
2 Press evenly at the spot between the eyebrows.
3 Place the thumb on the cheekbone, clench fingers loosely and massage fingers gently over the forehead.
4 Place the second knuckle of each finger over the eyebrows and make a circular movement just above the eyes.
5 Using the thumb, grip the arm tightly just below the wrist, then apply pressure with the other fingers at the back of the arm.
6 Place thumb firmly in the small hollow at the side of the wrist immediately under the hand and massage with a firm circular movement.

Optional activity

Ask students to bring in similar pictures taken from a magazine or instruction booklet of physical exercises, dance steps, etc.

GROUP WORK Students could describe the pictures and / or write a list of instructions as to how to perform the activities.

PAIR WORK Students could instruct each other – one student could read the instructions, the other 'perform' (if suitable).

WRITING

For and Against

• *sample composition p10*

This first composition is in a style that should be familiar to students who have done First Certificate or the Cambridge Advanced, and should make them feel more confident about writing compositions at this level. Allow students to read through the model, which would get a grade A in the examination.

K Suggested answers

1 A possible title is *Should research into human embryology and genetic engineering be banned?*
2 The five sentences that provide a reasonable summary are the first five sentences of each paragraph, ie
  1 Recent advances in human embryology and genetic engineering have raised the issue of how this knowledge ought to be used, and it is now a matter of considerable public concern and debate.
  2 There are two main areas in which such research is widely regarded as being beneficial, and the first of these is in the field of conception.
  3 The second area is that of research into genetically transmitted diseases.
  4 On the other hand, there is deep-rooted hostility towards scientists who interfere with nature and human life.
  5 In conclusion, it can be said that research in these areas needs to be regulated rather than banned.

Emphasize the relevance of questions 1 and 2. The first question stresses that a composition will not get good marks if it is off the subject and is irrelevant. This is a very common failing in Paper 2. Students need to develop the skills of writing paragraph headings that relate directly to the title and to write compositions based on these.

The second question points to a very simple way of organizing compositions by using lead sentences. Each paragraph begins with what is essentially a summary of the central point, which is then illustrated with examples. This means that students who do not have very much experience of the world only have to think of four or five ideas, illustrate them with examples, and they have a perfectly acceptable composition.

The next exercises introduce in detail the five-stage composition process which is recommended throughout the book, and explained in the Introduction on page iii.

● *stage 1 general approach p10*

A Question interpretation and outline planning. Explain to students that the first stage involves deciding which approach to adopt, in other words, whether it will be a 'for and against' composition or whether a different format would be more suitable.

Draw students' attention to the sample plan. Explain that this would only take a minute to write down, and that it sets the framework for writing.

B Ask students to write four-line plans for the next three titles. Each sample answer should have essentially the same format, ie

K
1 introduction
2 points in favour
3 points against
4 conclusion

Ask selected students to read out the paragraph plans they have noted down or to compare plans in groups.

● *stage 2 brainstorming p10*

Explain to students that in this phase of the writing process, they need not note things down in order; the aim is simply to write down as many ideas as possible which can be organized later.

The technique presented here can be used by students who have difficulty in coping with abstract ideas. Encourage them to think of abstract ideas in terms of what different people they know (eg their brothers, sisters, parents, teachers, etc.) might say about a given topic.

Draw students' attention to the composition title, then ask them to discuss the issues raised in statements 1–10.

K
1 a Possibly said by a doctor at a conference.
b It raises the issue that not all diseases have physical causes, and that many real illnesses are caused by psychological conditions.

2 a Possibly said about an alternative medical practitioner.
b It raises the point that while the training for conventional medicine is rigorous, the training given to alternative medical practitioners is sometimes (but by no means always) rather slight.

3 a An individual giving some positive evidence about the effectiveness of alternative medicine.
b It raises the point that there are often successes in areas such as hypnotism.

4 a This is said by a herbalist, explaining their general approach to illness.
b Generally speaking, conventional medicine addresses the symptoms of disease, and alternative forms of medicine try to look at the underlying cause that has enabled the disease to take hold in the first place.

5 a A cynic talking about alternative medicine.
b It raises the point that many people are deeply sceptical about the claims of alternative medicine. *Mumbo jumbo* is a colloquial phrase that means 'nonsense', particularly in relation to jargon.

6 a An individual talking about a recognized disease.
b It raises the point that conventional medicine is by no means able to cure all known diseases; it can often alleviate the symptoms but not solve the underlying problem.

7 a Possibly said by a doctor talking about a disease.
b This underlines the point made in **6**. (In fact, this comes from a government advertisement warning about AIDS.)

8 a This could be said by a believer in conventional medicine who is having an argument with a herbalist.
b It raises the point that if the 'cures' of alternative medicine could be proven scientifically to be reliable, they would be used in conventional medicine.

9 a A patient talking about the effectiveness of conventional medicine.
b Conventional medication is, of course, very efficient at curing a wide range of conditions extremely rapidly with drugs.

10 a This could be said by a fan of alternative medicine or health food.
b It raises the point that some people believe that natural things are good for you and that artificial things are bad for you. This is based on a very optimistic view of nature.

● *stage 3 organization p11*

Paragraph planning. Explain to students that they should arrange their thoughts carefully after the brainstorming process, using the outline plan they first thought of. Important ideas should be allocated to the correct paragraphs; less important ideas could be mentioned only briefly or discarded.

Ask students to look again at the statements in the brainstorming session, and to say which paragraph would mention the issues that were raised.

K Suggested answer
Introduction
Points in favour of conventional medicine and against alternative: 2, 5, 8, 9
Points against conventional medicine and in favour of alternative: 1, 3, 4, 6, 7, 10
Conclusion

Ask students to comment on the plan and to suggest additions or changes; ask what they might write for the introduction and for the lead sentences to paragraphs 2 and 3.

stage 4 writing p11

This can be set as homework or done in class, but talk briefly about Stage 5 as well. Draw students' attention to the exam tip under Stage 5.

stage 5 checking p11

Remind students that checking is important and that, at Proficiency level, you can get away with far fewer basic grammatical errors than at First Certificate. Ask them to try checking their work by reading random sentences from their finished compositions. This may help them to look at the language more objectively, as they will not be distracted by the content.

Always ask students to keep their compositions after they have been corrected. If time permits, at a later stage look through each student's work and see if there are any kinds of errors that are continually repeated so that you can give the student an individual check-list of things to concentrate on when checking his or her work.

OVERVIEW 1

vocabulary p12

K 1 D 2 C 3 B 4 D 5 C 6 A 7 A 8 D 9 C 10 D

transformations p12

K
1 It's high time you made an effort to get out and about more.
2 His physical condition seems to be deteriorating slightly.
3 Whether you are rich or poor, happiness is elusive.
4 That commentator, whose name I've forgotten, is very well-known.
5 The leisure industry can be said to be the money spinner of the future.
6 He suggested inviting / that we should invite the Marshalls to a barbecue on Sunday.
7 If he hadn't overeaten, he wouldn't have had a heart attack.
8 Some people are completely mystified by alternative medicine.
9 The hypnotherapist suggested to Annie that she / that Annie should think about how she was going to play the character.
10 Sports such as gymnastics and skiing need regular practice.

blank-filling p13

K
1 is to be carried out
2 there was a lot of opposition initially
3 he decided to try / he started having / he took up
4 to give
5 feel
6 I arrived
7 looking forward
8 about going (out) / coming round
9 came to / made
10 was / would have been treated

rewriting p13

K
1 Tooth decay can be prevented by brushing your teeth regularly.
2 I'd (much) rather cycle than walk.
3 He is widely regarded as being the best man for the job.
4 There is a ban on smoking on the tube.
5 They have a lot of hobbies and interests in common.
6 Eating fewer sweets will save you having to visit the dentist so often.
7 The football match had to be put off because of / due to a sudden downpour.
8 He cannot come to terms with the fact that he will never race again.
9 In terms of education his childhood years had been well spent.
10 The tone of his voice brought (it) home to me how serious the situation was.

First Impressions

READING

Master of the Universe

Write the title *Master of the Universe* on the board, and ask students what they think this section will be about.

● *talking points p14*

A Ask students to look at the four photographs on page 14 and to work through the first three questions, which are about first impressions in abstract terms. Remind them if necessary of the patterns commonly used with the word *look*, eg

	interesting. (adjective)
She looks	like an interesting person. (noun)
	as if she would be quite interesting. (verb)

B Work through Questions 1 to 3, which are more related to students' own experiences; a useful phrasal verb here is *come over (as)*. Give students an example of this:

How do you think you *come over* in interviews?
(ie What impression do you give?)
I think I *come over* as rather shy and nervous.
(ie I appear to be ...)

Question 4 relates to prejudice and related language items. Explain to students that 'lookism' is a term from the American 'Politically Correct' movement which aims partly at removing discrimination from language. Ask students to guess what similar terms might mean – eg ageism, handicappism, weightism, sexism, racism; point out that new words for prejudices are continually being made up.

GROUP WORK Ask students to make up new words for prejudices, for example against people with freckles (which would be *freckleism*). The word is unlikely to be in a dictionary.

Point out that the suffix *-ism* does not always refer to prejudices, and is more commonly used to refer to philosophies, theories, beliefs, etc. Ask them for examples: Buddhism, Thatcherism, empiricism, Impressionism, etc.

● *reading p14*

A Ask students to skim read the passage for the answer.

K Professor Hawking, picture **1**.

B **Comprehension.** Ask students to scan the article and complete the matching exercise.

K **1** f **2** i **3** e **4** g **5** h **6** a **7** b **8** c **9** d

NB **6** *sucker* is an American colloquialism.

> **Note**
> Paragraph 1 mentions that 'Heisenberg undid the certainties of particle physics'. This is a reference to the theory that sub-atomic particles do not behave in an entirely predictable way.

C **Multiple-choice questions.**

K **1** D **2** A **3** C **4** B **5** D **6** C

● *vocabulary p16*

Expressions. Go through the list of expressions, asking students to explain their meaning where possible, before completing the exercise that follows. Some of the expressions are colloquial and would be found mainly in speech rather than in formal writing. The main example of this is **5**.

K
1 all in good time
2 in the nick of time
3 a bit pressed for time
4 at the best of times
5 Now's a fine time
6 to kill time
7 on time
8 to buy time
9 for the time being
10 time and time again

STRUCTURE

The Hawking Story

Ask students if they think that people with radically different beliefs (ie political, religious, etc.) can have a lasting relationship. Ask them why / why not.

● *cloze development p16*

The cloze gives further details about Professor Hawking and his wife; the content relates to the previous discussion about relationships. The photographs on page 16 are of Cambridge University and of Hawking with his wife. You may wish to inform students that the couple have since divorced.

The cloze leads into the grammar section on the use of simple and progressive tenses and stative verbs.

A Ask students to answer the true / false questions without completing the cloze test, as this will encourage them to read the whole passage first.

K **1** F **2** T **3** F **4** T **5** F **6** T

B

K **1** in **2** as **3** however **4** funds **5** longer **6** responsible **7** to **8** voice **9** None **10** with **11** held **12** without **13** find **14** with **15** to **16** theory **17** What **18** for **19** reaches **20** door

Optional activity

Many English words are derived from Greek or combinations of Greek and another language. An example from the text is *it seems like an agnostic slamming a door in her face*. The word *agnostic* derives from the Greek *a-*, meaning 'not' and the word *gno*, meaning 'know'. Write the following sets of words on the board. Ask students to work out what the constituent parts of each word are and what the words might mean.

NB This exercise is likely to be more useful to those students who do not have similar words in their own language.

1 agnostic amorphous atheism
2 theology anthropology psychology
3 psychopathic psychosomatic psychotherapy
4 aromatherapy chemotherapy hydrotherapy
5 hydrophobia xenophobia Anglophobia
6 anglophile gastrophile bibliophile
7 philosophy philanthropy philology

● *progressive aspect p17*

A If necessary, explain to students that the term 'progressive' is the same as 'continuous'. When we talk about the progressive **aspect** we are essentially talking about features that all the progressive tenses share.

This section looks at the progressive aspect, and at the link which exists between all of the progressive tenses. In general terms the progressive aspect can be used in **any** tense to talk about the following:

– an action happening at a particular moment in time
– an action or activity that is seen as temporary
– an action that is incomplete
– a series of repeated actions.

PAIR WORK Ask students to read through the pairs of sample sentences, and to discuss any differences in meaning.

K Suggested explanations

1 The first sentence refers to something that is always or generally true (*are done*). The second sentence refers to something **happening at a particular moment in time**.

Ask the students to give you an example of this same feature in another tense. For example, *This time tomorrow I'll be sitting on the beach.*

2 In the first sentence the progressive is used to talk about an activity that is only seen as **temporary**. The second sentence refers to an activity that is seen as permanent.

Ask students to give you an example of this same feature in another tense. For example, *You'll be working here until the new office is ready.*

3 In the first sentence, the activity is complete. In the second sentence the progressive form is used to indicate that an activity is still in progress and **is not complete**.

Ask students to give you an example of this same feature in another tense. For example, *I'm learning English.*

4 In the first sentence the progressive form is used to talk about **a repeated series of actions**. The use of the simple form in the second sentence suggests the action is habitual.

Ask students to give you an example of this same feature in another tense. For example, *I've been trying to ring you all morning*.

B This exercise continues the work from the introductory section and introduces another two features of the progressive aspect, which are to emphasize that a repeated action is rather irritating (**e**), and to talk about a future arrangement (**f**). These two features are most commonly shown by the present progressive.

The use (**e**), eg *You're always leaving the top off the toothpaste*, requires an adverb such as *forever* or *always*. The meaning in the example would be changed if the word *always* was omitted.

Ask students to read through the sentences and to indicate which of the features **a** to **f** are the most prominent. The following answers are correct, but there may be a little room for debate.

K **1** f **2** c **3** e **4** a **5** c **6** d **7** e **8** d **9** f **10** b **11** b **12** a

● *avoiding the progressive aspect p18*

A Ask students to look at the six sentences and to select the ones that sound the most natural.

K **1b**, **2a** and **3b** sound natural. Sentences **1a**, **2b** and **3a** sound unnatural because of the sound clash of *been being*.

Explain to students that, while perfect progressive tenses exist in the passive and are used very occasionally, they are generally avoided. Point out that the avoidance of the passive can be achieved in different ways:

1 by using the active instead of the passive as in **1b**. The use of the active makes the sentence slightly less formal.

2 by using a prepositional phrase as in **2a**, *under review*. Ask students if they can think of any other prepositional phrases that have a passive meaning. Some common examples are:

under | *consideration, construction, discussion, observation, pressure, repair, review, stress, supervision, surveillance*

on | *loan, order, sale, trial.*

However the use of prepositional phrases to avoid the present perfect progressive is limited, and sometimes entails the use of different lexis.

eg *The bridge has been being built for two years. The bridge has been under construction for two years.*

3 by changing the lexis, and changing the verb to a noun as in **3b**.

B Ask students to rewrite the sentences using the words that have been given.

K 1 When they finished the meeting, the matter had been under discussion for hours.
2 Christmas cards have been on sale since the beginning of September.
3 She was unaware that she had been under (police) surveillance since her arrival.
4 He was tired when he left because he had been having interviews all day.
5 A number of scientists have (recently) attacked the theory of relativity (recently).
6 She has been having a hard time at school, because of her new glasses.

● *stative verbs p19*

A Direct students' attention to the extracts from the text and ask them what they can tell you about verbs which are not generally used in the progressive. As a general rule, 'stative' verbs (eg *love, know, want*) describe states and 'dynamic' verbs (eg *drive, hit, fight*) describe actions. Stative verbs are either rarely used in progressive forms or show a difference in meaning between the simple and progressive forms.

Tell students to look through the list of common stative verbs below and classify them into the groups suggested. This activity serves to remind students of the most common stative verbs, and may be omitted if you feel they are already very familiar with them.

K Suggested answers
1 Verbs related to the senses – feel, hear, smell, sound, taste.
2 Verbs related to thinking – believe, doubt, guess, imagine, know, realize, regard, remember, suppose, understand.
3 Verbs related to possession – belong to, have*, own.
4 Verbs related to emotional states – dislike, hate, like, love, mind, prefer, want.
5 Verbs of appearance – appear, seem.
6 Others – contain, depend on, find, involve, mean.

*NB When *have* means 'possess' it is a stative verb; in other phrases such as *to have a bath*, it may be used in the progressive.

B **Meaning changes in stative verbs.** This section looks at the differences in meaning between the simple and progressive forms in a variety of tenses.

K 1 *would have thought* – Establish that *think* in its simple form means ' to have an opinion'.
2 *had been thinking* – Here it is in the progressive because it refers to thinking as the process of making a decision.
3 *is* – normal use of the verb *to be* for something that is generally true.
4 *was being* – *To be*, in the progressive like this, is normally used to refer to behaviour on a particular occasion or over a particular period (ie temporary state). Compare *He is very kind*, which is generally true and *He is being very kind*, which refers specifically to one occasion or set of circumstances.
5 *have been imagining* – The verb here means to dream up or create pictures in the mind. With this meaning, *imagine* may be used in either the progressive or simple, depending on the context.
6 *don't imagine* – Here the verb in the simple means 'to think' or 'to have an opinion'. With this meaning, *imagine* can only be used in the simple form.
7 *was appearing* – Used in the progressive, *appear* often means to act in a play or opera.
8 *appeared* – Used in its most common form in the simple, *appeared* means 'seemed'.
9 *have always felt* – When the verb *feel* means 'to have an opinion' it can only be used in the simple form.
10 *haven't been feeling* – When the verb *feel* refers only to one's state of health or mind, it may be used in either the simple or, as here, in the progressive.

Point out to students two important and common expressions that seem to contradict the rules about stative verbs. These are *want* and *mean* in the present perfect progressive. For example, the following would be considered correct:

I've been wanting to have a chat with you for some time …
There's something I've been meaning to talk to you about …

NB In the first sentence the meaning of *want* doesn't change. In the second *meaning* means 'intending'.

Remind students of the four main functions of the progressive aspect listed in *progressive aspect* above.

Most of these stative verbs refer to states that are clearly thought of as permanent rather than temporary – for example, *I know Jane very well.* When one of the stative verbs is used in the progressive it is being used with a change of meaning, or to show something is temporary.

EXAMPLE
I love chocolate. (permanently true)
I'm in Corfu for my two-week summer holiday and I'm loving every minute of it. (stresses the temporary nature of the activity)

SUMMARY SKILLS

The Theory of Inequality

● *talking points* p20

GROUP WORK Allow three to four minutes for students to reach a conclusion about the statement, then invite one member from each group to report back to the class on the group's decision.

Conduct a 'straw poll', asking the students to raise their hands if they feel that the statement is a) true, b) untrue, c) partially true.

Suggested prompts for further class discussion
- Traditional roles of men and women in society.
- Difficulties of creating equal opportunities for men and women.
- The importance of physical strength needed for some jobs.
- Jobs traditionally considered as suitable for men / women.
- Who looks after the children?

● *summary 1* p20

Notes
Thomas Vaughan (1622–65) – British alchemist and mystic, who regarded himself as a philosopher of nature. His published writings deal with magic and mysticism. He died inhaling fumes from mercury.
Sir Isaac Newton (1642–1727) – British natural philosopher, famous for his universal law of gravitation and his laws of motion.
Robert Boyle (1627–91) – British natural philosopher and scientific investigator who carried out a series of experiments on the properties of air.
Charles Babbage (1792–1871) – British mathematician and mechanic whose great 'calculating engine' was never completed.

Refer the students to the illustrations on page 21 of Robert Boyle's air pump (line 46) and to the drawing of Ada Lovelace (line 74).

Ask students to skim read the article.

K **2** best sums up the point the writer is making.

● *comprehension* p20

A

K **1** d **2** e **3** h **4** b **5** g **6** a **7** c **8** f

B Multiple-choice questions.

K **1** B **2** D **3** C **4** B **5** A

C Reference devices.

K
1 a rebel
2 modern science
3 science
4 some other form of (knowledge)
5 the time of Newton
6 the 19th century
7 the reasons for women's inadequacy in science

● *summary 2* p21

A

K
Exclusion of the 'opposite sex' – paragraph 4 (l. 34–55)
Fear of the unknown – paragraph 2 (l. 7–22)
The 'weaker sex' – paragraph 6 (l. 67–86)
The male / female divide – paragraph 3 (l. 23–33)
Defining terms of reference – paragraph 1 (l. 1–6)
A Scientific family – paragraph 5 (l. 56–66)

B

K
Margaret Cavendish was the first female to gain access to one particular all-male domain / was a woman of aristocratic birth. (3 and 5)
Caroline Herschel basked only in reflected glory / was a worthy member of a scientifically-minded family. (2 and 6)
Ada Lovelace caused her tutor much anguish / seemed unnaturally scientifically minded. (1 and 4)

C Linking sentences.

K **1** and **2** contain non-sequiturs – conclusions that do not follow on logically from the information in the first part of the sentence. The sentences would make sense if the second parts of both sentences were exchanged.

1 Mary was never able to achieve the success she craved despite the fact that she studied so hard.
2 Mary was able to achieve the success she craved on account of the fact that she studied so hard.

Combined sentences from B.

Margaret Cavendish was the first female to gain access to one particular all-male domain on account of the fact that she was a woman of noble birth.

Caroline Herschel basked only in reflected glory despite the fact that she was a worthy member of a scientifically-minded family.

Ada Lovelace caused her tutor much anguish on account of the fact that she seemed unnaturally scientifically minded.

Optional summary

Ask students to write 40 to 60 words on the reasons for women's supposed inadequacy in science. Their answers should include these points:

1 Women's reputed associations with the devil.
2 Men's unassailable belief in their own superiority.
3 The weakness of the female constitution.

LISTENING AND SPEAKING

Best Sellers

This section picks up the theme of Stephen Hawking and extends it to the topic of books. It ends with a humorous listening passage.

● *listening 1 p22*

K 1 C 2 D 3 A 4 B 5 B

Tapescript
(**A** = Presenter, **B** = Critic)

A Were you at all surprised by the success of *A Brief History of Time* – and when it came out, would you have anticipated it?

B Well, I think the honest answer would have to be no to both questions. Before it came out, I think most people were fairly confident that it would do well, but it has really succeeded beyond anyone's wildest dreams … I mean after all, it is now the best selling general book of all time, if you'll pardon the pun! It has been on the best seller list for longer than any other book, apart from things like the Bible or dictionaries … and that is no mean achievement.

A I don't suppose he had very much difficulty in getting it published then.

B None at all. In fact the idea was suggested to him by the head of the Institute of Astronomy, and he'd been offered an advance of about £10,000. But just at the same time, an American literary agent heard about the book and decided to hold an auction, the upshot of which was that he was offered a quarter of a million dollars up front.

A So they must have had a fair degree of confidence in the book.

B Oh yes, and there'd been similar books such as *The First Three Minutes* which had done well and, so to some extent they were on fairly safe ground. And all of these books about Black holes and time and space have a very long lasting appeal because they, they in the end, are addressing those nagging questions about life, the universe and everything, which are basically the old religious questions about God in a new form. There seems to be a fairly essential human wish that some hermit or wise man, somewhere, should actually understand everything, and, er, should know the solutions. And Hawking, of course, has the air of someone who actually does have the answers – whether or not you can actually understand what he is trying to say is almost beside the point – what's important is that these questions are intellectually soluble, and that's what's comforting. Most people are happy to leave the mathematics to the experts and take their word for it.

A But presumably in any book like this, there must be a fair amount of mathematics and rather complicated equations?

B No, no, no, there's none of that, and he was told by his publishers that every equation would halve the sales of the book, which must have been rather frustrating. What he has attempted to do is to explain everything in absolutely straightforward ordinary English, that anyone can understand.

A Could a book like this be accused of vulgarization?

B In a sense, I suppose it could … I mean there is that story about a Russian physicist, Andre Linde, who was flying to America for a conference, and he was sitting next to a businessman who was reading the book. So Linde asked him what he thought of it, and the businessman said he thought it was fascinating. 'Oh, that's interesting,' said Linde. 'I found it quite heavy going in places and didn't fully understand some parts.' So the businessman closed his book, and leant across with a compassionate smile and said 'Let me explain …'.
But there are always diehards who say that popularizing and simplifying complex ideas is a bad thing, and there are always experts who are afraid of losing their mystique. But Hawking's not one of them, and I think what comes over in the book is a genuine attempt to teach and explain as much as possible, and to concentrate on the main facts that can be grasped, without getting bogged down in too much technical detail. And to my mind at least, that seems like a very useful and worthwhile thing to do.

● *speaking p22*

A Ranking. Remind students that in the examination, there is no 'correct' answer to any of these ranking exercises. The focus therefore, during the lessons, should be less on which feature is the most important, and more on the explanations and reasoning.

Go over some examples of ways in which these factors can be compared:

A using nouns as subjects, eg *I think that an attractive cover is more important than favourable reviews.*

B Using *the fact that* + verb, eg *I think the fact that it has an attractive cover is more important than the fact that it has favourable reviews.*

C Using the gerund, eg *I think (its) having an attractive cover is more important that (its) having favourable reviews.*

B Picture discussion.

Ask students to look at the pictures on page 22.

K **1–3** have no set answers.

4 The first picture (*Eothen*) – extract A
The second picture (*Guide*) – extract B
The third picture (*Easy Prey*) – extract C

5 This question concentrates on style, and provides an introduction into an area of language awareness that is important at this level. Ask students to provide justification for their answers by quoting extracts from the text.
In extract A, the vocabulary is formal (*ascended, fanciful, florid grace*); there is extensive use of adjectives, and the repetition of the phrase *drawn westward* has an almost lyrical quality.
In extract B, the most obvious informal or slang

words are 'boozer, oddish, gatecrash, get thrown out'. Explain the following:
boozer = someone who drinks a lot (of alcohol)
oddish = slightly odd
gatecrash = to go to a party without being invited
get thrown out = be made to leave forcibly
NB The suffix *-ish* is common in speech and serves to modify the adjective as in *goodish* (quite good), *greenish* (slightly green), *coldish* (quite cold), etc. It is used mainly with common, short adjectives, less so with longer and more formal ones.
Extract C follows patterns very similar to everyday speech. The sentences are divided up by commas into short phrases, some of which have the effect of afterthoughts, as in ... *such as a cosh*, ... *almost certainly*. It also avoids formal language, for example, the use of ... *but there weren't any* as opposed to ... *but there were none*. In a more formal context it would be possible to rewrite the passage in a single sentence as opposed to three.

6 This question can be done in pairs as a short writing activity.

7 This question picks up the theme from the start of the unit; you may wish to develop it further, or discuss other proverbs students can think of.

● *vocabulary p23*

A **Expressions.** PAIR WORK Ask students to discuss the meaning of the expressions before doing the exercise.

Tell students to write out the sentences in full, as some of the expressions themselves need to be modified to fit into the blanks.

K
1 throw the book at you
2 take a leaf out of her book
3 turn over a new leaf
4 speaks volumes about her
5 I am in Mrs Lawson's good books
6 does everything by the book

B **Story telling.** Give students an example, if necessary.

I'm a bit worried about Ken – and I think he's taking a lot of risks. He's in England at the moment, and he's got a forged British passport. Now that's bad enough, but the thing is, he has got a flat from the council at a very low rent, but he's staying with friends and he's renting it out to other illegal immigrants. He's also claiming unemployment benefit, but in fact he's got a day job in a hotel and he drives a minicab at night. So far he's got away with it, but if they catch him they'll throw the book at him.

Do the activity in pairs. Allow students up to five minutes to prepare their small anecdotes and encourage them to use one of the expressions in the last sentence of their story.

● *listening 2 p23*

K 1 F 2 F 3 T 4 T 5 T 6 T 7 F 8 F

Tapescript
(**N** = Narrator)

N Inside the building, the room was much as Slartibartfast had described it. In seven and a half million years it had been well looked after and cleaned regularly every century or so. The ultramahogany desk was worn at the edges, the carpet a little faded now, but the large computer terminal sat in sparkling glory on the desk's leather top, as bright as if it had been constructed yesterday. Two severely dressed men sat respectfully before the terminal and waited.
'The time is nearly upon us, Phouchg.'
'Seventy-five thousand generations ago, our ancestors set this program in motion, and in all that time we will be the first to hear the computer speak.'
'An awesome prospect, Phouchg.'
'We, Loonquawl, are the ones who will hear the answer to the great question of Life ...!'
'The Universe ...!'
'And Everything ...!'
'Shh, I think Deep Thought is preparing to speak!'
There was a moment's expectant pause whilst panels slowly came to life on the front of the console. Lights flashed on and off experimentally and settled down into a business-like pattern. A soft low hum came from the communication channel.
'Good morning.'
'Er ... Good morning, O Deep Thought, do you have ... er, that is ...'
'An answer for you? Yes, I have.'
The two men shivered with expectancy. Their waiting had not been in vain.
'There really is one?'
'There really is one.'
'To Everything? To the great Question of Life, the Universe and Everything?'
'Yes.'
Both of the men had been trained for this moment, their lives had been a preparation for it, they had been selected at birth as those who would witness the answer, but even so they found themselves gasping and squirming like excited children.
'And you're ready to give it to us?'
'I am.'
'Now?'
'Now.'
They both licked their dry lips.
'Though I don't think that you're going to like it.'
'It doesn't matter! We must know it! Now!'
'Now?'
'Yes! Now ...'
'Alright.'
The two men fidgeted. The tension was unbearable.
'You're really not going to like it.'
'Tell us!'
'Alright. The Answer to the Great Question ...'
'Yes ...!'

'Of Life, the Universe and Everything ...'
'Yes ...!'
'Is ...'
'Yes ...!'
'Is ...'
'Yes ...!!! ...?'
'Forty-two.'
It was a long long time before anyone spoke.
Out of the corner of his eye Phouchg could see the sea of tense expectant faces down in the square outside.
'We're going to get lynched, aren't we?'
'It was a tough assignment.'
'Forty-two! Is that all you've got to show for seven and a half million years' work?'
'I checked it very thoroughly, and that quite definitely is the answer. I think the problem, to be quite honest with you, is that you've never actually known what the question is.'
'Look, alright, alright, can you just please tell us the question?'
'The Ultimate Question?'
'Yes!'
'Of Life, the Universe and Everything?'
'Yes!'
Deep Thought pondered for a moment.
'Tricky.'
'Yeah, but can you do it?'
Deep Thought pondered this for another long moment.
Finally: 'No.'

WRITING

The Descriptive Composition

● *introduction p24*

A Ask students to look at the photographs on page 24 and compare them. Then ask them to comment on the different descriptions; **A** is more down to earth, and is rather flat and uninteresting; **B** shows more imagination and insight. **A**, although it is perfectly grammatically correct, is what you might expect at FCE level; **B** is more what you would expect at CPE.

B **Practice.** Ask students to complete the task. If time is short, this can be done in pairs, with one student writing a factual description of someone and the other student writing the 'character' description.

● *character adjectives p24*

A Compositions requiring character description in part or in whole frequently occur in the Proficiency exam.

Draw students' attention to the exam tip. Students need a good range of vocabulary at their disposal at CPE level, and should show that they have one. The words on the left would demonstrate this to an examiner, and the words on the right are relatively simple. More complex vocabulary, however, must only be used where appropriate.

Ask students to match the words with their definitions.

K **1** d **2** f **3** e **4** g **5** a **6** b **7** c **8** l **9** n **10** m **11** h **12** j **13** k **14** i

B **Word-building.** This exercise could be done for homework.

K
callous – callousness
placid – placidity
sullen – sullenness
vivacious – vivaciousness
listless – listlessness
irksome – irksomeness
boorish – boorishness
self-effacing – self-effacement
retiring – retiredness (*retirement* usually refers to the state of no longer being employed)
frivolous – frivolity
condescending – condescension
gregarious – gregariousness
petulant – petulance
frank – frankness
(*retiredness* and *irksomeness* are arguably used very rarely)

● *features p24*

A Allow students to read the example carefully.

B **Practice.** This activity can be done in pairs or groups of three: each student completes one task and reads out his / her description to the other.

● *significance p25*

A PAIR WORK Each student will select a number of important features to describe someone they know well, and can then explain to a partner why these features are important.

B **Practice.** This short description serves as a model composition, although it is not of the length required in the exam.

K The items from the list that have been included are:

age
facial features
problems (although these are not explained in detail)
things he does
his hands
his relationships (lack of communication with the other orphans)
gestures and reactions
furniture (lack of it)
walls
clothes
skin
habits

Emphasize to students the central point that when writing a description, you do not need to restrict yourself to the traditional description of facial features (wavy hair, straight nose, etc.)

Students should aim at bringing out character, and this can be done either explicitly or by using a range of external features that can be used as props.

● *writing task* p25

This can be done in class or set as homework. Advise students to look at the title very carefully as it needs some interpretation to be answered fully. The question needs not only a character description, but also an explanation of the history of the relationship between the student and the subject in the composition.

OVERVIEW 2

● *vocabulary* p26

K **1** C **2** D **3** C **4** A **5** A **6** B **7** C **8** C
9 C **10** B **11** D **12** D **13** A **14** D **15** D

● *blank-filling* p26

K
1 in spite of the fact
2 without which
3 to having / to doing
4 for the time
5 throw the book
6 ever since / since then
7 of the fact that
8 on to
9 have been trying to get
10 and time again

● *transformations* p27

K
1 The government's immigration policy has been under review for some time now.
2 They have been trying out / testing a new flu vaccine since the beginning of the year.
3 He is the most likely person to succeed in solving the problem.
4 He met Jane, who was later to become his wife, when he was at Cambridge.
5 I am beginning to get more and more annoyed by his behaviour.
6 It was only when I met her husband in France that I heard his side of the story.
7 He said he was a bit pressed for time, but that he would ring me the following day.
8 I would have thought that she would have liked her present.
9 Few students listened to / took note of what the teacher was saying.
10 Her work resulted in the discovery of eight new comets.

UNIT 3

SAFETY AND DANGER

READING

War and Peace

• *talking points* *p28*

GROUP WORK Refer the students to the pictures on page 28. Allow about five minutes for groups to discuss the points in their books.

• *reading* *p29*

Notes
NB Allow students to skim read the passage and answer the question before giving them this information.

The passage comes from a story written in the form of a journal by William Boyd and entitled *Transfigured Night*. It is about the Second World War. It appeared in a collection of writings by modern authors.
F. W. Nietzsche (1844–1900) A German philosopher whose philosophy was the rejection of the accepted absolute moral values, and the 'slave morality' of Christianity.
Charles Dana Gibson (1867–1944) An American illustrator famous for his pictures of the typical 'American young woman', known as the 'Gibson Girl'.

A Ask students to skim read the passage and answer the questions.

K The passage is set in the Second World War.

B Multiple-choice questions.

K 1 C 2 D 3 C 4 B

Optional activity
Ask students if they have read any novels / seen any films about war recently. What sort of experiences did they depict? Were the images of war positive or negative?

• *vocabulary* *p30*

A Words which create atmosphere.

K (a) saved elation glad pleased kind of love
(b) rigours reluctant harsh impasse impossibility morbid despair cold dark detest lonely pollute

B Similar but different.

K 1 A 2 C 3 D 4 B 5 D 6 D

C Use your eyes! Related word groups.

K 1 d 2 f 3 e 4 b 5 i 6 c 7 a
8 h 9 j 10 g

D Expressions

K 1 doing the donkey work
2 do it up
3 I can do it with my eyes closed.
4 does a lot of harm / does no good
5 do me a good turn / favour
6 does wonders for
7 did time
8 A life of hardship won't do you any good.

STRUCTURE

Minimizing the Risks

• *talking points* *p31*

Ask students to look at the picture on page 31.

Notes
O.S.H.A. – an American organization entitled 'Occupational Safety and Health Administration'.

The Calgary Stampede – an annual exhibition held to celebrate the customs of the Old West.

• *cloze development* *p31*

Notes
This passage was written in a 'tongue-in-cheek' style by someone connected with the theatrical world. The writer approaches the subject from an unusual angle, ie when you go on holiday, choose a place where it will be raining! The images he conjures up are both colourful and amusing.

K
1 more
2 course
3 though
4 had
5 more
6 dogs
7 as
8 do
9 excuse
10 Besides
11 likely
12 times
13 apologizing
14 taken
15 everybody
16 wake
17 predicament
18 claimed
19 raising
20 doubt

• *vocabulary* *p32*

Synonyms and paraphrases.

K
1 dissolve
2 stir
3 cultivate
4 sodden
5 grumbling
6 marred
7 persecuted
8 revelation
9 havoc

1 havoc 2 marred 3 dissolved 4 revelation
5 grumbling 6 sodden 7 stirred 8 persecuted
9 cultivating

● *uses of have* p32

A

K **1** The construction is frequently used when we arrange for something to be done for us by someone else. There is often payment involved. In **b** the plumber has been paid to put the central heating in, whereas in **a** they have done it themselves.

2 Although the construction in **1b** is the same, ie *have* + object + past participle, the meaning is different. You did not arrange the event, rather you were the victim of the event.
NB The subject does not have to be a person.
eg *Someone smashed the car windows.*
The car had its windows smashed.

3 Sometimes *have* can be replaced by *get*. *Get* retains the same meaning as *have* in **1b** but the sentence construction changes quite considerably.
eg *We had the house painted by Gilbert and Son.*
We got Gilbert and Son to paint the house.
NB *Get* can sometimes replace *have*, eg *to get one's fingers burnt* or *If you say that once more, you'll get your teeth knocked out*, etc.

4 *had my clothes dissolve* is an example of a construction which usually expresses the idea of causing something to happen or be done without your control or volition. It often conveys the idea that this kind of event is unusual or has never happened before.
eg *The car has never broken down on a long journey before.*
I've never had the car break down on a long journey before.
Notice the structure *had* + object + the infinitive without *to* is different from the structure in **1**, **2** and **3**. In **1**, **2** and **3**, if the sentences were rephrased, *central heating*, *car* and *house* would be the objects of the transitive verbs *put in*, *stole* and *painted*. However, if this sentence were rephrased, *clothes* would be the subject of the verb *dissolved*.

5 *have* + object + *-ing*, or the 'bare' infinitive are variations of the construction in **1**, **2** and **3**. This use of *have* means 'I won't allow you to do this'.
NB In the first sentence *have* + *staying* / *stay* means 'tolerate'. In the second sentence *have* + *know* means 'insist'.

6 The same construction appears in **5**, *have* + object + *-ing*, and is used to predict what might happen (and it is often unpleasant). The use is colloquial.

7 Another use of *have* + object + *-ing* (as in **5** and **6**) is when we have been instrumental in helping / persuading / teaching someone to do something.

B

K **1** **a** We've never had the police arrive on our doorstep in the middle of the night before.
b I've never had my hair fall out in handfuls before!

2 **a** All the shops had their windows blown out by the gas explosion.
b I had my pocket picked (by a thief) on the tube.

3 **a** We had a new carpet laid yesterday.
b We're having the windows fitted tomorrow.

4 We got the builders to put in double glazing.

5 I won't have them smoking in my classroom.

6 We'll have them all staying the night if we don't ask them to leave now.

7 With a little encouragement I had her walking round the room.

● *rewriting* p34

K **1** It never occurred to me / entered my head to go to Iceland for my holidays. (Also: Going to Iceland for my holidays never entered my head.)

2 His holiday insurance scheme failed because no one was prepared to back it up / he was unable to find any backing for it. (Also: … prepared to back him up)

3 The holiday ended in disaster. / catastrophically.

4 It was raining cats and dogs / came down in torrents all day.

5 In all probability / The odds are that the company will fold.

6 I won't have anybody playing football in front of my house. / Playing football … is forbidden.

7 No one shares my point of view. / No one is of the same opinion as I am / me.

8 Physical exercise is nothing new / is as old as the hills. / (Also: There is nothing new about physical exercise.)

9 I hope you haven't taken offence at my remarks / my remarks amiss.

10 Not everybody agreed with the decision. / The decision was not unanimous.

Ask students to look at the illustration on page 34 and to match it with one of these expressions.

SUMMARY SKILLS

Taking a Chance

● *talking points* p35

GROUP WORK Before referring students to the list in their books, ask them to list what they consider to be the greatest risks we are exposed to in our modern-day lives. Allow two or three minutes, then put a master list on the board. Allow a further three or four minutes for them to rank the risks listed in their books. Then refer them to the key on page 215.

Ask students to compare their lists with the official statistics.

● *summary 1* p35

K The passage discusses modern society's response to risk, looking at several criteria which influence our perception of what risk is.

● *comprehension* p36

K **1** B **2** D **3** A **4** C **5** D **6** B

● *summary 2* p36

A

K
1. Chauncey Starr claimed that some theories about societal risk can be proved by experiments.
2. People are prepared to accept 1,000 times more voluntary than involuntary risk.
3. Starr proved the above to be true through experiments which showed that we are more likely to die doing an activity we have chosen to do, ie a voluntary risk.
4. Starr also proved that the greater the number of those sharing the risk, the less serious the risk is considered to be.
5. Advertising can convince us that the risk taken is not as great as it appeared to be.
6. The amount of voluntary risk we are prepared to take seems to be on a par with the risk of dying from disease.

B Connecting ideas.

K Voluntary risks are those which (you seek out for yourself), whereas / while / however involuntary risks are those (over which you have no control).

However could also be placed after *involuntary risks*, ie *involuntary risks, however, ...*

Suggested answer
Boldness means bravery while foolhardiness means hot-headedness.

Optional summary
Ask students to write a summary of 30 to 40 words explaining how humans decide on the level of voluntary risk they will take. These points should be included:

1. the chance of dying from disease
2. the risks involved in sporting activities
3. our inbuilt sense of how far we should expose ourselves to risk.

LISTENING AND SPEAKING

Just my Luck!

Ask students what things are considered lucky / unlucky in their country.

● *talking points* p37

Ask students to look at pictures **1–4** on page 37. Refer them to the exam tip before doing the speaking activity.

A

K Suggested explanations

1. a broken mirror – unlucky – the person who breaks the mirror is meant to have seven years' bad luck.
2. a black cat crossing someone's path – lucky
3. walking under a ladder – unlucky
4. Number 13 (particularly Friday the 13th) – unlucky

B Expressions.

K **1** c **2** b **3** d **4** a **5** e

Ask students to think of occasions when these expressions might be used, eg

1. finding gold
2. winning your first game on a roulette wheel
3. constantly driving over the speed limit and hoping you won't get caught
4. winning a prize in a raffle
5. choosing a holiday hotel from a brochure with no illustrations.

● *listening* p37

A

K
1. final / ~~university~~ college
2. third / five
3. nearly 100
4. almost a miracle

Tapescript
(**P** = Presenter)

P Hello, and welcome to *Young hero or heroine of the week*. The subject this week is Cindy Talbot, a final year college student who was on the third day of her five-day solo-hiking trip through Colorado's National Forest, when she was struck by lightning. Lightning kills nearly a hundred Americans each year, more than hurricanes or tornadoes, and to survive a direct hit is almost a miracle. We are fortunate to have Cindy with us in the studio today.

B Which option should I choose?

K **1** A **2** C **3** B **4** C **5** C

Tapescript
(**P** = Presenter, **C** = Cindy, **R** = Rod, **M** = Mark)

P Luckily, Cindy was rescued by Rod and Mark, who are also in the studio with us today. So, welcome, all of you.

C, R, M Hi, hello.

P Tell me Cindy, what were you actually doing when the lightning struck?

C Well, I'd noticed the thunderclouds gathering and I was, er, resting on a rocky peak people call Middle Bald Mountain, when I heard the thunder rumbling in the distance, so I thought 'Cindy, you'd better get moving' ... you see I didn't want to get caught in the storm. But I was too late, I guess. The downpour must have lasted for about an hour, so I sheltered under some trees. But eventually the sun came out, so I came out from under the trees to dry off a little bit.

P And what happened then?

C Well, I'd just put my backpack on – it has a metal frame by the way! – when the whole world exploded, and I felt an electrical charge surging through my body. It was literally a 'bolt out of the blue'! But I realized that I was still alive and had to get help but I couldn't move my legs, so I had to crawl! It sure was heavy going, but after about an hour I reached a wet, muddy kind of dirt track.

P And it was there that you were rescued by Rod and Mark, right?

C Uh huh.

R Yeah, that's right. We happened to be driving back home in the pick up, 'cause we have a timber business, and we'd been cruising around searching for a particular kind of wood in the area …

C I don't think they believed my story at first!

M We sure didn't. We saw this weird looking object – seemed to be kind of sprawling across the road, not moving, but it looked kind of human. Anyway, we jumped out of the truck to get a closer look and we found Cindy here. We got her to the nearest hospital, and, er, in a few days she was on her feet again.

C Yeah, thanks to these guys, but I've still got the scars on my back, … on my hips and on my foot too, and I'm scared to death of lightning now, but I learned that I'm a lot tougher than I thought. I'm not really a quitter and I'm determined … really determined to go on hiking.

R Yeah, but not in electric storms, huh?

C I can't promise you guys that, I'm afraid!

C **Sound discrimination.** If students have difficulty reading the words refer them to a dictionary which gives the phonetic sounds of the words, eg the *Advanced Learner's Dictionary* or the *Concise Oxford Dictionary*.

K **1** B **2** B **3** A **4** B **5** A **6** A **7** A **8** B **9** B **10** A **11** A **12** A **13** B **14** A **15** A **16** B

● *vocabulary p38*

Expressions.

Ask students to look at the picture on page 38 and match it with one of the expressions.

K
1. bright and breezy
2. the calm before the storm
3. it's an ill wind that blows nobody any good
4. makes heavy weather of doing his homework
5. under the weather
6. get wind of it
7. under a cloud
8. a storm in a teacup

● *speaking p38*

Coping in a crisis. Refer students to the exam tip under *speaking* before doing the simulation.

Optional activity
Ask students to tell the class about their own personal experience of coping in a genuine crisis. Allow students two to three minutes to describe what happened and what they did.

WRITING

Task-based Composition

● *introduction p39*

The task-based composition in this unit presents more background information than would normally appear in the exam. The aim of this is to allow them to concentrate on style rather than on content, and they are presented with a model which they can imitate for the purposes of their own composition.

Allow students to read through the introduction. Ask them what they would find easy or difficult about this kind of composition.

Give examples of the kind of questions that have come up in past papers. These include

– a letter of application for a job based on an advertisement
– two statements of opinion by separate parties in an industrial dispute, based on some short notes
– a letter to an estate agent
– sets of instructions
– explanation of the advantages of a burglar alarm system
– a newspaper report based on a number of short faxes.

● *sample composition p39*

A Allow students to read through the newspaper report, and explain any unknown words. The standard of vocabulary, and particularly the journalistic language, is higher than would be expected at Proficiency, but the underlying structure is something that examiners would expect.

B **Language focus.**

K **1** Possible paragraph headings
Introduction.
Details of the progress of the storm.
Local details, reactions and eye witness reports.
Criticism of the authorities.
Action being taken.

2 The main progression is indicated by the following words and phrases: *Yesterday evening*, *just after eleven*, *by 2 a.m.*, *Later*, *eventually*, *in the early hours of the morning*.

3 There are eight examples: *has been hit*, *was flattened*, *were littered*, *had been blown off*, *was woken*, *has been raised*, *had been forecast*, *had been caused*.

4 There are a large number of verbs and phrases that describe the wind, including: *buffeted*, *to pick up*, *storm force winds*, *hit*, *increased in violence*, *reached hurricane force*, *lashing*, *gusts*, *flattened*, *blast*. Point out to students that this variation in vocabulary is something they should attempt in their own work.

5 The writer's viewpoint is not made clear; however, the personal opinions of other people are mentioned.

● *writing task p40*

The photograph at the bottom of page 40 will help the students to understand the situation before they start to do the task. This can be set as homework, but the information needed for the composition may be discussed in class. It is important to note that students would probably not get so much information in the exam.

Emphasize to students that they should attempt to follow the same paragraph model as the sample composition, as this will help them considerably in producing an authentic-sounding piece of work.

OVERVIEW 3

● *vocabulary p41*

K **1** C **2** D **3** C **4** B **5** D **6** B **7** D **8** D **9** B **10** C

● *transformations p41*

K
1. We have had the whole of the first floor decorated.
2. If I had been in such a situation, it is difficult to know / I don't know what I would have done.
3. I asked Cindy (to tell me) what she had actually been doing when the lightning struck.
4. The children are under a cloud because of their bad behaviour.
5. I've never had my car break down on a motorway before.
6. She has no intention of giving up her hobby.
7. The hurricane which devastated the area was the result of / caused by freak weather conditions.
8. Considerable concern has been caused by / expressed at the failure of the authorities to provide adequate warning.
9. The first priority for the council is the restoration of communications and essential services.
10. I've had all my crops completely wiped out by the storm.

● *blank-filling p42*

K
1. only had it
2. had been in that
3. did him no / did not (seem to) do him any
4. good / use grumbling / complaining about
5. people parking
6. without
7. frightened / scared to
8. rumbling
9. under the
10. afford to have them

● *rewriting p42*

K
1. His outrageous conduct did great harm to the regiment's reputation.
2. You could hardly make out the ships through the thick fog.
3. It was raining cats and dogs.
4. In all probability a treaty will be signed soon.
5. Defence alliances are as old as the hills.
6. Everyone shares the same opinion regarding ...
7. The disagreement is a storm in a teacup.
8. The world press got wind of the story from a government official.
9. They were loath to come to our aid.
10. Organic vegetables are said to do wonders for your / one's health.

UNIT 4

STRANGER THAN FICTION

READING

Suspension of Belief

The section title will be discussed in an optional activity following the multiple-choice questions.

● *talking points p43*

The aim of this exercise is to look at a number of important vocabulary items which are relevant to the topic, as well as to lead into the theme. Consequently the vocabulary level of the sentences for discussion is high.

Pre-teach some of the vocabulary with the class. Where possible, ask students to explain the meanings of the more difficult words and phrases, and help them if they are unable to do so. The vocabulary that may need to be highlighted is as follows.

Notes

a figment of the imagination – an image or idea that only exists in the imagination

Compare this with *an optical illusion* (a visual image which is interpreted wrongly by the brain) and *a mirage* (an optical illusion often seen in the desert, which is a reflection caused by light and heat).

déjà vu – the feeling that one has been in exactly the same place and situation before; from French, literally meaning 'already seen'

reincarnation – the belief that after death, the spirit returns and lives again in another body

clairvoyant – a person who can see things in their mind that are happening elsewhere or at another time

charlatan – an impostor who pretends to have important knowledge, but does not

medium – a person who is able to communicate with the spirit world

séance – a meeting of a small group of people attempting to contact the spirit world

pre-determined – in a pre-determined world, the future has already been fixed (possibly by God or fate); mechanistic worlds are pre-determined

mechanistic – a mechanistic world is one like a machine, where atoms collide with each other in predictable patterns

prediction – a statement describing what will happen in the future; ask how this differs from the more limited word *forecast*, which is usually a partly scientific statement about what will happen to the weather or economic trends

sceptical – inclined to doubt claims, given to questioning the truth of supposed facts

telepathy – communication from one mind to another, but not through known senses

dabble – literally means to splash about in water, but here it means to engage in a pursuit or hobby in an amateur fashion

occult – the supernatural, mystical or magical

Ask the students to complete the task. Act, if necessary, as a neutral mediator and make students explain and justify their opinions.

● *reading p43*

A Ask students if they know anything about Harry Houdini, then ask them to read the first paragraph and answer the questions below. Refer them to the picture on the left of page 43 which shows him padlocked in a milk churn (line 13). If the group is small enough, ask each student to choose one of Houdini's feats and say how he might have accomplished it. This will provide motivation for reading the rest of the text, as students will want to see if their predictions were right.

Optional activity

Write the following words and phrases on the board, then ask students to read through the passage to find a word or phrase that means the same.

		ANSWERS
1	a garment for restricting arm movements	strait-jacket
2	a large metal container for holding milk	churn
3	a small burrowing animal with velvety fur	mole
4	acceptable and in order	kosher
5	a perfect model	paragon
6	achievements	feats
7	quoted	cited
8	making smaller	contracting
9	manual skilfulness	dexterity
10	a saw for cutting metal	hacksaw
11	outer ring	rim
12	unorthodox opinion	heresy

B Multiple-choice questions.

K **1** C **2** A **3** D **4** B **5** C **6** B

Optional activity

Now that students have read the passage, ask them to discuss the implications of the title of this section.

Suggested answer

The title simply means 'don't believe what you see', with a pun on the word *suspension*, as many of Houdini's tricks involved being suspended in mid-air (refer students back to the central picture on page 43). There is also an ironic reference to the literary term 'suspension of disbelief'.

● *language focus p45*

Could, was able to, managed to. Explain that these three verbs are similar in meaning but there are some differences. *Could* is a full modal verb and has a general use (see the next section); *was able to* means 'had the ability or opportunity to' and may imply success; *managed to* means 'tried and succeeded'. One main difference is that *was able to* can be used with involuntary actions, whereas *managed to* cannot.

Sentences **1–10** show the following.

K
1. Both *could* and *was able to* can be used to talk about general ability in the past.
2. It is not possible to use *could* to refer to a single voluntary action which took place; however, if the sentence had been in the negative, *couldn't* would have been possible (eg *They once hung him upside down but he couldn't break free in time.*)
3. Both *could* and *was able to* can refer to involuntary actions (eg the verbs of the senses).
4. There is no present perfect form for *could*.
5. *could* cannot follow another modal.
6. *managed to* is not used for general ability.
7. *managed to* can be used for a specific voluntary action; *could* is again not possible, because the sentence refers to one occasion only.
8. *managed to* is not used for an involuntary action (eg verbs of the senses).
9. *manage to* is an infinitive form.
10. *managed to* can be used in perfect forms.

Write the following table on the board and ask students to help you complete it by examining sentences **1–10**.

	could	be able to	managed to
General ability (past)	✓	✓	✗
Positive voluntary action	*✗	✓	✓
Involuntary action	✓	✓	✗
Perfect forms	✗	✓	✓
Infinitive forms	✗	✓	✓

* This can only be used with specific voluntary actions in the negative, eg *I couldn't get into the house because it was locked.*

● *vocabulary p45*

A **Expressions.** The exercise picks up the use of *tie* in the text and extends it.

K **1** c **2** d **3** b **4** e **5** a

B

K
1. tying up
2. being tied down
3. got tied up
4. to tie in with
5. is tied up

STRUCTURE

The Camera Never Lies

Ask students if they believe the cliché *The camera never lies* is valid. Do they know of any famous photographs that have been tampered with?

● *cloze development p46*

Before doing the cloze, briefly discuss the exam tip with students.

Write *Titanic* on the board and brainstorm students' associations with the word. Ask them to skim read the cloze passage to see if their associations were accurate.

K
1. similarities
2. later
3. had
4. crew
5. lacked
6. number (not amount)
7. on
8. matter
9. was
10. place
11. great / full / top
12. sails
13. were
14. survived
15. down
16. but
17. until
18. damaged
19. having
20. Out

The information in the passage is true. Invite students to comment on the accuracy of this premonition and to say how many of the premonitions mentioned came true.

1. The names of the ships were almost identical – *Titan* and *Titanic*.
2. Both ships were the largest ever built.
3. Both had the very latest equipment.
4. Neither had a sufficient number of lifeboats.
5. Both were believed to be unsinkable.
6. Both ships sank in April.
7. Both ships hit an iceberg
8. Both disasters resulted in a large loss of life.

● *discussion p46*

A PAIR WORK Ask students to examine the photograph on page 46 and answer the questions. The photograph showing the man, who was seen as a bad omen, is genuine, taken in Queenstown harbour on April 11 1912, but the boiler in this funnel had in fact been shut down to allow for maintenance work.

B This part serves to remind students of six common forms of the infinitive. In this exercise the meaning of *might* remains constant whatever infinitive is used. Ask students to classify the infinitives as to whether they are present or perfect, simple or progressive, active or passive. Write the table below on the board and as students complete the transformations, ask them where to place the infinitives on the table.

K
1. be
2. be standing
3. have tampered
4. have been repairing
5. be solved
6. have been superimposed

The finished table should look like this.

Infinitive	Active	Passive
present	be	be solved
present progressive	be standing	
perfect	have tampered	have been superimposed
perfect progressive	have been repairing	

Remind students that although progressive passive forms exist, they are normally avoided.

Refer students back to Unit 2, *Avoiding the progressive aspect*.

must, mustn't and variations p47

Students need to be clear about the various uses of *must*, as they are commonly tested. The sentences explore different ways of expressing obligation and deduction.

A The sentences are as follows.

K **1** c **2** f **3** d **4** a **5** h **6** g **7** b **8** e

As students answer questions 1–6, invite them to suggest other similar sentences of their own.

1 definite positive deduction = 1, 4, 8
2 present or future obligation = 2, 3
3 past obligation not fulfilled = 5, 7
4 past obligation fulfilled = 6
5 Plain infinitive with both active and passive sentences can follow *must* (obligation). (Refer students back to the table)
6 All six forms can follow *must* (deduction). (Refer students to the table)

B **Transformations.** Explain to students that this exercise practises the grammar taught above.

K **1** You must get to the airport on time.
2 There must be some mistake with this bill – it's astronomical.
3 You were supposed to get / have got here over an hour ago – what kept you?
4 You must have been speeding, or the police wouldn't have stopped you.
5 We had to go to church every Sunday when we were at school.
6 You should have come to the party because you'd have loved it.
7 You mustn't tell anyone about our plans.
8 You should have called the doctor at once. (Note that 'You should have . . . ', implies a certain amount of criticism for failing to do something.)

necessity and lack of necessity p48

If necessary remind students of verbs of obligation and necessity in the present.

A ***Need* and *should*.** The use of *needed to* and *didn't need to* should be familiar; the use of *needn't have* and *should have* may require clarification.

Work through the sample sentences with the class. Invite them to comment on the differences in meaning between the sentences before answering the questions in B.

1 *needed to do* is followed by the plain infinitive and implies that there was a need to do something. However it does not indicate whether or not that action was carried out.
OTHER EXAMPLES
I needed to buy some more milk, so I went to the shop.
I needed to buy some more milk, but they had run out.

2 *didn't need to do* implies there was no need to do something. Again, it does not indicate whether or not the action was carried out.
OTHER EXAMPLES
I didn't need to get new tyres, but they had a special offer so I got four.
I didn't need to get new tyres, so I got in the car and drove home.

3 *needn't have done* uses the perfect infinitive and implies that an action has / had already been carried out but it was unnecessary.
OTHER EXAMPLE
I needn't have arranged a loan from the bank because in the end we decided not to move house.

4 *should have done* uses the perfect infinitive and implies that an action has not been carried out despite the necessity to do so.
OTHER EXAMPLE
You're too late to apply for that job – you should have answered by last Sunday.

5 *shouldn't have done* uses the perfect infinitive and implies that an action has already been carried out but that it was wrong to do so.
OTHER EXAMPLE
It's your own fault that you've forgotten the time of the meeting – you shouldn't have lost your diary.

B

K **1** needn't have
2 should have
3 shouldn't have
4 didn't need to
5 needed to

C

K **1** didn't need to take
2 needn't have booked
3 should have booked
4 didn't need to get
5 shouldn't have borrowed
6 needed to get
7 needn't have spent
8 shouldn't have been driving

can, could, may and might p48

A This part concentrates on some of the variations in meaning of these modal verbs. Ask students in pairs to look through the sentences, and to say what each of the sentences expresses. Those which refer to **e** (irritation) and **f** (an unfulfilled possibility) are likely to be the most difficult.

K **1** e – Read out this sentence to the students, using the correct intonation.
2 f and a
3 c
4 b
5 c
6 a
7 e
8 d
9 b
10 d

B Ask students to look through the five openings of sentences on the left. Explain that each of the five openings must be matched up with two endings on the right and run through the example. Allow students to work out all the answers before checking round the class.

K **1** d, h **2** c, i **3** a, g **4** b, e **5** f, j

Ask selected students what the function of the modal verb is in each of the sentences. If students come up with acceptable alternatives to the solutions above, use the opportunity to ask them to justify their choice.

2c *You may see Peter tonight ... as long as you do all your homework first.*
This could be rephrased as: *You have my permission to see Peter tonight.*
Here *may* expresses permission. *Can* would also express the same idea.

2i *You may see Peter tonight ... because he said he'd try and come to the party.*
This could be rephrased as: *There's a chance that you will see Peter tonight.*
Here *may* expresses possibility. *Might* would also express a similar idea.

3a *My car can't be stolen ... because it's impossible to open the door without the right key.*
This could be rephrased as: *Nobody can steal my car.*
Here *can't* expresses (lack of) ability.

3g *My car can't be stolen ... because I bought it from a reputable dealer.*
This could be rephrased as: *I am certain that my car is not a stolen car.*
Here *can't* expresses deduction. *Couldn't* also expresses the same idea, although it would sound more natural with a past infinitive.
The words *be* + past participle often create ambiguity with modal verbs; this is because *be* + past participle can sometimes be a passive infinitive, as in the first example; sometimes the past participle can act as an adjective, as in the second example. The ambiguity is normally cleared up by the context.

4b *You might have written to us ... because we went to a lot of trouble preparing for your visit.*
This could be rephrased as: *We're annoyed that you didn't write to us ...*
Here *might* expresses irritation. *Could* would also express the same idea.

4e *You might have written to us ... but our filing system is in a mess, so I have no record of it.*
This could be rephrased as: *It's possible that you have written to us.*
Here *might* expresses possibility. *Could* and *may* would express a similar idea.

5f *He could have caught an early train ... so he might be here in half an hour or so.*
This could be rephrased as: *There's a chance that he has caught an early train.*
Here *could* expresses possibility / speculation. *May* and *might* would express the same idea.

5j *He could have caught an early train ... but he decided to spend the night in London instead.*
This could be rephrased as: *He had the opportunity (which he didn't take) to catch an early train.*
Here *could* expresses unfulfilled opportunity.

C **Discussion.** GROUP WORK Ask students to suggest possible explanations for the various photographs on page 49. Concentrate on their use of modal verbs of deduction, and correct them where necessary. Allow them also to use adverbs freely, for example *Maybe it's a spotlight*, as these forms are also perfectly acceptable. The pictures are of the following:

1 a ghost **2** corn circles **3** an angel **4** a UFO

SUMMARY SKILLS

Good and Evil

● *talking points p50*

A

K The picture on page 50 is *The Garden of Delights* by Hieronymus Bosch (c. 1450–1516). Good and evil are symbolized through the animals, birds and fruits, which were all well-known medieval images.

B GROUP WORK Allow four to five minutes for this activity, then after students have compared with another group, put a master list on the board to see how all the students' lists compared.

● *summary 1 p50*

Notes

The Inquisition was a tribunal organized by the Roman Catholic Church and was made responsible for the suppression of heresy. It was active from the 15th to the 18th century, and executed people it found guilty.

neurological – connected with the scientific study of the nerve systems

exorcism – the expulsion of an evil spirit by using a holy name

pharmacology – the science of the action of drugs on the body

K Suggested answers for paragraph descriptions

1 Descriptions of three cases of abnormal behaviour.
2 The temptation to attribute these types of behaviour to the forces of good or evil.
3 A more logical explanation of the first type of neurological disease, Tourette's syndrome.
4 A more logical explanation of the second disorder, epilepsy.

● *comprehension* p50

A

1 devout
2 horror
3 jerk and twitch
4 attributed to
5 self-injurious
6 paranormal
7 racial and ethnic epithets
8 monograph (a separate treatise on a single subject)
9 infamous
10 gross misdiagnoses
11 At the other end of the spectrum
12 impending terror and revulsion

B Suggested explanations
Point out to students that single-word answers are not sufficient.

1 (there is) really no light there at all
2 some hostile power from elsewhere / not of this world
3 sacred stimulation / stimulation coming from God
4 the officials of the Inquisition (see background notes), whose job it was to decide whether a person was a heretic or not. *Inquisition* is a proper noun, hence the capital letter.
5 did not respond to outside provocations, or happenings. – *i* is the Latin plural of – *us*.
6 the sufferer experiences an atmosphere of fear and hatred just before the seizure happens.

C **Reference devices.** Below are some of the reference devices used in the passage. *Do* / *did* do not occur here but are the most familiar to the students.

1 *In all these cases …* (line 19), *… to control them.* (line 23)
2 *This being the case …* (line 23)
3 *This would be especially likely …* (line 28)
4 *… in the first two cases …* (line 29)
5 *In the final case …* (line 33)
6 *… these three diseases …* (line 44)
7 *… a rare disease …* (line 48), *its strange symptoms* (line 51), *reported in that volume* (line 60)
8 *… , these are similar …* (line 70)
9 *Such gross misdiagnoses …* (line 76)
10 *… their disorder …* (line 82)
11 *… the process.* (line 83)
12 *The second case described above …* (line 88)
13 *At one end of the scale …* (line 93)
14 *At the other end of the spectrum …* (line 98)
15 *… , as in the case described.* (line 100)
16 *… , immediately following this, …* (line 105)
17 *… an easy one …* (line 110)

● *summary 2* p51

A Ask students to answer the questions about the first case orally before reading the summary in their books. Then they should compare their answers with what is in the summary.

B
Suggested summary
The second case illustrates a person who first experiences a feeling of extreme fear, then seems to be knocked over with some force. The individual then makes violent body movements, which often result in serious injury or death. This lack of body control might suggest that this is the work of the devil. In fact, the person is probably suffering from a neurological disease called epilepsy, whose symptoms can manifest themselves in many different ways. (approx. 70 words)

In the third case the individual seems to be overwhelmed by an intensely bright light, which is not there at all. The light can have various forms and patterns. This behaviour could easily be ascribed to some inexplicable but external god-like power trying to communicate with the individual. In fact the symptoms indicate that the person is suffering from a neurological disease (unnamed in the article). (approx. 60 words)

Optional summary
Students could write a summary of 80–100 words on the research carried out into Tourette's syndrome, and the conclusions reached.

Points to include

– Beyerstein – relationship of the three diseases – Friedhoff and Chase – symptoms, causes and treatment of Tourette's syndrome – Shapiro and Shapiro – connections with the Inquisition – attempts at exorcism – neurochemical causes – not demonic possession.

LISTENING AND SPEAKING

The Magic Kingdom

● *talking points* p52

The aim of this part is to discuss myths, legends and folk tales and to stimulate students' imaginations by reminding them of aspects of their childhood they may have forgotten.

A Remind students of the cliché *The camera never lies.* The photograph at the top of page 52 was believed to be genuine for many years, but modern analysis has revealed that it is a fake. You may invite students to speculate as to why someone would want to do this.

B The first question is designed to get the students to talk about mythical creatures in precise terms. Questions **2** and **3** broaden the discussion as students are invited to discuss the value of these folk tales in terms of the psychological insights they offer, and their role in education. In a multi-national class it may be interesting to ask which fairy stories they are familiar with. There may be a shared tradition of the more common stories such as *Cinderella* or *Snow White*, which are well known in Europe.

● *listening 1 p52*

A The interview is with an authority on fairies; his general attitude is rather unusual.

K **1** A **2** C **3** D **4** A **5** D **6** B

Tapescript

(**I** = Interviewer, **P** = Peter)

I … And *Giants and Dwarves* will be available in book shops at the end of this month. And now I'd like to welcome Peter Wilson, who has just written a book on fairies.

P Good morning.

I The first thing I suppose I ought to ask you is well, why a book on fairies?

P Well, a great deal of the motivation stemmed from my own personal experiences of the fairy kingdom and my own sightings …

I Sightings?

P Yes, naturally, and initially I was curious to find out more … but the more I looked into it, the more confused and confusing the picture seemed to be …

I Why was that?

P Er, because there is a mass of sentimental fiction, such as, you know, the 'Once upon a time' syndrome with the inevitable happy endings, and delightful as they are, they do not properly represent the fairy kingdom …

I In what way are these, I suppose you would call them fairy stories, how are they wrong?

P Because the fairy represents power. Magical power. And because it is incomprehensible to humans, it is also inimical. Now we all accept that the fairy kingdom is more or less dependent on humans, but the danger is that we think that they must be like us as well, but of course they aren't. They are alien creatures, and their values and ethics are far removed from ours.They don't think like us, and perhaps more importantly they don't feel like us … and in fact that is precisely the core of much of their envy of mortals …

I So are fairies in general not very well disposed towards people?

P I don't mean to be rude, but one of the problems of talking to people who don't know about fairies, sorry, but people like yourself …

I No, no, no, please, I don't mind at all.

P It's that you suffer from a lot of misconceptions. For a start, people tend to bundle all sorts of fairies together, but in fact there are all sorts of different kinds … I mean there are Pixies, Brownies, Kelpies, water fairies, Boggarts, to name but a few, and they are about as different as you could imagine …

I I see … but are there basically good fairies and bad ones?

P Well again, you are running the risk of being a little too anthropomorphic again … but to get back to your point … take goblins, for example. Now generally they are immensely ugly creatures, and are intensely malicious and like nothing better than to lure people to their doom with forbidden fairy fruit … and yet the Knockers, which are the Goblins that live in the mines in Devon and Cornwall are, generally speaking, fairly favourably disposed towards miners and usually lead them to the richer seams of tin. And they're fine, as long as you leave them some food, but even they can be intensely capricious.

I So it's best to treat them with a certain amount of respect.

P Yes, certainly. They're nearly all capable of being mischievous and spiteful, and Brownies for example, who are very helpful, can quite easily turn into a quite different kind of fairy, such as a churlish and troublesome Boggart when they have been teased or are angry, and their revenge can be terrible …

I And how would you know if you had angered a fairy?

P Well, the evidence is all around you … rheumatism and cramp, for example, have long been thought to be caused by being pinched by fairy fingers, and something like infantile paralysis is, of course, due to the baby in reality being a changeling.

I A changeling?

P Yes, there are times when fairies steal human babies, for various reasons, but they replace it with a piece of wood or something like that, and under a fairy spell it looks exactly like the human baby that has been stolen … but these changelings tend to be very sickly, and generally don't live long.

I I see … there is one thing I was wondering though … where is one likely to meet fairies … at the bottom of the garden?

P No, the difficulty with mooning about in misty woods, or communing with nature, is that it isn't likely to bring about anything very much other than a general sense of damp … they live in rivers and trees, and of course in ancient earthworks and hills, though it is extremely inadvisable to go disturbing them, because there's nothing that annoys them more than having curious humans blundering about in their domains like ill-mannered tourists, and there's always a chance that one of them might turn nasty. The fact is that fairies will either accept you and let you see them or they won't, and there's not much that can be done about it.

I Well, thank you very much for coming in to talk to us today … it's been quite an eye opener … and as I said earlier, Peter Wilson's book, *Fairies*, is now available in all good bookshops.

P Thank you.

B **Listening and note-taking.** Ask students to read through the text, then listen to the tape again and fill in the blanks. It is important for students to listen again, as the missing words are all adjectives. The correct answers depend on the information on the tape.

Check that students are familiar with the vocabulary items listed under **Notes**, and ask them to explain their meanings where you can.

Notes

alien – strange, not familiar, unknown
capricious – wilful, changeable, guided by whim
churlish – displaying bad manners, not well-bred
favourably disposed – benevolent, behaving kindly towards
inimical – harmful, hostile
magical – wonderful, something that cannot be explained
malicious – full of ill will, wanting to harm
mischievous – naughty
spiteful – vindictive, eager to hurt or annoy
troublesome – annoying

K
1 magical
2 inimical
3 alien
4 malicious
5 favourably disposed
6 capricious
7 mischievous
8 spiteful
9 churlish
10 troublesome

● *listening 2 p53*

A Visions of the future. Introduce the subject very briefly by asking whether the students have heard of Nostradamus. If they have not, tell them that he lived during the Middle Ages, and made a number of prophecies that some people believe have come true.

K **1** T **2** T **3** F **4** F **5** T **6** F **7** T **8** F **9** T **10** T

Tapescript
(**P** = Presenter, **N** = Nostradamus)

P One of the names most commonly associated in the collective consciousness with augury and foreknowledge is that of Nostradamus, although the facts about this man and his prophecies are less widely known. Born in Provence in 1503, the Frenchman Michel de Nostredame studied medicine at Montpellier University and began a lifetime of seemingly dedicated caring for the sick. He particularly cared for the victims of the Black Death, a virulent plague that had reached epidemic proportions. After the death of his first wife and her two children, ironically victims of the disease, he wandered widely, at one period having to evade the infamous Inquisition because of some injudicious remarks he had made concerning a statue. Eventually he remarried, this time to a rich widow, and settled down in Salon.

It was there that he began to write almanacs and his book of prophecies. Each prophecy is written in the form of a four line verse or 'quatrain' and they are given in groups of 100 called 'centuries', although they are not in chronological order. He intended to write 100 quatrains, but the seventh century is not complete, so there are 942 in all.

The first two quatrains are not prophecies but describe the divining technique. Nostradamus used a method recorded by Imblichus, a fourth century Neoplatonist, details of which had been republished in a book in 1547. A bowl of water was placed on a brass tripod, and the seer stared into the water until images of the future appeared. The prophecies became very popular all over Europe and Nostradamus was given a royal audience with Catherine de Medici on three occasions. After his death in 1556, his fame continued to spread.

There are a number of his quatrains which appear to refer to historical episodes with an uncanny accuracy. The following quatrain is believed to be about the rise of Hitler and the Second World War, and the prophecy even predicts the name almost exactly:

N Beasts ferocious with hunger will swim across rivers
The greater part of the region will be against Hister
The great one will cause it to be dragged in an iron cage
When the German child will observe nothing.

P In another quatrain he is believed to have predicted the rise of the emperor Napoleon, who was born in Corsica:

N An Emperor will be born near Italy
One who will cost his Empire at high price
They will say that from the sort of people who surround him
He is to be found less prince than butcher.

P Nostradamus is also credited with foreseeing the fighter aircraft and the atomic bomb; one of the quatrains has also been interpreted as predicting a nuclear war, with its origins in the Middle East, at around the end of the millennium.

Sceptics would argue that the quatrains are vague and are open to many different interpretations. They would suggest, too, that almost any historical event could be made to fit one of the 940 randomly ordered prophecies, and also that there were bound to be some apparently spectacular predictions with such a large base. But whatever the millennium brings, Nostradamus and his apocalyptic visions are certain to remain a subject of fascination and controversy for the foreseeable future.

Optional activity

Copy the left hand column of definitions below onto the board. Tell students to listen to the tape again. Ask them to find a word for each definition as they listen. Point out that the answers are in the order in which they appear on the tape.

		ANSWERS
1	foretelling the future by omens	augury
2	predictions	prophecies
3	poisonous and malignant	virulent
4	notorious	infamous
5	unwise, ill-judged	injudicious
6	calendars with astronomical data	almanacs
7	ordered according to time	chronological
8	person who sees visions	seer
9	formal meeting	audience
10	unnerving	uncanny
11	period of 1000 years	millennium
12	imprecise	vague

B Discussion. Questions **1** and **2** allow students to react to the passage they have heard.

The quotations in Question **3** are said to predict the atomic bomb (the sun at night) and the jet fighter.

Questions **4** and **5** relate to students' personal experiences of premonitions and predictions. With an entirely sceptical class, you could ask them whether they would wish to know their future if a new, reliable and scientific method was developed that could do this.

● *speaking p54*

Possibility and probability. Allow adequate time for this activity, as this area of language is commonly tested in the examination. None of the words or phrases should cause students difficulty. It is important, however, to stress that accuracy is essential, and that they need to be clear about the different ways of talking about possibility and probability.

Look through the model sentences and point out that the same sentence can be rephrased using the patterns in **A–E**.

Give students an example of what they are to do in the pairwork exercise. For example, read out the first sentence, *It's a foregone conclusion that you're going to pass your exam.* Ask students how they would say it using Pattern B, or Pattern D, etc.

Ask students to carry on the activity in pairs or small groups, rephrasing the sentences orally. Monitor and correct where necessary.

Optional activity
Role play: Ask students to work in pairs. One student could be a fortune-teller (with a crystal ball, or tarot cards, or tea-leaves, etc), the other student is a customer. The fortune-teller foretells events in the other student's life, using the patterns from A to E. Once they have finished, the roles can be reversed.

WRITING

Telling a Story

● *introduction p54*

Point out that in this kind of question in the exam the composition title will often be a sentence or part of a sentence that they must incorporate unchanged into their narrative. The sentence will have to occur either at the beginning or at the end of a story.

Ask students to look at the title and say what the most important feature is.

ANSWER The question asks for a 'fairy' story.

Normally the question will not be so specific and will simply say 'story'; however, if the question asks for a story and they write a dialogue, they will lose substantial marks.

● *planning and writing p54*

The following notes refer to the five stages in the Student's Book.

Stage 1 Allow students to read through the information. After they have read the basic plot refer them to the exam tip.

Stage 2

1 You may ask students to work out some answers to these questions and invite comments.
2 They can then write five questions of their own based on the rest of the plot in Stage 1, and compare these with a partner. Ask selected students for examples of what they have noted down.
3 Let students read through the words and images. Invite further suggestions.

Stage 3 Ask students to read the suggested paragraph structure. The aim is to encourage them to jot down ideas when they are planning and then assign them to paragraphs.

Remind them of the words and images in Stage 2, and ask them to suggest which paragraphs they would appear in.

They can read the story to see if they were correct. The final version is not definitive, as many words and images could have appeared elsewhere.

Stage 4 Allow students to read through the composition. Invite comments as to their reactions to it.

Stage 5 Ask students not to look at the story and to correct the passage. They can check their corrections by looking back at paragraphs 3 and 4. The errors are: *entry, who's, were rising, was cleared, did he go, were used to, face menacing, sat, from, by.*

● *focus on narrative tenses p56*

The importance of the correct use of tenses cannot be stressed enough; students who are not able to do this properly will require additional remedial exercises. See *Practical English Usage* by M. Swan or *A Practical English Grammar* by Thomson and Martinet.

1 the simple past; the five other verbs that carry the action forward are *saw, left, stood, went, sat.*

2 the simple past; the other example is: *rose*. The verbs are in the simple past because they are describing permanent features, and are not describing an activity of any kind. Compare:

The path led to the cave.
The guide who was leading the group along the path slipped and fell.

The sides rose to a ceiling high above his head.
Smoke was rising from a fire in the centre of the cave.

3 past progressive (or past continuous). Other examples are: *was making*, *were racing*, *was throwing*.
4 past perfect. The other example is: *had been cleared*.

● *writing task p56*

Set the task as a writing activity in class or as homework. Remind students to pay particular attention to the use of tenses when they check their work.

OVERVIEW 4

● *vocabulary p57*

K **1** D **2** A **3** C **4** A **5** C **6** D **7** A **8** A
9 A **10** D

● *blank-filling p57*

K
1 must have
2 impossible to
3 haven't been able to get / haven't managed to get
4 managed to / were able to
5 supposed to
6 needn't have
7 didn't need to / didn't have to
8 have let me
9 can't have
10 chances are

● *rewriting p58*

K
1 He was bound to fail his exams.
It was inevitable that he would fail his exams.
2 He must have missed the eleven o'clock train.
He can't possibly have caught the eleven o'clock train.
3 You might have phoned me to say you'd be late.
Why on earth didn't you phone me to say you'd be late?
4 I doubt (very much) whether she will agree to giving you a pay rise.
There's little likelihood of her giving / that she will give you a pay rise.
5 Davis is / seems certain to win the gold medal.
There's no doubt that Davis will win the gold medal.
6 The only thing the house lacks is a large garden.
The house has got everything apart from a large garden.
7 I'm afraid to say that we've used up all the oil.
I'm afraid to say that we've run out of oil.
8 The film bears some resemblance to Shakespeare's Hamlet.
The film has much in common with Shakespeare's Hamlet.
9 The chances are that the project will be finished on Thursday.
The project shouldn't take longer than Thursday to finish.
10 The Embassy said I didn't need to get a visa.
The Embassy said a visa wasn't required.

UNIT 5

IT BROADENS THE MIND

READING

Traveller or Tourist?

● *talking points p59*

Ask students to look at the captions on page 59.

K **Explanations**
Turin – touring (Europe)
Genoa – do you know (a better way to travel)
Pisa – piece of (cake) (a very easy task to do successfully)
Cannes – can do (we / you can do it)
Rome – roam (wander)
V(ery) nice – Venice
Votre Dame – French, meaning 'your wife / lady friend' (the reference is to 'Notre Dame' or 'Our Lady', the cathedral in Paris)
Paris – Pa (father) is, Ma (mother)

● *reading p59*

A After students have decided on a suitable title for the text, write their suggestions on the board and ask the class to vote for the one they think is best.

After they have chosen, refer them to the key on page 215.

> **Notes**
> *a pith helmet* (line 6) – a light-weight sun helmet made from the dried lining of, eg an Indian swamp plant
> *pensión* (line 33) – a Spanish word for a small, family run hotel or boarding house
> *council estates* (line 50) – low cost housing concentrated in areas provided by the local council
> *The Salvation Army* (line 74) – Founded in 1865, this is a Christian 'army' providing (amongst many other things) low cost food and lodgings all over the world for poor people.

B

K **b** disparaging (bringing discredit on)

C Multiple-choice questions.

K 1 B **2** A **3** D **4** C **5** A **6** B

● *vocabulary p60*

A Unfavourable adjectives. Ask students to guess the meaning of each word from its context in the passage, before going on to sentences **1–7**.

K 1 f **2** d **3** b **4** e **5** a **6** c **7** g

B Negative prefixes. Tell students that *ignorant* cannot be used without the negative prefix.

K discomfort uncomfortable ignoble uninteresting misunderstanding unprovoking

C Suffixes.

K useful / less careful / less worthless pointless hopeful / less youthful motionless stressful resentful meaningful / less

D Expressions.

K *run off with* – steal and run away with
look down on – feel superior to
caught up in – involved in (often unwillingly)
run – d, e, g; look – c, f, h, i; catch / be caught – b, i

1 catch someone's eye
2 run for it
3 look on the bright side
4 look a gift horse in the mouth
5 run out of
6 catch someone red-handed
7 look down your nose at
8 run short of
9 run a business
10 look like a drowned rat

> **Optional activity**
> Ask students to select one idiom and either draw it, or write a sentence using it.

STRUCTURE

The Intrepid Explorer

Discuss the meaning of the title (*intrepid* – fearless), and ask students to predict what this section might be about. Ask students to give some examples of intrepid explorers.

● *talking points p61*

Ask students to look at the photographs on page 61.

K **1** cable-car **2** bicycle-rickshaw **3** sandmobile **4** reindeer sleigh **5** monorail **6** paraglider

Ask students if they can think of other unusual forms of getting around.

cloze development p62

Remind students to read the cloze through once, before starting the exercise. Explain that this is a true story written by the nephew of August Courtauld.

K
1 was
2 the
3 hidden / buried / covered
4 out
5 last
6 get
7 followed
8 over
9 saw / described
10 after
11 had
12 member
13 possibility / establishment / setting-up / feasibility
14 see / establish
15 more
16 an
17 of
18 appearance / air
19 in
20 use

vocabulary p62

A Shades of meaning.

K Suggested answers

Negative	Neutral	Positive
running out	volunteered	youthful
deceptive	appearance	volunteered
ordeal	significantly	adventure
incarceration	alone	clubbable
alone	contrast	
appalling	feasibility	
confused		

Encourage students to comment on the words which they might place in more than one column, eg *volunteered, alone.*

B Describing attitude.

K Suggested answers

resigned (line 7 – *But August never saw / described it as an ordeal, never said he wished he hadn't gone*)

laconic (of speech or writing, brief, concise) (line 4 – *had just decided that he would have to walk back on 1 June if he could get out)*

courageous (line 13 – *there was a clubbable spirit of youthful adventure among them*)

practical (line 3 – *he was smoking tea-leaves in his pipe*)

Ask students to explain why the other adjectives do not describe August's attitude and find references to the text to justify their answers.

rewriting p62

K
1 Initially they had supplies to spare / spare supplies / supplies left over / surplus supplies.
2 After such an experience nowadays, Uncle August would have been forced to undergo counselling / to submit to counselling / to go through counselling.
3 He was looking forward to / excited at the thought of seeing his fiancée again.
(Also: He couldn't wait to see his fiancée again.)
4 Their marriage / wedding took place a year later.
They celebrated their wedding / marriage a year later.
They became man and wife a year later.
5 The reporter asked him to express his feelings about his experience.
The reporter asked him how his experience had affected him / for his reaction to his experience.
6 He returned from the treacherous Antarctic expedition hale and hearty / safe and sound / alive and kicking.

wishes and regrets p63

K **A** It means that August never said he regretted going on the expedition.

1 **a** Both sentences express a regret for something which happened in the past and there is no difference in meaning. *Regret* followed by *(not)-ing* is a simpler and more often used structure than *regret* followed by *(not) having (done).* Popular use has moved away from *having done* because the sequence of events is unambiguous in *(not)-ing*. In addition the future time reference with *regret / remember*, etc. is shown by the infinitive, not the gerund.

b *regret* with *to* is used with the infinitive to express regret for something we are about to say.

2 **a** *I wish I could sing better.*
I wish I had a car.
We wish we were living …
All these sentences imply that none of these things are true at the moment, eg the speaker cannot sing, does not have a car, and is not living in the countryside.

b *I wish to know exactly what happened.*
The infinitive form follows when *wish* introduces a request.

c The tone is neutral; the facts are contrary to the speaker's wishes.

3 *I wish he wouldn't / didn't smoke cigars in the house.*
See **2c** above for explanation of *didn't smoke. I wish he wouldn't smoke* expresses either concern for him, ie *he's my husband and I know how harmful smoking is*, **or** concern for myself / irritation, ie *it's disgusting, what about my health?*

I wish they would tell me what's worrying them.
Would is used when people / other things might change.
Remind students that we never say *I wish I wouldn't* or *We wish we wouldn't.*
It is more usual to say *I / We wish I / we could* when referring to the first person singular or plural.

4 *I wish we hadn't told him the news. He was very upset.*
The past perfect is needed.

K 5 *If only I didn't have to do so much homework.*
If only I had applied for the job … !
If only he wouldn't / didn't interrupt when I'm speaking …
If only is more emphatic than *wish*. It gains its emphasis from the unvoiced second half of what is effectively a conditional sentence.
eg *I wish I hadn't taken the car (I wouldn't have got stuck in the traffic jam).*
If only I hadn't taken the car (I wouldn't have had an accident).

B

K **1** **a** He regrets saying / having said those terrible things.
b We regret to inform you that your job application has not been successful.
2 **a** I wish I weren't / wasn't a chain smoker.
NB Both *was* and *were* can be used to describe an unreal past. However *were* is used more than *was* to express unreality or doubt, and *was* is used more in conversation than *were*.
b We wish you were teaching next year.
3 **a** I wish it would rain soon; everything's so dry.
b I wish she wouldn't phone me at work.
4 I wish they had let us know they were moving house.
5 They wished they had bought the land.
6 If only he didn't fall asleep / wouldn't fall asleep in the middle of dinner.
7 If only I had taken up his offer of a job.

SUMMARY SKILLS

A Necessary Evil?

● *talking points p64*

Ask students to look at the headlines on page 64. Explain any vocabulary or references students might not know.

Notes
brawl – a noisy quarrel or fight
No room at the inn – According to the story in the Bible, when Mary and Joseph were looking for accommodation in Bethlehem, they had to sleep in a stable, where Jesus was born.
Under cover – protected from the weather by glass or plastic
dreaded – to be feared
theme park – a fun park where all the rides and exhibits relate to one theme

● *comprehension p65*

Refer students to the exam tip before they complete **a–g**.

K **a** Tourism is instrumental in providing jobs.
b To result in traffic jams / blocked roads.
c Devoted to the preservation of the countryside.
d Boats discharge untreated human waste straight into the lake.
e The constant pressure of thousands of walkers has eroded the paths, leaving them uneven and slippery, which could result in people falling and injuring themselves.
f A bus service depends on the number of fare paying passengers it can attract. In a country area where not many people live, the number of passengers would be very small and the bus service would make a huge financial loss. The company can afford to subsidize the service out of the tourist season because it makes enough money in the high season.
g Wildlife shelters would be out of bounds to tourists who have caused damage to the environment. If tourists were denied access, they could not destroy the vegetation.

● *summary p66*

A

K Suggested headings

Advantages	**Disadvantages**
1 Economic benefits	**2** Traffic congestion
3 Environmental help	**4** Pollution
6 Amenities provided	**5** Erosion of walkways
	7 Threatened habitats

Students' sentences should be a combination of their headings and their own words.

B **Linking additional and contrasting information.** Emphasize to students the importance of linking words, and that summaries must always be clear and concise.

Optional summary
Students could write a summary of 60 to 80 words on how tourists to this area spend their time.

Points to include
Tourists:
1 spend money locally, eg on souvenirs
2 park their cars and go for (long) walks
3 enjoy facilities for watersports and take out boats on the lakes
4 travel around the area by bus
5 picnic and land their boats on the lakesides.

LISTENING AND SPEAKING

Time Traveller

● *talking points p66*

Ask students to look at the pictures on page 66 and to suggest an approximate date for each pair. The pictures are in the same order as the names of the periods listed below. If students prefer, they can choose a time of their own to travel back to.

● *listening 1 p67*

Ask students to read the description and guess the type of information required (ie name, number, date, etc.) before listening.

K
1 800 years
2 Oxford University
3 sights, sounds and smells
4 famous former students
5 a scholar's desk / scholars' desks
6 a major tourist attraction in
7 November to March

Tapescript
(**P** = Presenter)

P Thank you for calling the Oxford Story information line. The Oxford Story is a permanent exhibition which brings to life the 800 year history of Oxford University.
Visitors experience a ride combining sights, sounds – and even smells – from the past. As they slowly travel through the Oxford Story's three levels, they are drawn into a world of academics, eccentrics, scientists, and great writers from the University's history.
A visit, which can last an hour or so, includes a look at student life today, with a roll call of famous former students. The ticket price includes *Scribe's Lane* (a recreated 1950s Oxford street scene), a short audio-visual presentation on student life today, and the 'ride', during which visitors sit at a scholar's desk for 24 minutes as they travel through time.
The Oxford Story is now established as one of the city's major tourist attractions. It is open every day of the year, except for Christmas Day.
Opening times are: April to June 9.30 to 5, July and August 9.30 to 7, September and October 9.30 to 5, November to March 10 to 4.
Enjoy your visit!

● *listening 2 p67*

K **A Note-taking.**
1 graduates who were principals
2 the students
3 at 10am and 5pm / eg meat, bread, butter
4 Latin and some English (with strong regional dialect)
5 in squalor (in the halls or hostels)
6 were extremely poor / strained / ∴ led to violence
7 drinking too much ale, ie beer
8 1355, St Scholastica's Day / ∵ lasted 3 days / argument between students and landlord → students set fire to the town

Tapescript
(**N** = Narrator)
Commentary 1

N Just as a master had the right to teach, so a graduate could establish a hall or hostel for a small number of scholars. Under the supervision of the principal the students shared the expenses of food and heating. Dinner was at 10 a.m. and supper at 5 p.m. Meat, bread, butter and beer were the staples of their diet. Latin was the language of meal-times although English was spoken, often with a strong regional dialect.
Most scholars were extremely poor and supported by donations from their parish and friends. Richer students did exist: graduates who could afford to rent lodgings in private houses and employ poorer students as servants. Such lodgings often amounted to no more than a single chamber in a house. Chaucer describes one such student in his *Canterbury Tales*. The squalor of the halls contrasts with his herb-strewn rooms furnished with his own belongings.

Commentary 2

N The number of teachers and students increased steadily during the 12th century. By 1200 the masters and scholars had formed themselves into associations, like guilds, to protect themselves from traders in the town. Whilst students were scattered about the town, the area around St Mary's Church became the focus for the early university. The Congregation House in the Church was the first meeting place for the masters.
The student population divided into two main groups, the Northerners and the Southerners. Rivalries between them added to the friction that existed between the student body and the townsfolk. Assault was a common crime, exacerbated by the large quantity of ale that was brewed and sold by many Oxford householders. The earliest riot recorded was in 1209 and such events continued for a century and a half until the great riot and massacre of St Scholastica's Day, 1355, which went on for three days. The dispute arose from a disagreement between a landlord and some students in a tavern near Carfax. It resulted in the students setting fire to the town, the townsfolk plundering the students' hostels and sixty-three scholars being killed.

B Group discussion. Tell each group to appoint a 'secretary' to report on the group's decisions.

C Homophones.

K **1** a **2** b **3** b **4** b **5** b **6** b **7** b **8** b **9** a **10** b **11** b **12** a **13** a

Explanations for words on the right

1 *rite* – a ritual or religious act
2 *haul* – (noun) an amount gained or acquired; (verb) pull or drag forcibly
3 *principle* – (noun) fundamental truth or law
4 *bred* – reared or brought up
5 *bier* – a movable frame on which a coffin, or corpse, is placed
6 *tails* – hindmost part of an animal; the other side of the coin (the monarch's head is on the other)
7 *plaice* – a European flatfish
8 *mane* – long hair growing in a line on the neck of a horse or lion
9 *ail* – (archaic) trouble or afflict in mind and body, only used in the third person, eg *What ails you?*
10 *brood* – (noun) the young of an animal produced at one hatching, sometimes the children of a family; (verb) followed by *about*, to worry or ponder over
11 *soled* – had new soles (undersurfaces) put on shoes
12 *grate* – (noun) recess of a fireplace; (verb) reduce to small particles by rubbing on a serrated surface; utter in a harsh tone; have an irritating effect on
13 *daze* – (verb) to stupefy, bewilder; (noun) a state of confusion or bewilderment

Tapescript

1 You have no right to tell me what to do!
2 The fishermen's haul far exceeded their expectations.
3 He sticks to the rules – he's a man of principle.
4 He was born and bred in Scotland.
5 The President's body lay in state on a red bier.
6 Head I win, tails you lose!!
7 The meat's a bit tough here but they do a nice plaice and chips
8 The horse's mane was plaited for the procession through the streets.
9 I enjoy a sandwich and a glass of old-fashioned real ale once in a while.
10 Mrs Jones watched over her brood like a mother hen.
11 I must have these shoes heeled and soled.
12 What's the real difference between big and great?
13 We never see him for days on end.

● *speaking p67*

A time video

Allow four to five minutes for this activity. When students have finished, ask them to tell the rest of the class what they decided to include on their video.

WRITING

The Narrative / Descriptive Composition

● *introduction p68*

Allow students to look through the information. Explain that sometimes a question may ask for a simple description. Past questions have asked for a description of the perfect teacher, or a description of a nurse's day in a busy hospital. Other questions have been rather more complex than this. For example, one question asked students to describe someone who had greatly influenced their life and to examine the reasons for this influence. Students must therefore look carefully at the question to see if it is as straightforward as it appears.

● *sample composition p68*

A Tell students to read the question and the sample composition, but do not comment on it as yet.

B **Grading.** Help students to see that although in terms of language the composition is good, it does not answer the question fully, so would not get an 'A'. The last paragraph about Emma is an afterthought which has just been tacked on at the end, whereas it should have been incorporated in the main body of the composition.

C **Paragraph planning.** Go round the class while students are doing this, asking them for their ideas and helping them where necessary. Allow reasonable time for this activity, as it is important for them to get into the habit of dissecting questions carefully. When they have finished, ask selected students for their ideas.

● *style improvement p69*

A The problem with the sample is that the verb *go* is repeated far too often. As was mentioned in the composition in Unit 3, it is important to vary key items of vocabulary and to avoid repetition.

B

K Suggested answer

We drove down the rough track towards the jungle until we reached the river that cut across the road. We parked the Land Rover in the shade of some rubber trees and got out. We waded across the river, which fortunately was not too deep, and then, as we were in no hurry, walked through the rice fields on the other side towards the forest. The path that led through the trees was entirely overgrown, so we hacked our way along it with considerable difficulty. It was nearly mid-afternoon when we finally emerged from the thick undergrowth and arrived at the bottom of the mountain. Although we were all by now feeling exhausted, we clambered up the steep slope and reached the rendezvous point just as the sun was going down.

● *writing task p69*

The writing task can be set as homework, as there are fairly extensive notes to guide the students. As this is quite a complex composition, you could run through the notes with the students in the class.

When marking the students' compositions, apart from correcting grammatical errors, comment on:

A How well they have managed to combine the two elements of the composition, the journey itself and why it was nostalgic.

B How well they have varied key items of vocabulary; this is a description of a journey, but they should use other verbs of travel and movement apart from *went*.

OVERVIEW 5

● *vocabulary p70*

K **1** B **2** C **3** B **4** B **5** D **6** C **7** C **8** A **9** C **10** B

● *transformations p70*

K
1 If only I had bought that car.
2 I wish I had realized how cheap it was.
3 Contrary to what we had expected (them to be), / our expectations, they were seasoned travellers.
4 I wish I could understand the language when I go to France.
5 It took tremendous strength of character to trudge through malaria-infested swamps.
6 If only I could pass my driving test first time!
7 He couldn't wait to go home again.
8 I wish you weren't leaving so soon.
9 I wish he would phone me.
10 Being able to find a *pensión* in Spain doesn't mean (that) you can understand Spaniards.

● *blank-filling p71*

K
1 look on the
2 caught
3 wouldn't leave
4 hadn't
5 arose
6 to our own
7 if we wanted to
8 were exhausted / tired / weary
9 to inform
10 they were not supported

● *rewriting p71*

K
1 The police caught the thieves red-handed. / The thieves were caught red-handed.
2 We are running out of sugar.
The / Our sugar is running out.
3 His birthday celebrations took place last Saturday.
4 In addition to their money, they lost their passports as well.
They lost their passports, in addition to their luggage.
5 The flight was delayed due to bad weather.
6 They arrived at their destination safe and sound.
7 Travellers look down on those who lead a more sedentary life.
8 If only life weren't so difficult!
9 Someone has run off with my jewellery!
10 I don't care what you do with the money.

UNIT 6

ART FOR ART'S SAKE?

READING

Under the Hammer

Ask students what they understand by the term *under the hammer.*

ANSWER It is used to describe the method of selling at auctions. When an object is sold and bidding has finished, the auctioneer bangs his hammer.

● *talking points p72*

Ask students to look at the pictures on page 72.

A PAIR WORK Make sure that students take turns to select the items before they look at the values. Tell them to base their choices on what they think might be valuable. When they have made their selections, ask a number of students for their first choice, and ask them to explain why they have chosen it. Then ask them to look at the key on page 215. Ask for their reactions.

B **What makes items valuable?** PAIR / GROUP WORK Ask students in pairs or small groups to agree on a list of three factors that make things valuable; ask them for their suggestions and invite comments from the other pairs or groups.

Repeat the procedure for the next question, this time asking each pair or group to agree on only one object each. Invite the class to discuss the items that have been chosen.

● *reading p72*

A

Notes
The reading passage is by the columnist Bernard Levin, and taken from *The Times.*

Maori – the original inhabitants of New Zealand, believed to have emigrated there from Polynesia in about 1350

Bonham's – a large firm of auctioneers

escritoire – a writing desk

The Iliad – a Greek epic poem by Homer, describing the war against Troy over Helen, wife of Menelaus, whom Paris, son of King Priam of Troy, had carried off.

Autres temps, autres moeurs – a French expression meaning literally 'other times, other manners'. This basically means that customs and manners change over time.

cabinet de voyeur – a French expression meaning a cabinet for displaying curiosities

B Comprehension questions.

K Suggested answers

1. The writer does not know the details of when or where the woman acquired the head, but knows that she has broken no laws in obtaining it.
2. The writer is being ironical by using language that mirrors what the auctioneers would say themselves, particularly by using the phrases *in good condition, with tattoo.* The irony lies in the way this matter-of-fact descriptive language, normally used for ordinary everyday objects, is used here to describe a human head.
3. He thinks their objections are both well founded and well expressed.
4. The test defines whether a person is able to judge what is morally right and wrong, ie whether they have imagination or not.
5. One can feel this *sense of fitness* because Hector regains his dignity by being properly buried.
6. People who feel nothing at the burial of Hector lack imagination.
7. The writer is suggesting that we are blind when it comes to questions of morality, but that imagination will help to lead us in the right direction.

Optional activity
After students have answered the questions, you could encourage a wider discussion of the issues raised.

Ask students:
- whether they would find anything distasteful about buying or selling a human head.
- whether they would feel the same about an Egyptian mummy, and why
- whether there is anything else they would object to seeing sold at auction.
- whether they agree or disagree with the writer's opinions.
- how one can decide who 'owns' ancient items such as this. In what sense does the head 'belong' to the Maori people?
- how the principle of ownership applies to other art treasures, such as the Elgin Marbles originally in the Parthenon and now held in the British Museum).

● *vocabulary p73*

A

K
1. demur
2. desecration
3. succinctness
4. touchstone
5. roused to fury
6. boon
7. severed
8. ethics

B Adjectives.

Suggested answers

Negative	Neutral / Positive
impending	forthcoming
abhorrent	normal
degrading	recondite
wicked	victorious
pointless	noble
childish	rightful

C

1 impending
2 degrading
3 rightful
4 pointless
5 victorious
6 abhorrent / wicked

● *role-play* *p73*

PAIR WORK Allow students a few minutes to read their role and think of a few arguments to justify their position. During the role-play, monitor students, correcting where necessary, and listen out for any common errors or areas of difficulty.

STRUCTURE

Absolutely Abstract

● *talking points* *p74*

A Allow students to look at the painting on page 74 and react to the comments; the aim here is to review the various structures which are used with *look*. Initially, simply ask for students to give their comments about modern art in general and allow them to express their opinions or prejudices.

B The picture is less abstract than it seems, and by looking carefully, one can make out forms and figures that have been distorted. This is one of the earliest 'abstract' paintings, and still bears some resemblance to the real world.

Ask students to answer the questions. Ensure that the correct structures with *look* are being used.

Suggested answers

1 There are two parts of the painting that are arguably relatively calm, the rainbow in the centre and the birds in the top right-hand corner. On the whole, it is a violent and dramatic picture. In the bottom left-hand corner there are a series of black lines which represent the lances of the soldiers and the reddish-brown cloud of smoke represents an explosion.

2 The birds can be seen at the top of the picture, in the centre, and on the right; the castle on the hill is the image in the top right-hand corner, drawn with a black outline; in the bottom right-hand corner there are three Cossacks standing. They are dressed in white and have red hats. Two of them are holding long black lances and the third is holding a sword.

3 The horses are slightly more difficult to see. They are in the top left-hand corner, and again they are white with a black outline. They are both rearing up, with their front legs interlocked. The rider of the horse on the left has a curved back, a red hat, a yellow uniform and is holding his sword outstretched in his right hand; the other rider has a red hat and yellow uniform and is holding his sword above and behind his head. The battle is going on in the centre of the picture and in the left-hand corner. There are ranks of soldiers where the rainbow begins on the left, and there are further ranks of soldiers on the blue hill where the rainbow ends on the right. The sun is shining under the rainbow, slightly obscured by the smoke of battle.

● *cloze development* *p74*

The doctrine of Expressionism provided a great impetus for experimentation in the field of art. One of the central tenets of this doctrine was that what mattered in art was not the imitation of nature but the expression of feelings through the choice of colours and lines; this naturally led to the idea that art might be made more pure by doing away with all subject matter and by relying exclusively on the effects of tones and shapes. And it was the example of music, which gets on so well without the crutch of words, that had suggested to artists and critics the dream of a pure visual music. However, it was one thing to talk about such possibilities in general terms and quite another to actually exhibit a painting without any immediately recognizable object. It appears that the first artist to do this was the Russian painter Wassily Kandinsky (1866–1944). He was essentially a mystic whose dislike of the values of progress and science made him long for a regeneration of the world through a new art of pure 'inwardness'. In his somewhat confused and passionate book *Concerning the Spiritual in Art*, he stressed the psychological effects of pure colour, the way in which a bright red can affect us like the call of a trumpet. His conviction that it was possible and necessary to bring about in this way a communion from mind to mind gave him the courage to exhibit these first attempts at colour music in paintings such as *Cossacks*, which really inaugurated what came to be known as abstract art.

● *intensifiers* *p75*

This part looks at the use of intensifiers, which are a prominent feature of native-speaker conversation, but are less common in written English. (One recent study has shown that the word *really* is six times more common in speech than in writing.) It shows how some intensifiers, eg *very*, can only be used with gradable adjectives like *good*, and how others, eg *absolutely*, can only be used with ungradable adjectives like *brilliant*. From a purist's point of view, the prevalence of intensifiers in normal speech is a sign that language is being debased, and that adjectives are being devalued. For example, *wonderful* does not need an intensifier when used as it should be, and the word *absolutely* to intensify it is, in theory, redundant.

Nevertheless, the guidelines presented in this part (and they are guidelines rather than rules, because everyone's individual speech patterns vary) should enable students to sound more natural and fluent; in addition, this area of language is tested in the exam.

A **Very and Absolutely.** Present the example, and ask students if they can see a difference between the word *good* and the word *brilliant*. Establish that it is a question of degree, and that most ungradable adjectives like *brilliant* already have a superlative meaning in themselves.

Give students further examples of this by asking them to look through the list, saying which ones can be intensified by the word *very* and which ones can be intensified by the word *absolutely*. They can then identify which are gradable and which are ungradable. You may wish to point out that there are, of course, other intensifiers, but these will be dealt with later in this part.

Ask students for their answers and write them on the board in two columns.

K

	gradable		ungradable
very	good	absolutely	amazing
	attractive		brilliant
	pleasant		awful
	gloomy		incredible
	bad		astonishing
	expensive		perfect
	cheap		fine
	complicated		

Point out to students that this is not an exhaustive list of ungradable adjectives. Tell them that they need to develop ways of distinguishing between gradable and ungradable items, because there is a similar pattern with verbs as well. For example, you can say 'I absolutely loathe her', but not 'I absolutely admire her.'

B Ask students to go through the exercise individually or in pairs. Remind them that the odd one out in each set is either because the three others are gradable, or because they are ungradable.

K
marvellous (ungradable, the others are gradable)
poor (gradable)
pretty (gradable)
devastated (ungradable)
boiling (ungradable)
terrified (ungradable)
shattered (ungradable)
foolish (gradable)
large (gradable)
content (gradable)

● *listening p75*

This listening passage presents important grammatical information, and provides a table for intensifiers and the different classes of adjectives they can be used with. If you do not have access to a tape recorder, read out the tapescript or write the information on the board.

A Play the tape and ask students to fill in the blanks with the intensifiers that are used.

K

Ungradable		Gradable	
1	absolutely	2	pretty
3	absolutely	4	incredibly
5	totally	6	amazingly
7	just	8	terribly
9	utterly	10	very
11	really	12	really
13	quite	14	quite

Ask students for the answers to Questions **1–4**. Point out that the less *quite* is stressed, the stronger the following adjective / adverb becomes. The more *quite* is stressed, the weaker the adjective / adverb becomes.

1 The intensifiers that are only used with ungradable adjectives are *absolutely*, *totally*, *just*, and *utterly*. The latter is more common with pejorative adjectives.
2 The intensifiers that are only used with gradable adjectives are *pretty*, *incredibly*, *amazingly*, *terribly*, and *very*.
3 *Really* is used with both kinds of intensifiers and has the same meaning. If students wish to use an intensifier but are in doubt, this is the one to opt for.
4 *Quite* changes its meaning depending on the adjective. With ungradable adjectives (eg *amazing*) it means *absolutely* or *completely*. With gradable adjectives (eg *expensive*) it can mean *surprisingly*, *not very*, or *fairly* according to the stress and intonation of the sentence.

Tapescript
(**H** = Helena, **J** = Jane)

J Hello.
H Hi, it's me. How are things?
J Oh fine. The party on Saturday was absolutely fantastic … and the rest was pretty reasonable, I suppose, though nothing much happened. But where were you?
H On Saturday? I wasn't here – I went down to see that Impressionist exhibition …
J Oh, what was it like?
H Oh, it was absolutely wonderful. One of the best things I've seen in ages. Didn't I tell you about it? …
J No, I didn't realize …
H You really should've come, you'd've loved it. It was incredibly good. I was a bit worried about driving in London, you know, and I'd thought about getting the train or the bus, but in the end I thought I'd give it a try …
J Didn't Jerry go too?
H No, I went on my own, well, you know what Jerry's like when I try and make him do anything remotely to do with culture, he gets so bad-tempered … he's totally unbearable and it's just not worth the effort …
J That was very brave of you. Was it OK?
H Yes, it was fine. It could, I mean maybe it was because it was a Sunday, but getting there was amazingly easy, and I found a place to park, and it only took just over an hour I suppose …
J That's not bad.

H It was definitely worth doing ... and there wasn't anybody on the roads, it was just brilliant ... and then when I got there I just went straight in ...
J But I thought they said there were those enormous queues.
H No, I didn't have to queue at all, I was terribly lucky because you know Jenny.
J Yeah.
H ... well, she'd got a press ticket because she works for that magazine, and she didn't particularly want to go so she let me have it ... and it was just as well really because the queue was incredible – it went round the block about five times, and I would have been utterly devastated if I'd gone all that way and had to wait heaven knows how long to get in, and even then there's no guarantee ...
J Mm, you'd think they might have warned people, wouldn't you?
H Well, I think they did actually say something on the radio about turning up without tickets because it was very crowded inside as well, and that was just with the people who had tickets already ...
J Was it very full then?
H Yes, there were lots of people, but it didn't matter, because they let some people go through on their own, and then they had a kind of guided tour every ten minutes, and that sort of kept people moving, so the organization was really amazing.
J Did you get a guide?
H I did, actually, yes. I don't normally like that kind of thing but the one we had was really interesting and explained all sorts of things about the different pictures and made it all come together ...
J Oh nice ...
H ... and what they've got there that you'd really like, they've got those water lily paintings by Monet, you know, as seen on every chocolate box, but in fact when you actually see them for real, they are quite magnificent, they really are.
J So was that all free too, the guide and everything?
H No, I had to pay for that, and it was quite expensive ... it was about er five pounds I think, or something like that, but was worth it ... and, er, I mean are you thinking of going at all?
J I had thought about it but I wasn't sure ...
H Well, if you have the chance I really think you should ... I'll tell you all about it. Actually I was thinking of dropping round to see you at around four-ish. Will you be in?
J Yes, I'm here all day.
H Right, I'll see you then ... bye.
J Bye ...

B The second part of the listening looks at differences in stress, intonation and meaning when *quite* is used with both gradable, and ungradable, adjectives.

Play students the sentences.

K **1** c **2** a **3** d **4** c **5** b **6** d

If necessary, write the sentences with stress and intonation patterns on the board, and ask students to practise saying them.

1 Auctions of paintings are held quite regularly.

2 The prices for lesser-known works are quite reasonable.

3 The cost of Impressionist paintings is quite ridiculous.

4 Nowadays forgeries are becoming quite common.

5 The Modern Art exhibition was quite good.

6 The range of paintings in the National Gallery is quite magnificent.

C **Differences in meaning.** Invite students to comment on the differences between the sentences.

K In the first pair, the difference is one of meaning. *Your hair is very fine* refers to the thickness of the hair, but *Your hair is absolutely fine* means that the style, or haircut, or general condition is perfectly acceptable.

In the second pair the difference is mainly one of register. *I thought she was very beautiful* is formal or neutral, whereas *I thought she was absolutely beautiful* is informal, and would be more common in spoken English.

Further examples of differences in register are:
very great – very important or impressive, eg Napoleon was a very great general.
absolutely great – 100% all right or OK, eg I love your dress – it looks absolutely great.
very full – very crowded, eg We'd better hurry – the cinema's very full.
absolutely full – no room for any more, eg No second helping for me, thanks, I'm absolutely full.

D **Personal reactions.** Remind students of the point made in the exam tip on page 75.

Encourage students to reply to the questions with the right emphasis. This is best done as a class activity, as you can check that the stress and intonation are correct. This exercise should be light-hearted and should only take a couple of minutes.

● *collocations p76*

This final exercise focuses on an area of vocabulary rather than grammar. Students are asked which adverbs and adjectives collocate, ie sound right together.

A The correct answer depends on the adverb collocating with all three items in a set.

K *highly* – amused, trained, qualified
deeply – hurt, offended, moved
bitterly – disappointed, resentful, cold
greatly – changed, different, mistaken

seriously – ill, injured, wounded
fully – aware, insured, conscious
perfectly – simple, fair, reasonable
most – kind, generous, helpful

B

K 1 seriously wounded
2 perfectly simple
3 greatly mistaken
4 bitterly cold
5 most kind / generous
6 fully conscious
7 deeply moved
8 highly qualified

SUMMARY SKILLS

Traditional Values

● *talking points p77*

Ask students to look at the picture on page 77. It contains each of the objects described in **A**.

A

K 1 a carved chest from Zanzibar, decorated in a pineapple pattern with brass studs
2 one of a pair of wood dancers from southern Sudan, with a plaited raffia collar
3 an Indian oil jar made from beaten iron
4 carved figures from West Africa
5 a tall Japanese porcelain vase
6 a dolphin skull and a fish skull
7 turtle shells hanging on the wall
8 a three-legged tribal stool from Ethiopia

B Allow students three to five minutes to discuss the question. Write these prompts on the board: *works of art, ornaments, furnishings.*

● *summary 1 p78*

Notes

Coptic churches – *Coptic* means relating to the Independent Egyptian Church

Haile Selassie – Emperor of Ethiopia, exiled in 1931 by the Italians, returned in 1941. Deposed by the army in 1974, died in 1975.

Baker Street – a London street made famous for being the fictitious home of Conan Doyle's detective Sherlock Holmes

Icon – a devotional painting or carving, usually on wood, of Christ or another holy figure, especially in the Eastern church

The Commonwealth – a free association of independent nations originally consisting of Britain and countries which were formerly part of the British Empire

The West End – the area of London where shops, theatres, cinemas, museums, restaurants, etc. are to be found

yurt-dwellers – nomadic people who live in felt tents

dowry – property or money brought by a bride to her husband

Verbal summary.

K 1 Arts and crafts / Development projects in poor countries
2 France, Ethiopia and other parts of Africa, India (Nepal) and the Caribbean, Kazakhstan (formerly part of the USSR), and London
3 She has been:
– advising people to sell their products more effectively (marketing the black mushroom)
– encouraging people to diversify, eg make paper out of banana fibre (Caribbean) and water hyacinth (Nepal)
– encouraging people to resume old, traditional crafts which had almost been forgotten (Kazakhstan).

● *comprehension p79*

A

K 1 B 2 C 3 A 4 B 5 C 6 A 7 C 8 B
9 C 10 C

B Reference devices.

K 1 restoring people
2 the beggars hanging around the church
3 of exotica
4 her flat / base in London
5 financial help from the West
6 paper made from the water hyacinth
7 the people of Nepal
8 of the black mushroom
9 a drawing on vellum from a Coptic bible
10 the crafts which survived in the remote areas

C Discussion. GROUP WORK Allow two to three minutes for students to discuss Questions **1** and **2**, then ask two groups of students to compare their ideas.

● *summary 2 p79*

K Points to include

Mara's attitude	**The attitude of the Western world**
– very practical	– too theoretical
– believes traditional skills can be used to produce items people want to buy	– they try unsuccessfully to help other countries out of guilt
– believes people should resume old skills	– projects too vast and unwieldy

LISTENING AND SPEAKING

In the Picture

As an introduction ask students about galleries and museums in their country. Ask them about the type of art and exhibits displayed, and whether they think entry to see these exhibits should be free. What are the advantages and disadvantages of free entry?

● *listening p80*

A Tell students that the first listening passage is connected with the painting of *King Cophetua and the Beggar Maid* on the right of page 80.

K **1** D **2** B **3** C **4** C

Tapescript
(G = Guide)

G If we could move along now … thank you. Here we have an example – and of course the painting is now very well known – of a pre-Raphaelite painting from the later part of the century, in the 1880s and the 1890s, and, er, I think you can see that there is a reaction here against some of the earlier concerns, such as the doctrine of truth to nature.
This painting by Burne-Jones, completed in 1884, is a very good example of his philosophy of what painting ought to be about, and … er … unlike some of the other painters of his generation who felt that art should have practical lessons for modern industrial society, Burne-Jones felt, as he said himself, that a painting should be 'a beautiful romantic dream of something that never was, never will be, in a land that no one can define or remember, only desire.'
… This painting, it seems to me, completely encapsulates that philosophy, and *King Cophetua and the Beggar Maid*, as it is titled, was felt by his wife to be the most distinctive of all his paintings. The story of the King is based on an old legend, in which a King fell in love with a beggar girl and found that his love for her was greater than his wealth and power. In all probability, Burne-Jones knew of the story from his reading of Tennyson's poetry, and so it is another example of what I was saying earlier about the links between the Romantic movements in literature and poetry, and the movements in art.
The artist imagines the King sitting at the girl's feet, and gazing at her in adoration. The artist said himself that he was determined that the King should look like a King and the beggar like a Queen, and he had certain details such as the crown and maid's dress specially made for him so that he could capture the detail. You will probably notice, too, that the setting has very strong echoes of fifteenth-century Italian art, particularly of Mantegna and Crivelli … and it is very sumptuously and elaborately decorated, and it is all enhanced by these very highly-wrought textures and jewel-like colours. You can see what I mean in the woodwork, … and also in the clothing if you look at it. The two characters in the background have got these very rich flowing clothes that hang down very opulently, and there's that same richness in the soft cushions and the King's flowing cloak … There's also, in this painting, a great deal of personal feeling, as there is in much of Burne-Jones' work, in fact, and it is very likely that the King represents Burne-Jones and the beggar maid is Frances Graham, a girl he was in love with. Frances Graham, in fact, married someone else at the time Burne-Jones was working on the painting, and it was an event which affected him very deeply. It is significant that the maid is holding a bunch of anemones, and some of them, if you look closely, have fallen on the steps by the King. Anemones are symbolic of rejected love, and so Burne-Jones could well have intended the painting to be an expression of his own feelings at the loss of the woman he loved.
Of course to the wider public, at the time it was exhibited in 1884, it would have had another meaning which would have been recognized quite easily, which is that they would interpret the painting as being about the rejection of worldly wealth and the elevation of love above everything else. It was a message that was very dear to Burne-Jones' heart, and very relevant for late Victorian Britain.

B Tell students that the second listening passage is connected with the painting of *The First Cloud* on the left of page 80.

K **1** F **2** F **3** T **4** T **5** F **6** F **7** T **8** F

Tapescript
(G = Guide, **P** = Peter, **L** = Laura)

G … so in many ways Orchardson's *The First Cloud* is a typical example of late Victorian painting, and deals with serious concerns. If we could all move along now, I'd like to show you some of the modern paintings in the collection … You can get all of the paintings, in fact, as postcards at the shop and there are posters of some of them …

P Are you coming?

L I'll be along in a minute. I'd just like to look at this one a bit longer. I'll catch you up in a moment.

P OK. See you in a minute.

Man It went well, don't you think? They seem to have enjoyed the evening. I said, Amelia, it went very well, don't you think. They seem to have enjoyed the evening.

Woman Yes, very well.

Man Come and sit by the fire.

Woman I am quite content by the window, thank you …

Man You may catch a chill.

Woman Really, Edward, I am quite capable of deciding whether or not I am warm or cold. Thank you.

Man Yes, I would say that the dinner went very well, very well indeed. The cook performed magnificently in my opinion and at least the servants gave no cause for concern.

Woman No.

Man Or indeed for embarrassment. And I enjoyed the strawberries – they could perhaps have been a little sweeter, but it would be unkind to complain about so minor a matter. Is there an interesting view from the window?
Woman It is quite dark.
Man So it is. I am surprised that you seem to find it so fascinating. But then again, the entire evening seems to have been one of fascination.
Woman I am not sure that I know what you mean.
Man Well, then, let me make myself clear. Was it the housekeeper who arranged the places at the dinner table?
Woman No, I arranged the seating myself.
Man That comes as no great surprise. And you positioned everyone so that you would sit next to Captain Richardson.
Woman It was my duty as a hostess.
Man Have you met Captain Richardson before?
Woman Well, I may have done, I think. He is Henrietta's cousin, and he is staying with them at the moment as you well know. But what has this to do with anything?
Man You take my breath away … How dare you bring that man into this house! How dare you parade him in front of all our friends. What is it? Do you think that we didn't notice? That everyone didn't notice? Those affectionate glances, those soft smiles, those shining eyes of yours? Good God! How can you be so shameless and bring your scandal into our very home? ...
Woman Edward, Edward, control yourself … you are imagining all of this, and there is nothing to be said, I have done nothing. You must stop. Your rages are building a wall between us, and I cannot always be the one to pull it down …
P Are you OK?
L Oh hello, sorry, I was just getting carried away.
P The guide was wondering where you were.
L Oh dear, well, we'd better hurry up then. It's a good painting, that.
P Yes. I hope it doesn't remind you of me.
L Of course not. No, not at all …

C Dialogue writing. This activity can be set for homework or done as a pairwork activity in class. The main purpose of the exercise is to develop creative and imaginative skills for the writing section of the exam.

Give students a time limit of thirty minutes to complete the exercise. Tell them that there is no 'correct' answer, but that they need to decide what is going on in the picture at the top of page 81 and base a dialogue on that. Encourage students by asking them a few questions about the painting.

Suggested questions
What is the relationship between the man and the woman?
What mood is the man in?
The title of the painting is *The Awakening Conscience*, so what may the woman have just thought of?
What may have prompted this thought?
Does the man know what the woman has thought of?
What might happen to their relationship as a result of this?

Students can be given a few lines of dialogue to help get them started.

EXAMPLE
Woman That song – I haven't heard it since I was a child, when the world was so innocent and full of hope.
Man Don't go away.
Woman Oh, but I must, don't you see? I can see so clearly now …

When students have completed their dialogues, allow them to read them out to other pairs of students in the class.

Notes
William Holman Hunt was one of the seven artists who formed a group called the 'Pre-Raphaelite Brotherhood' in 1848. It was a reaction against contemporary art, and was inspired by the art of Italy and Northern Europe before the time of Raphael. Hunt used his art to moralize on the spiritual ills of contemporary society in paintings such as *The Awakening Conscience*. This picture is full of symbols (eg the sunlight in the garden outside versus the darkness of the room) which illustrate the theme of the 'fallen' woman, whose conscience is suddenly awakened to the innocence of her past and the present error of her ways.

● *speaking p81*

Ask students to look at the picture at the bottom of page 81.

A Role-play. PAIR WORK Give students a few minutes to look through the notes and prepare what they are going to say. Refer Student B to the instructions on the left of the painting.

Notes
Black on Maroon was painted by Mark Rothko in 1958, and was originally painted to hang in the Four Seasons Restaurant in the Seagram Building, New York. At the time Rothko was one of the leading Colour Field painters of the Abstract Expressionist School. He worked on the commission for eight months, but at the end of this period decided to withhold the paintings as they were unsuitable for such a luxurious and worldly setting.

Rothko's works were visionary in their aim. Through their large scale, which dominates the spectators' field of vision, the artist seeks to draw them into the painting, which becomes an object of contemplation. The floating rectangles can be seen as 'doors' or 'windows' leading to a transcendental reality.

B **Picture discussion.** GROUP WORK Remind students of ways of expressing reactions using present participles and verbs.

EXAMPLE
I find paintings like this rather annoying.
Paintings like this really annoy me.

Ask students if they can think of any other examples of words that can be used in both of these patterns. Further examples are: *bore*, *irritate*, *shock*, *amuse*, *interest*, *fascinate*.

WRITING

Task-based Composition

● *introduction p82*

This is the second of the task-based compositions, and looks in detail at the stylistic differences between formal and informal letters. Emphasize the point made in the introduction that this kind of question requires students to:

– analyse and extract information
– write in an appropriate style.

Explain that the degree to which they need to extract information varies considerably; in most composition questions there will be very little material to analyse, and they will have to make up the content of the letter themselves. In this composition most of the content is given to the students because the emphasis is on style.

● *sample composition p82*

A Ask students to read the sample question. Then ask them how they would feel if a so-called professional photographer took terrible photos of their wedding, what they would do about it, and how they would go about complaining.

B Ask students to read through both of the letters. Students should realize that both letters are bad examples. Ask them to explain why. Encourage them to say that although the letters are fine in terms of their content, the styles are entirely wrong. The first letter should be informal, but has been written in a formal, business style; the second has been written in a chatty, informal style whereas it should be a business letter.

C **Formal and informal vocabulary.** Draw students' attention to the exam tip, which emphasizes the importance of writing in the correct style. Ask students to complete the table of formal words and expressions and their equivalent informal expressions. The completed table should look as follows:

Formal	**Informal**
out of focus	fuzzy
to compensate for	to make up for
(some of them were) poorly composed	they've got bits chopped off
entirely unacceptable	absolutely awful
(can be) compiled	put something together
to forward	sending (your bill) back
I look forward to hearing from you	Hope to hear from you soon

D **Formal and informal styles.** Discuss the example with the students, and then allow them to analyse the letters on their own. When they have finished, ask students for their ideas. They should be able to work out the following areas where formal and informal styles often differ.

1 Abbreviations and contractions
Informal: These are used in informal letters, eg *I'm*, *they're*, *there's*, *isn't*, etc.
Formal: Not used; the full form is necessary, eg *has not*, *I would be*, etc.

2 Use of the passive and active
Informal: Most of the verbs are in the active unless there is a good reason to use the passive, eg *I'm sending your bill back .... I'm going to try and put an album together*, etc.
Formal: The passive is much more common, for example: *... his fee will not be paid ... so that an album of the guests' photographs can be compiled.*

3 Use of the first person singular
Informal: This correlates with the use of the active, so is very commonly used, eg *I'm terribly sorry*, *I think*, *I'm going to send ...* .
Formal: Partly because of the more extensive use of the passive, this is less common. In addition we would avoid saying *I think ...*, and would present a personal opinion as a fact. For example, instead of saying *I think the pictures were awful*, we would say *The pictures were unacceptable*.

4 Use of intensifiers
Informal: Intensifiers are far more common in speech than in formal writing. Informal letters, which mirror speech, are therefore more likely to use these, eg *absolutely awful*, *completely fuzzy*, *really upset*, *absolutely dreadful*.
Formal: Intensifiers are less common, and if they are used, they tend to be more formal, as do the adjectives, eg *entirely unacceptable*. The more informal intensifiers such as *totally*, *incredibly*, *amazingly* would sound out of place.

5 Use of phrasal verbs
Informal: These are commonly used, eg *make up for*, *put (an album) together*.
Formal: Verbs deriving from Latin are more common, eg *compensate*, *compile*.

6 Link words
Informal: The simpler linking words and phrases tend to be used, eg *Anyway*, *what's more*.
Formal: More formal link words are used, eg *but*, *therefore*. Words such as *anyway* or *basically* would be out of place.

7 Set phrases and idioms
Informal: Phrases and idioms that are found in speech are more common, eg *Thanks very much, make a mess of, not going to pay you a penny, hope to hear from you soon.*
Formal: Idiomatic expressions are usually avoided and in addition there are a number of set phrases that are commonly found in formal letters, eg *Thank you for ... I would be most grateful if you could ... the above address ... I look forward to hearing from you.*

8 Rhetorical questions (ie direct questions addressed to the reader)
Informal: These are possible, for example, *... this isn't the kind of thing you expect, is it? Is that OK?*
Formal: These are best avoided. Even direct requests are often rephrased in embedded questions, eg *I would be grateful if you could forward the photographs you have to the above address ...*

9 Expression of personal feelings
Informal: Personal feelings can be readily expressed, eg *I think ... I'm really upset.*
Formal: Personal feelings are usually kept out of formal letters. Even letters of complaint should avoid expressions of anger and resentment. The message can still be conveyed by rephrasing personal feelings as facts, for example, *the pictures were entirely unacceptable.*

10 Ellipsis (missing out words)
Informal: Pronouns and the verb *to be* are sometimes omitted, for example: *Hope to hear from you soon.* Other examples might be: *Lovely party! Great to see you again. Will ring next week.*
Formal: Ellipsis would be out of place in a formal letter.

• *writing task p83*

Set the writing task in class or for homework. Explain to students that the writing task is directed, and that they should feel free to copy elements of the two sample letters into the new, corrected versions. Emphasize that it is style rather than content that you are interested in.

K **Stage 3**

	Letter to a friend	**Letter of complaint**
Paragraph 1	c	b
Paragraph 2	e	d
Paragraph 3	f	a

Points to include
When correcting the compositions, the following check-list may be useful, and you may like to tick the compositions where they show the following features.

Informal letter

informal vocabulary
abbreviations
use of the active rather than passive
use of the first person singular (especially *I think ...*)
use of phrasal verbs
use of informal link words (*anyway*, *basically*, etc.)
set phrases and idioms
avoidance of formal letter phrases
rhetorical questions
expression of personal feelings
ellipsis

Formal letter

formal vocabulary
full forms, no abbreviations
more extensive use of the passive
avoidance of the first person singular for expressing opinions
use of the formal equivalent of phrasal verbs
more formal link words (*nevertheless*, *however*, etc.)
formal set phrases (*With reference to your letter of ...*, etc.)
avoidance of rhetorical questions
avoidance of direct expressions of anger and recrimination
avoidance of ellipsis

OVERVIEW 6

• *vocabulary p84*

K **1** D **2** D **3** A **4** B **5** A **6** A **7** A **8** B **9** A **10** C **11** D **12** B **13** D **14** D **15** B

• *rewriting p84*

K
1 It's pointless / It would be pointless trying to change his mind.
2 Peter was left a large sum of money by his uncle. / Peter's uncle left him a large sum of money.
3 The fans were deeply disappointed by the results (of the match).
4 The thieves seem to have got into the museum through the roof.
5 Her paintings are a source of income. / One source of income is her paintings.
6 The price of Impressionist paintings these days is quite ridiculous / ridiculously high.
7 He struck me as (being) a very capable person.
8 Mara used to work as / be a picture restorer.
9 These products are now sold at all large supermarkets.
10 She is half-Italian on her father's side.

• *collocations p85*

K **1** C **2** D **3** A **4** D **5** D **6** C **7** B **8** A **9** D **10** B

UNIT 7

Only Flesh and Blood

READING

Rich and Poor

● *talking points p86*

Ask students to look at the pictures on page 86.

K **A Descriptions.** The young and the old woman are the same person.

Suggested combinations
bushy eyebrows / moustache
fair / dark / greying hair
shabbily / elegantly dressed
receding hairline
straight / curly hair
a worried expression
staring eyes
an attractive smile

B Speculating. Encourage students to make as many suggestions as possible as to what might have happened, before going on to the reading.

● *reading p87*

Notes
Tell students that this is a true story, which appeared in a quality paper's Sunday magazine.

In 1893 in North America the Sherman Act was repealed (revoked) and silver was no longer legal tender so the silver boom collapsed.

Lily Langtry (1853–1929) – British actress, greatly admired by Edward VII, known as the 'Jersey Lily' as she was born on the island of Jersey.

Sarah Bernhardt (1845–1923) – the stage name of French actress Rosine Bernard. Lost her right leg as a result of an accident in 1915, but still continued to act.

Oscar Wilde (1854–1900) – Irish writer, famous for plays including *The Importance of Being Earnest* (1895), imprisoned for two years for homosexuality in 1895.

Benvenuto Cellini (1500-71) – Italian artist, sculptor, silversmith, famous for his autobiography.

nouveaux riches – French term for people who have recently acquired (ostentatious) wealth.

A

K **a** The story of Baby Doe and Horace Tabor.
b Leadville, Colorado in the late 1800s and early 1900s.

B Comprehension: reading for gist.

K Suggested answers

1 A strange combination of ostentatious wealth and the deprivation of the North American West.
2 He thought it was the most logical comment on 'art' that he had ever heard.
3 The story of Horace Tabor and Baby Doe.
4 He had failed to be elected to the position of US Senator and, in compensation, was made a senator for the last thirty days of the outgoing senator's term of office.
5 They had a very low opinion of his bride.
6 The silver boom collapsed in 1893.

C Multiple-choice questions.

K 1 C 2 D 3 A 4 C 5 C 6 B

● *vocabulary p88*

Similar but different.

K 1 C 2 A 3 B 4 D 5 C 6 A 7 B

● *listening p89*

K
1 working as a day labourer / postmaster.
2 moved back to Leadville and tried to work the silvermine.
3 a wild eccentric trying to raise money for the mine.
4 in a small, squalid shack at the minehead.
5 ran away, … died an alcoholic.
6 frozen to death in a blizzard in 1935.

Tapescript
(N = Narrator)

N 'Whatever happened to Baby Doe?' is a question often asked by visitors to Leadville and the answer, I'm afraid, is not a happy one! The Tabors were reduced to destitution. Horace worked as a day labourer to save his wife and two daughters from starving. In 1899 an old friend got him appointed postmaster of Denver and his fortunes briefly revived. But he died a year later. His last words to Baby Doe were, 'Don't give up the mine.'
This is where the story becomes tragedy. The former courtesan, who had spent 17,000 dollars on her daughter's christening robe and had given her 100 peacocks as pets, moved back to Leadville and devoted the rest of her life to working the Matchless. She became a wild eccentric, a bag lady who sallied forth every few months to try to raise money from the bankers in Leadville and Denver to reopen the mine.
Eventually, she moved with her daughters to a shack at the minehead, a small, squalid building exposed to the elements, whose walls she pasted with pictures of her days of glory, cut out from magazines. The oldest daughter ran away. The younger, Silver Dollar, who had inherited her mother's youthful morals but none of her later obduracy, died an alcoholic in Chicago in 1925. Still Baby Doe tried to work the mine, descending into the depths itself, well into her

seventies, trying in vain to find the new silver load which would restore her fortunes.
She finally died an old, mad recluse, frozen to death aged 80 in a blizzard in 1935.

STRUCTURE

Too Many or Too Few?

● *talking points* p89

The table on page 89 shows changes in the birth rate in five different regions of the world in two five-year periods between 1960 and 1990. In all countries the birth rate has fallen, in some regions only marginally (Africa) and in others quite dramatically (East Asia).

● *cloze development* p89

Refer students to the list of types of words omitted in a cloze exercise on page 4.

K
1 growing
2 fewer
3 figure / proportion
4 increase / rise
5 caused
6 between
7 as
8 no
9 having
10 well
11 take
12 meant
13 aged
14 have
15 straight / directly
16 last / past
17 grown
18 in
19 duty
20 being / existence

Note
Demography is the study of population trends. *Demographers* and *demographic* are related words.

● *vocabulary* p90

A Words which cause confusion.

GROUP WORK Students could do the exercise in groups of three, looking up one word each.

K Suggested explanations (more detailed explanations can be found in the *Concise Oxford Dictionary*)

1 *migration* – moving from one place to another
immigration – coming as a permanent resident to a country other than one's own
emigration – leaving one's own country to settle in another
2 *inverted* – turned upside down, reversed the order of something
converted – changed in form 'converted the attic into a bedroom'
diverted – turned aside, deflected 'diverted the river'
3 *converse* – opposite, contrary 'this statement is the converse of the other'
inverse – reversed in position, order or relation 'inverse proportion'
reverse – turn the other way round, up or inside out 'reversing light'
4 *decline* – deteriorate, refuse courteously
incline – be disposed, turn away from, bend
recline – assume or be in a horizontal position (when resting)
5 *subtract* – deduct a part, number, quantity from another
detract – take away, reduce, diminish
attract – draw or bring to oneself
6 *inquire* – seek information formally
acquire – gain by and for oneself
require – need or depend on for success or fulfilment

1 emigration
2 diverted
3 reverse
4 decline
5 detract
6 acquired

B Expressions 1.

K
1 no corresponding adjective
2 no corresponding noun
verb: *to short-change* – to give insufficient money as change
3 no corresponding forms
4 no corresponding adjective
verb: *to cut short* – to make shorter / more concise, or to interrupt
5 adjective: *short-listed*
verb: *to short-list* – to select candidates and place them on a list, from which a final choice will be made.
6 noun: *shorthand* – method of rapid writing for keeping pace with the speaker
no corresponding verb
7 no corresponding forms
8 no corresponding forms
9 noun: *short-sightedness* – ability to see clearly only what is near / lacking imagination or foresight
verb: *to be short-sighted*

1 short-listed
2 short-handed
3 made short work of
4 shortcomings (usually used in the plural)
5 short-changed
6 short cut
7 run short of
8 short-sightedness

C Expressions 2.

Ask students to look at the illustration on page 91 and match it with one of the expressions.

K **1** g **2** c **3** b **4** f **5** a **6** e **7** d

1 (just) take your pick
2 take a / the hint
3 taken down a peg or two
4 took its toll
5 taken for a ride
6 take pot luck
7 take it amiss

• *passive review p91*

A There is no difference in meaning between the pairs of sentences but the second sentence in each pair sounds more natural.

K Suggested explanations

1 a We do not know who *they* are. Leave out the agent if it's obvious, include it only if it's unique or unusual.

b The statement is more important than whoever is making it, therefore the person is not mentioned in the construction.

2 a We do not know who the murderer was.

b The crime is more important than the unknown criminal.

3 *an expert, etc.* is a very long subject, full of information. At the end of the sentence it has emphasis, while still making *a talk* the focus of the sentence.

4 In **b** the experiment is the main focus of the sentence, more so than the people who carried it out. The people are significant only to the extent that the liquid cannot pour itself.

Ask students where they might find frequent examples of the passive, eg in newspapers, on the TV, radio news, sets of instructions, accounts of experiments. Refer them to the note and point out that active and passive are therefore not necessarily interchangeable.

B

K **1 a** It is said that the Prime Minister is on the point of resigning.

b The Prime Minister is said to be on the point of resigning.

2 a It was said that the Queen was considering abdication.

b The Queen was said to be considering abdication.

3 a It was said that the Chairman of the Board had absconded with the funds.

b The Chairman of the Board was said to have absconded with the funds.

These sentences are typical of those read in newspapers or heard in news bulletins.

C

K **1 a** No final decision has yet been made on whether to adopt the new project.

b It has not yet been finally decided whether to adopt the new project.

D

K **1** Redundancy notices are being issued by the management and over half the work force will probably be sacked.

2 If people had been forced to stop smoking, more lives would have been saved.

E

K The meaning changes between **1** and **2**. In **1**, the plans were for staff to be taken on in the 1980s, but we don't know if the plans were implemented. In **2**, the plans were drawn up in the 1980s.

There is no difference in meaning between **2** and **3**.

4 a The students were given a talk by the leader of the opposition party.

b A talk was given (to) the students by the leader of the opposition party.

c *In the nineteenth century* can be followed by either of the above.

The third sentence would change the meaning, suggesting that the talk took place in the nineteenth century.

F

K Tenses which sound awkward in the passive are present perfect, past perfect and future perfect progressive, future progressive (see Unit 2 for more details).

• *transformations p92*

K **1 a** It is believed that the senator is well over seventy.

b The senator is believed to be well over seventy.

2 a It was thought that the old lady had been living in an abandoned shack.

b The old lady was thought to have been living in an abandoned shack.

3 Several coal mines have already been closed down by the government and more will be closed down in the near future.

4 A statement was issued by the aid agency saying that emergency food supplies would be sent to the famine-stricken area.

5 No official declaration of independence will be made until next year.

6 A petition which had been signed by 300 people, protesting against the proposed new motorway, was handed in yesterday.

7 a Large sums of money were given by various charities to the refugee fund.

b The refugee fund was given large sums of money by various charities.

SUMMARY SKILLS

Who Depends on Whom?

● *talking points* p93

Ask students to look at the pictures on page 93.

GROUP WORK Allow about five minutes for students to discuss who looks after whom, and other available options.

● *writing headings* p94

A Before students read the report ask them if they can imagine how demography could be useful to governments, organizations, etc.

PAIR WORK Students could discuss suitable headings for the paragraphs, then compare their headings with those of another pair. Allow three to four minutes for this and encourage students to skim read. Students can then compare their headings with the ones given in the book.

B

K
1 e **6** g
2 i **7** f
3 a **8** b
4 h **9** c
5 d

● *comprehension* p95

PAIR WORK Ask the students to complete the exercise. Refer them to page 215 for the explanations of why these answers are unsuitable, then ask them to make a list of the points criticizing the answers so that they can remember not to make the same mistakes themselves.

(A = suggested answer)

K
1 Repeats one of the words used and does not explain the meaning.
A: An important point to consider when drawing conclusions.
2 Similar to No 1, although slightly better as it explains *head*.
A: What each individual is earning on average.
3 A line reference is not sufficient, an explanation is needed.
A: The rise in population of 2.7 per cent a year in South Africa.
4 The answer is too narrow and needs clarification.
A: Ensuring that the income per head is equal to the rise in the population so that it can be supported by the work force.
5 Copies almost verbatim what is written in the text.
A: Because there are fewer people to support, growth in the economy has resulted in income per head rising, but not in equal proportions.
6 Doesn't explain *economically active*.
A: Generating money by being a member of the work force.
7 Only half of the explanation.
A: The mutual relation between those relying on others to support them and those who are capable of earning their own living.
8 Merely changes the order of the words.
A: Because the more dependants there are in the population (students, retired people), the harder it is for the state system to provide enough money to make sure they can be looked after by the state.
9 Too abrupt, no explanation.
A: The longer people live, the more money taxpayers will be required to pay in order to provide money for pensioners.
10 Too narrow, only half of the story.
A: Because not every member of society who could be employed actually has full- or part-time work.
11 Too abrupt, no proper explanation given.
A: Although attitudes have changed, the fact remains that far fewer women are employed in the work force than men, and those women with small children and full time employment are exceedingly rare.

● *summary* p95

K Suggested summary (120 words)

A rapid increase in the population results in a decrease in income per capita unless the economy grows quickly. However, a more gradual increase in the population leads to an increase in income per head, although benefits are not universal.

It is vital to know the numbers of the economically active, since the young, old and retired members of society are totally reliant on the above to support them.

It is worth noting that the dependency ratio, namely the relationship between the economically active and their dependents, can increase dramatically if more people go on to further education or take early retirement. The outcome, therefore, of an increased dependency ratio is a heavier financial burden for the state to bear.

Optional summary

Students could write a summary of 80–100 words on the dependency ratio, population growth and 'participation rate' in Britain only.

Points to include
- the dependency ratio over the last half century
- the effects of population growth over the last ten years
- the involvement of women in the work force.

LISTENING AND SPEAKING

Help!

● *talking points p96*

Ask students to look at the picture on page 96 and to describe what is happening.

GROUP WORK Encourage students to evaluate each item on the list, then choose three or four that they think would be the most desirable. Allow four to five minutes and put any other suggestions students may have on the board.

● *listening p96*

A

K **Speaker 1**
- volunteer
- social occasion (party)
- food, clothing
- Save the Children Fund
- beneficial

Speaker 2
- pop star
- live concert on TV
- money for food
- HELPLINE
- reasonable

Speaker 3
- reporter
- TV / radio programme
- bank loans for projects
- The World Bank
- disastrous

Speaker 4
- man / private individual
- making an appeal on the radio / TV
- sponsoring a child
- ACTIONAID
- beneficial

B

K **Speaker 1** – 3; **Speaker 2** – 6, 8; **Speaker 3** – 9; **Speaker 4** – 16.

Suggested corrected sentences

1 … an amazing experience.
2 … part-time fund raisers.
4 We wanted to bring the children back …
5 … round-the-clock.
7 … will reach their target.
10 The leaked report lends considerable weight to the long-running criticism of the World Bank for giving the wrong sort of help to poor countries.
11 … resulted in the destruction (razing) of some parts of the Amazonian forests.
12 … will displace (cause them to abandon their homes) hundreds of thousands of people.
13 We help an organization …
14 … reading an advertisement in our Sunday paper.
15 … stay in her own community.

Tapescript

Speaker 1 Honestly, it was the most amazing experience. I wouldn't have missed it for the world! We raised enough money in our spare time to fill two lorries with food and clothing – blankets, too, you know – all sorts of things – but we had to drive them ourselves – one thousand five hundred miles! The Save the Children Fund gave us a lot of practical help, too. But when we got there – just to see the faces of those children when we gave them some toys – they'd never seen anything like them. The trouble was – the compassion one feels – you really wanted to load up the lorry with all the kids and bring them back here! But at least they were being well cared for at that stage and we felt we'd done a really worthwhile job – and could always retrace our steps – once we'd re-financed another venture, of course!

Speaker 2 Tonight, I'm appealing to everyone out there – not just those of you who have come to hear us perform! This live HELPLINE round-the-clock special is in aid of the famine-stricken province we've been hearing so much about recently – and seeing on our TV screens night after night. And believe me, however little you pledge – we will make sure that it reaches its destination. Last year (in between concerts to raise money) I myself went out to supervise deliveries of foodstuffs and essential supplies to stricken areas, and we can never, never, send enough to help these people. But what we do send will reach its target, so it all depends on you. Pick up the phone – the number will be coming up on your … your TV screens shortly and will be announced for radio audiences throughout the performances. All you need to do is quote your credit card number or send us a cheque and you can sleep easily tonight knowing that you've done your bit for HELPLINE.

Speaker 3 In-Depth Report this afternoon looks at the World Bank's role in lending to the nations of the world. More than a third of World Bank projects completed last year were judged complete failures by its own staff, according to a leaked internal World Bank report. It lends considerable weight to long-running charges by critics that Bank loans have paid for wholesale environmental and social destruction in poor countries.

The World Bank lent $16.4 billion last year to developing countries and the former Soviet bloc, and was one of the largest sources of money for development projects like dams, roads and timber management.

Critics have long said that projects such as the Bank's forestry management plans have resulted in the razing of the Amazonian rainforest in Brazilian states like Rondondia. Projects for irrigating the Nile delta have destroyed the land because faulty designs allow the intrusion of sea water, and plans for major dam projects in India and China will displace hundreds of thousands of people.

Speaker 4 My wife and I sponsor ten-year-old Baindu from Sierra Leone. Doing something to alleviate poverty had been at the back of our minds for some time, but it was an advertisement in our Sunday paper that really spurred us into action. We chose sponsorship through ACTIONAID because of the personal links with a child and the fact that the money goes directly to help the child's family and village. With ACTIONAID you know exactly where your money goes – and the good it's doing. What really impressed us was how ACTIONAID works with the people themselves to decide how the money should be used to help the whole community. When we sent off our first donation we received a personal file on Baindu and her community, plus a photograph. They've sent regular reports on the community's progress ever since and a quarterly paper reporting on ACTIONAID's work world-wide. We see the donation as a realistic sum to pay out each month, especially with the convenience of direct debit. It's good to see that a small amount can achieve so much!

● *vocabulary p97*

A Expressions.

K 1 c 2 c 3 a 4 d 5 b

B

K
1 He's always ready to lend a helping hand, when we're busy on the farm.
2 Every time he opens his mouth he can't help saying something tactless.
3 She's tried not to lose her temper so often, but she can't help it / herself.
4 Help yourself to some olives.
5 We'll just have to make the best of this dreadful weather – it can't be helped.
6 When I was struggling to set up my small business, he helped me out.

WRITING

Telling a Story

This writing section includes a listening section which illustrates the 'brainstorming' process required in Stage 2. It should give students an indication of the kind of cohesiveness they should aim for. The work therefore needs to be done in class until at least the end of Stage 2.

● *introduction p97*

Draw students' attention to the fact that they may have to interpret a title.

● *stage 1 general approach p97*

A This part looks at the vital area of question interpretation and outline planning. Short titles such as this one are very common in the examination. Encourage students not to simply go for the first idea that comes into their head, but to try and think of two or three ways of interpreting a title like this, and to then choose the most promising approach.

Allow students to read through the three approaches to writing the composition called 'The Present', and to discuss the questions with a partner. When students are ready, ask for their answers.

K Suggested answers

1 Outline 2 would almost certainly guarantee a poor mark. It may seem at first like a rather ingenious and imaginative way of interpreting the question, but the instructions ask for a story, not an abstract discussion. If students are tempted to opt for a clever interpretation of the question, warn them that there are possible problems such as this.
2 Outlines 1 and 3 would answer the question.
3 Outline 3 has the greatest potential for emotional impact.
4 Outline 1 runs the risk of being repetitive; a description of someone going to shop after shop is unlikely to hold the reader's attention.

B Allow students a few minutes to write three quick outlines for 'The surprise'; when students have had a chance to discuss their outlines in pairs, ask selected students for their ideas.

● *stage 2 brainstorming p98*

Point out to students that the person on the tape is discussing how to write a composition based on Outline 3. Play the tape.

K 1 C 2 A 3 C 4 D 5 D 6 B

Emphasize that the main point that the writer is trying to make is that it is not necessary to think of the details of a story in a linear fashion. The writer goes backwards and forwards as ideas come, is prepared to make changes to earlier ideas, and it is only at the end that a final plan is arrived at.

Tapescript
(W = Writer)

W On the whole, the culture of the short story is to take a small incident that has some emotional impact and write something poignant and subtle. In general, it is worth avoiding anything dramatic or violent as it usually tends to be rather crude. In many ways, working out how to write a good short story is a bit like solving a puzzle – you start with an idea of where you want to start and finish, and the challenge comes from filling in all the details and making all the pieces fit together.

Now, let's take for example this story of the present, and the old woman at home. We can begin by establishing that it is her birthday and that she is on her own, as this emphasizes her emotional vulnerability and will increase the impact of any act of kindness that is shown to her. Let us then say that it is her eightieth birthday, and this would provide a perfect introductory paragraph, with a description of the woman at home, perhaps on a cold, rainy day, and there could be a description of some of the objects in her room.

Now we have to turn to solving the puzzle, bearing in mind that you want to avoid too many coincidences and that you want to provide motivation and link the different elements to the central theme. The first problem is that she has to receive a present of some sort, and the question is: what present is it and who does she get it from? Leaving aside the first question for the moment, there are two possibilities. She can get it from someone she knows or from someone she doesn't know. The problem with getting it from someone she knows is that it rather contradicts the idea of her loneliness, so it's probably better if it comes from someone she doesn't know.

Now if we choose the latter, this creates the difficulty of explaining how the person knows it is her birthday, but that's not insurmountable. The old woman could tell the person, or he could find out, or she could tell him. And we can make it a man rather than a woman because there's more of a romantic interest – well not romantic exactly because she's eighty but there are more opportunities there.

Now let's get back to the problem of how he knows it's her birthday. The best thing is probably if he finds out himself, perhaps by seeing a birthday card. So then there's the problem of who the card is from – because we don't want to undermine the main idea of her feeling lonely, so we can't have a card from someone in her family because she hasn't got one. The best thing would be to have the card from herself – this also underlines the feeling of loneliness, because she's gone to the trouble of writing herself a card so that she gets a card on her birthday.

So the person sees the card and gives her a present, but who is this person and what is the present? It could be something being delivered, like a chair or something … or something being sold, and the person gives it to her. Or it could be something in the post – but then there's the same problem as the birthday card. So really it has to be something being delivered or sold. But who by?

I know what – instead of making this visitor a man, we could make the person a child – in fact a young girl – and the present in itself can be worthless – a bunch of wild flowers or forget-me-nots – that she can pick from a field, so we get round the problem of the stranger having to buy anything. But from the point of view of the structure it's better if the child doesn't have to go away to get the present, and already has it with her.

She could be a gypsy child – selling violets for pocket money – and there would be a good contrast too between the general suspicion people have of gypsies and the kindness of the girl.

So now what remains to be done is to organize all this and put it into paragraphs.

● *stage 3 organization p98*

A Ask students to organize the six elements of the story into the right order. Do not check the answers at this stage.

B Ask students to read the model composition.

Invite comments about the composition and go through the answers to the previous exercise.

K **1** c **2** f **3** b **4** a **5** e **6** d

Remind students of the punctuation of direct speech. Ask them to come up with a list of the most important rules, which should include the following.

1. A new paragraph every time there is a change of speaker.
2. Inverted commas at the beginning and end of the words spoken.
3. A comma at the end of a piece of speech if there is a verb like *said*, *replied*, *answered*. For example, *'I don't understand,' she said.*
4. There is no need for a capital letter immediately after a piece of speech even if the words spoken form a complete sentence or a question. For example, *'May I come in?' she said.*
5. If the verb precedes the item of speech, there is either a comma or a colon. For example, She said, *'Can I come in?'* or *She said: 'Can I come in?'*
6. If a sentence is interrupted by *he said*, *she replied*, etc. there is no need for a capital letter to introduce the second part. For example, *'I'm glad you're here,' he said, 'because there's something I've been wanting to talk to you about.'*
7. If the words after *he said*, *she replied*, etc. form a new sentence, then a capital letter is required. For example, *'Please come in and sit down,' he said. 'What is your name?'*

Remind students also that they should avoid saying 'she said' all the time. The problem can be solved by either not having any such word, because the paragraph changes indicate that the speaker is changing, or by using other words such as *replied*, *enquired*, *asked*, etc.

● *writing p99*

The writing task may be set for homework or done in class. Students should follow the notes and use one of the outline plans they have discussed.

If students would like a different title, suggest the following.

The Stranger
The Letter

Refer students to the exam tip, which underlines the importance of checking.

OVERVIEW 7

● *vocabulary p100*

K 1 D 2 C 3 C 4 B 5 B 6 A 7 C 8 A
9 D 10 C

● *transformations p100*

K 1 The drop in the number of school leavers is said to have been caused by the fall in the birth rate between 1964 and 1977.
2 The welfare benefits in this country must be paid for by those at work.
3 Population forecasts have often been proved wrong by unexpected demographic change.
4 Emergency plans, later abandoned, were drawn up to build new cities.
5 Plans had to be made for extra places in schools in the 1970s.
6 The damage caused by the lack of technical knowledge is said to have been partially repaired.
7 The forecasters are felt to be doing an unsatisfactory job.
8 Any unsold perishable goods are disposed of at the weekends.
9 The first scheme was given our approval.
Our approval was given to the first scheme.
10 It is said that Napoleon died from asbestos poisoning.
Napoleon is said to have died from asbestos poisoning.

● *blank-filling p101*

K 1 estimated
2 attended by
3 In her
4 to provide
5 short work
6 per
7 will never
8 been charged
9 have been a
10 to have been

● *rewriting p101*

K 1 He's done his best.
2 They have short-listed three applicants.
3 I'd rather have silver than gold.
4 He attempted to buy the company (but) without success.
5 According to the long-term economic forecast, the prospects of recovery look bleak.
6 Smoking is frowned upon in this restaurant.
7 When she sold the jewellery at such a low price she was taken for a ride.
8 We'd been thinking about giving them our backing / backing them up for some time.
9 I wouldn't have missed the concert for (all) the world.
10 You'll just have to take pot luck.

UNIT 8
WORDS SPEAK VOLUMES

Refer students to the unit title. Point out that if you say something 'speaks volumes', you mean that it gives you a lot of background information. For example, *The look she gave him spoke volumes about their relationship.*

READING

The Tower of Babel

This section deals with language change and examines the similarities between ancient explanations of language change and modern theories about the origin of language.

● *talking points p102*

A **Language change.** Ask students to match the texts with the approximate dates; tell them not to worry about words they do not know.

K Circa 8th century – 5
Late 14th Century – 4
Early 17th century – 1
Late 18th century – 3
Late 20th century – 2

B Ask students to discuss their answers in groups.

Notes

Text 1 comes from the Authorized version of the Bible, written in 1611 and the similarities with modern English are very close.

Ensure that the students are aware of the story of the Tower of Babel; briefly, the people of Babel started to build a tower and wanted to reach heaven. God was not pleased by this display of arrogance and therefore made them all speak different languages so that they would not be able to communicate with each other, thus putting an end to the plan. This is interesting, in the light of the article that follows, in that some modern theories trace languages back to an original language that was spoken in the Middle East, and the remains of the Tower of Babel are believed to be in Iraq.

Text 2 Late 20th century. This light-hearted extract challenges the notion that communication is always a good thing. You may like to ask students for their reaction to this.

Text 3 This text is from a lecture given by Sir William Jones in 1786. It was the first time that anyone had suggested that Sanskrit (from India), Greek and Latin had a common ancestor in the distant past which had since died out. Ask students whether they know what languages their own is related to.

Text 4 is from the 'General Prologue' in Chaucer's *Canterbury Tales*. A translation is as follows:

And she spoke French well and elegantly
As she'd been taught it at Stratford-at-Bow,
For French of Paris was to her unknown.

It raises the point that after the Norman conquest of England in 1066, French began to have a significant influence on English which has lasted to the present day. Ask the students what other languages have had a similar effect upon their own languages.

Text 5 is the most difficult to understand; it comes from the Anglo-Saxon *Beowulf* (lines 1384–6), and at first would appear to bear no resemblance whatsoever to modern English. However, if you look at a translation, you can see that some of the words are related to modern English:

Beowulf spoke, the son of Ecgtheow:
'Sorrow not, brave one! Better for man
To avenge a friend than much to mourn.'

● *reading p103*

K **A** Nostratic is older than proto-Indo-European.

Note

As this text is relatively complex, it may be necessary to explain to students that it is based on two main ideas. The first is that many modern languages are related to each other, so that languages as apparently diverse as English, Greek, German, French, Bulgarian, Pashto and Punjabi all come from the same source. The second idea – and one which is less universally accepted – is that proto-Indo-European itself is only one member of a much older family that descended from Nostratic.

B **Comprehension.**

K
1. The goal is *tantalizing* in that the process of achieving it is complex and frustrating because language is intangible and has changed so much over the centuries.
2. The phrase means 'the historical relationships between the many languages of the world'.
3. Indo-European.
4. *Proto-* means 'original'.
5. It shows that they were farmers, and also shows that their cultures were male-dominated, and that their religious beliefs were a reflection of the way they viewed themselves.
6. The passage suggests that language spread as farming communities moved to new lands.
7. Nostratic has undermined the theory by suggesting that proto-Indo-European is not the original source of many of the world's languages; the original source existed far further in the past.

8 The lack of any words for crops indicates that Nostratic was not spoken by agricultural communities; the lack of different words for wild and domestic animals suggests that it was spoken by people who did not look after animals; therefore the language was spoken by much more primitive people.
9 The majority of linguists agree that language could come from a single source.
10 The writer implies that language may have played a key role in the survival of our species and that the Neanderthals' lack of language was responsible for their extinction.

● *discussion p104*

Questions **1**, **2** and **4** can be done as a class activity. Question **3** can be done in groups, and members of the group can be asked to explain their conclusions.

STRUCTURE

Figures from Literature

● *cloze development p104*

Ask students to look at the photograph of Charles Dickens on page 104.

Dickens and his public. The cloze passage gives a number of biographical details about the life of the Victorian writer Charles Dickens (1812–70).

The passage differs from a standard cloze in that all the missing words are nouns. Students therefore will need to concentrate on the context to find the correct answers as there are no blanks that rely, for example, on adjectives and dependent prepositions. Ask students to read the passage first for general comprehension.

K

1	prophecy	**11**	perception
2	novelist	**12**	champion
3	success	**13**	abuse
4	bread	**14**	love-affair
5	diffusion	**15**	foray
6	adaptations	**16**	relations
7	copyright	**17**	longings
8	characters	**18**	range
9	dialogues	**19**	culture
10	responsiveness	**20**	matter

● *language study p105*

A Emphasis. The two examples show how there is a considerable degree of flexibility in English word order with the use of adverbials, ie adverb and prepositional phrases, and that these can be placed at the beginning of sentences. It is less easy to alter the basic sentence patterns of subject + verb + complement or subject + verb + object.

Ask students to read the two model sentences and see if they agree that the two parts that are emphasized are:

above and beyond such eager responsiveness to his art
out of his non-understanding and also his needs and fears, his disappointments and his longings

Simplify the first sentence as follows and ask students to say what the various parts of the sentences are.

Beyond this / there / was / a special relationship.
Prepositional phrase / subject / verb / complement

Point out that the main sequence of subject + verb + complement cannot be altered, but that the prepositional phrase can come at the beginning of the sentence, after the verb or at the end.

Simplify the second sentence as follows and ask students to say what the various parts of the sentence are:

Out of this unhappiness / Dickens / created / many characters.
Prepositional phrase / subject / verb / object

Again, the main sequence of subject + verb + object cannot be changed, but the prepositional phrase can come at the beginning or end, and arguably after the verb as well.

(The main focus of this section is on emphasis. For details of the rules governing normal word order, refer students if necessary to either *Practical English Usage* by M. Swan, or *A Practical English Grammar* by Thomson and Martinet.)

B Point out to students that in spoken English it is possible to emphasize parts of a sentence using techniques other than changes in word order.

1 Stress. Ask students to underline the relevant parts of the sentences in the exercise to emphasize the words in brackets. The underlined words should be as follows.

K **a** I **b** have **c** most **d** Dickens' **e** novels

Ask selected students to read out a sentence of their choice, and ask others in the class to say which part of the sentence is being emphasized.

2 Point out to students that one of the ways of emphasizing certain parts of the sentence in written or spoken English is through the use of cleft sentences.

a Ask them to look through the three pairs of sentences and to say what difference in focus there is in each.

Dickens captured the imagination of Victorian England.
It was Dickens who captured the imagination of Victorian England.

The second sentence emphasizes that Dickens rather than any other novelist captured the imagination of Victorian England. In sentences like this, the normal rules governing the use of relative pronouns apply. For example, *I saw Peter in town yesterday*, could be re-phrased as:

It was Peter who I saw in town yesterday. (not technically correct, but common in spoken English)
It was Peter whom I saw in town yesterday. (rather formal)
It was Peter that I saw in town yesterday.
It was Peter I saw in town yesterday.

Dickens devoted so much time to writing because his personal life was unhappy.
It was because his personal life was unhappy that Dickens devoted so much time to writing.

The emphasis in the second sentence is on *because his personal life was unhappy* and could emphasize that he devoted so much time to writing because of his unhappiness rather than in spite of it.

Dickens published Pickwick Papers in 1836.
It was in 1836 that Dickens published Pickwick Papers.
The second of these sentences emphasizes the date. Point out to students that the relative adverbs *when* and *where* are not used with prepositional phrases of time and place. Give students the following examples.

It was in London that they met. (not *where*)
It was on October 15th that they signed the treaty. (not *when*)

Point out to students that it is not possible to emphasize the action with this structure. For example, it would be wrong to say *It was published Pickwick Papers …* .

Additional layers of emphasis can be made clear in spoken English by using stress. For example, *It was in 1836 that Dickens published Pickwick Papers* might imply that he published the book (rather than started writing it) in 1836 (as opposed to 1834).

b Ask students to read through the two sentences. Point out that in both of the sentences with *what*, the emphasis is on Dickens' style even though the word order is different. Ask students to rephrase the following sentences in the same way.

1 *I didn't like the ending of the film.*

ANSWER What I didn't like was the ending of the film.
or The ending of the film was what I didn't like.

2 *His joke about career women annoyed me.*

ANSWER What annoyed me was his joke about career women.
or His joke about career women was what annoyed me.

As in **a** above, additional layers of emphasis can be made clear in spoken English using stress. For example *What critics have always admired is Dickens' style* could suggest that critics (rather than the general public) have always admired his style (rather than the plots of his books).

c Ask students to look at the sample sentence, and explain that the focus is on *travel round the country.* Point out that this rather repetitive structure is found more commonly in informal spoken English when telling a story, rather than in good written English. Ask selected students to rephrase the following.

1 *I'd lost my keys, so I broke a window.*

ANSWER I'd lost my keys, so what I did was (to) break a window.

2 *They wouldn't answer the phone, so I wrote to them.*

ANSWER They wouldn't answer the phone, so what I did was (to) write to them.

3 *We couldn't afford a hotel, so we went camping.*

ANSWER We couldn't afford a hotel, so what we did was (to) go camping.

d Ask students to look at the first example and to say what it implies. The sentence suggests that in the class, the only activity that took place was the reading aloud – there was no discussion of the style of the book, the characters, the background to the text, etc.
The structure *all* + subject + *do* + *be* + infinitive can express two different ideas. Give students the following examples and ask them to explain the differences in meaning.

I don't know what's wrong with the computer. All I did was switch it on.

Jack wasn't very good company at Christmas. All he (ever) did was play on his Nintendo Gameboy.

In the first sentence, the speaker is absolving himself from blame, and implying that he didn't drop the computer or knock it or anything else.
In the second sentence the speaker is making a critical remark and implying that the action was carried out to the exclusion of everything else.

Give students some more examples, and ask whether the function being expressed is criticism or lack of blame.

1 I don't know what's upset her. All I did was ask how her driving test went. (Lack of blame)
2 The handle's come off the suitcase, but all I did was pick it up. (Lack of blame)
3 I can't stand her. All she ever does is talk about herself. (Criticism)
4 I'll never go on holiday with you again. All you have done since we arrived is complain. (Criticism)
5 It's not surprising she doesn't like you. All you ever do is shout at her. (Criticism)
6 It's most unfair that they've sent him to prison. All he did was steal a little money. (Lack of blame)

Ask students to look at the second example of *all* in the Student's Book which focuses on the complement. Explain that the sentence means 'I found a second-hand paperback and nothing else'.

Ask students to rephrase the following using this structure.

1 *It was a terrible accident, but he broke an arm and nothing else.*

ANSWER All he broke was an arm.

2 *He's very dull. He talks about himself and nothing else.*

ANSWER All he talks about is himself.

3 *You've got to do something about your child's diet. She eats bread and nothing else.*

ANSWER All she eats is bread.

4 *I've had a rather unsuccessful day's shopping. I've bought one shirt and nothing else.*

ANSWER All I've bought is one shirt.

Before going on to the transformations in **C**, discuss the exam tip briefly. Underlining and the use of capital letters are not acceptable in good written style. If a student wishes to emphasize a part of a sentence, a cleft sentence, as long as it is suitably formal, may provide a solution; at other times different techniques, such as subject-operator inversion (see Unit 14) may be useful. However, over-use of any technique of emphasis should be avoided.

C Practice.

K
1 I wasn't in the office yesterday, so it must have been my assistant (that) you spoke to. (*my assistant to whom you spoke* is rather too formal here.)
2 What I can't understand is why you didn't come and see me earlier.
3 The doctor said that I wasn't ill and that all I needed was a good holiday.
4 What put us off buying the house was the busy main road.
5 She hardly sees her husband. All he (ever) does is work.
6 It was you(r) lying / the fact that you lied about your past that upset her.
7 He knew he would never be able to afford a Mercedes, so what he did was (to) steal one.
8 I've no idea why she is crying. All I did was smile at her.
9 It is his arrogance that I find irritating / irritates me.
10 It was only when he mentioned his surname that I realized we had been at school together.

● *vocabulary p107*

A Negative prefixes.

K **1** b **2** e **3** i **4** j **5** f **6** a **7** h **8** g **9** k **10** d **11** c **12** l

These words are of Latin origin. Sometimes both the adjective and its negative form are present in modern English, sometimes only the negative form has survived. The words commonly used without the negative prefix are: *auspicious*, *plausible*, *appropriate*, *coherent*, *logical*, *edible*, *vulnerable*, *reverent*.

The remaining words exist only in other forms, for example as nouns or verbs: *incessant – cessation*; *indelible – delete*.

B Expressions.

K
1 take it as read
2 read between the lines
3 word for word
4 in a word
5 word perfect
6 not to mince words
7 lost for words

Ask students to look at the illustration on page 107 and match it with an expression.

Sentences

1 word for word
2 in a word
3 mince words
4 Reading between the lines
5 word perfect
6 lost for words
7 take it as read

SUMMARY SKILLS

Reading between the Lines

Ask students if they can remember what the title of this section means.

ANSWER Understanding or sensing more than the actual words say, or having insight into a situation.

● *talking points p108*

The reviews appeared in the *Financial Times Weekend*.

GROUP WORK Divide the class into four groups and give each group one review. Ask each group to read their review in preparation for telling the rest of the class what the book is about. Allow about five to ten minutes for the whole activity, then conduct a 'straw poll' to see which book students would prefer to read.

Once students have decided, ask them

a how each newspaper title compares with the original title of the book.

b why the newspaper should have written another title to replace the original one.

Ask students whether they prefer the newspaper titles or the original titles of the books, and ask them to explain why.

Suggested explanations

a Titles **1** and **3** are similar but explanatory. Title **2** is playing with the words to explain the subject-matter. Title **4** is very different and possibly more difficult than the original but also adds to the interpretation of the contents of the book.

b Possibly to give the reader more information about the subject-matter of the books.

Notes

2 *pyre* – a heap of combustible material for burning a corpse

3 *grime* – soot or dirt ingrained in a surface

4 *literati* – 'men' of letters, the learned class

tyro – also *tiro*, a beginner or novice

Suggested discussion prompts for ingredients of a best-seller (if needed)

– well-known author
– good story-line
– interesting characters
– excitement
– well-written
– colourful setting / location
– interesting relationships between the characters
– a happy ending
– an unexpected ending
– right length
– right price
– good marketing

● *summary 1 p108*

K Although **A** and **B** are correct, they are too narrow in scope. **D** is incorrect and **C** best sums up the point the writer is making.

● *comprehension p108*

K Suggested explanations

1 totally lacking any ability to speak English properly
2 A test whose results could not be validated led to the most recent 'scare' about reading ability.
3 It is not surprising that it was heavily criticized for being academically unsound.
4 reveal difficulties in the ability to read
5 in contrast to the scare-mongering in the press
6 get to grips with ideas
7 come across a piece of continuous writing
8 confused / puzzled when there is no story-line to facilitate their understanding of the text
9 when putting forward / expressing a reasoned thought-process
10 exist in / occupy
11 need a clear-cut syllabus for teaching reading

● *summary 2 p109*

A

K **Answers for A**

1 If children are found to have traces of lead, aluminium or zinc in their bodies then they are less proficient readers.
2 Children with either a very strong right- or left-hand skill often have poorer reading skills.
3 We stop developing reading skills except in the field of literature.
4 Readers wrongly expect to be carried along by a story-line in a text explaining facts or arguments.
5 Sentences are often twice the length in 'non-literary' writing.
6 Sentence structure is less complex in narrative writing.
7 Paragraphs are more difficult to follow in 'non-literary' writing.
8 Signal words are used differently in 'non-literary' writing, and therefore misunderstood.
9 Non-narrative writing often uses words derived from Latin or Greek, which pupils rarely study.

Answers for B

1 Children are not being taught to read.
2 We should concentrate more on phonics when teaching reading.

Answers for C

1 We should have a clear-cut syllabus for teaching reading.
2 We need to broaden and develop reading throughout a pupil's education.

B The summary should include the 9 points listed under **A** above.

LISTENING AND SPEAKING

Loud and Clear

● *speaking p110*

A Allow students a few minutes to look at the photograph on page 110 and discuss answers to the questions that follows. Encourage students to use cleft sentences in some of their replies.

EXAMPLE
It's the English who are the worst culprits.
What really annoys me about them is the way they don't even try to speak our language.

B **Ranking.** GROUP WORK Ask students in groups to list the criteria in order of importance, and to give reasons for their choice. When the groups have finished, ask the class as a whole to agree on a list.

The only vocabulary item that might be unfamiliar is *lingua franca*; this means a language with which people of different nationalities can communicate.

If students have difficulties in choosing an order, remind them that a simple technique is to go through the list quickly, and note down whether each item is A very important, B fairly important, C not very important.
They can then rank the items in these three smaller groups and come to a final conclusion. A technique like this is useful in the exam, where they may not have much time to come to a decision.

C Students can approach this activity as a balloon debate. Divide the class up into four groups. Explain that each group represents one of four spokespeople in a balloon that is too small to hold all of them. In order to keep the balloon airborne only one of the people can stay on board. This person is the winner of the debate. Ask each group to select a language, and ensure that each group has a different one. Allow each group to prepare a short speech explaining why the language they have chosen is the best. This activity should take fifteen to twenty minutes.

When the students are ready, one student from each group should give a short speech to the class. When all the groups have finished, the class as a whole should vote for the language they think should be chosen, though they cannot vote for the language their group has chosen.

● *listening 1 p110*

Wordwatch.

K 1 T 2 T 3 F 4 T 5 F 6 F 7 F 8 F

After the listening, ask students whether there is any organization that decides what is right or wrong in their own language. See whether they think such an organization is, or would be, a good idea and why.

Tapescript

(P = Presenter, A = Amanda)

P Hello. Now we have in the studio today Amanda Reddaway, who is the head of *Wordwatch*. Amanda, firstly, could you tell us a little about *Wordwatch* and what it is you do?

A Yes, of course … well the original idea of *Wordwatch* came up because we had a lot of people who wanted to know things about grammar and pronunciation … pronunciation mainly … and in an organization like ours, with our broadcasting and publishing interests … it seemed reasonable to set up an in-house department to deal with those sorts of queries, er, to give you an example, um, a newsreader might have to read a report … let's say the report has just come in … and it has a word like say, er, Azerbaijan … now, I mean, if it's a newsflash and this is just the beginning of a story, let's say there has been an earthquake there or something, it's perfectly possible that they won't know how to pronounce it, so what we do, what we have to do in our department is to be able to say at once what the correct pronunciation is …

P I see … and is that basically what your role is … mainly pronunciation?

A Oh, no, not now … that was the way it started, in-house as I said, but over the last twenty years or so, our publishing division has grown a great deal, and when you're dealing with written English you have to be a bit more careful, because obviously if something's in print it's there for all to see, and you can't get away with anything …

P Do you have, er … what do you have then, a kind of grammar book?

A We call it a guide, a style guide, and it covers some of the more controversial points … there are the old chestnuts like split infinitives …

P Surely people don't still worry about them, do they?

A Oh, absolutely. You can guarantee that if one of the newsreaders says something like, um, 'The Security Council have called upon Iraq to immediately implement United Nations resolutions' instead of 'to implement United Nations resolutions immediately', we'd be deluged with calls from irate viewers … yes, really. But, as a matter of fact, I don't personally think there's anything particularly wrong with split infinitives, and the guide actually says that too … because, although the pedants and the traditionalists might get very upset about it, what we do in *Wordwatch* is to try and reflect what is generally considered to be acceptable in the community …

P But if that's true and what you're saying is that you basically keep up with trends, then where will it end? I mean, I know someone who gets very upset when people say 'less' instead of 'fewer', so, er, … 'there were less people on the streets yesterday evening' – I mean, is that wrong?

A I think probably yes, though that particular point is in a state of flux, and I should imagine that in fifty years time a word like fewer will seem almost archaic, but I think for the moment I would say that was not acceptable, certainly in print …

P Now there might be people listening who would say 'Well, who are you to tell what to say and what not to say? What gives you the right to impose your prejudices … ?'

A Oh, we are not …

P But you just said it yourself. You said it was 'not acceptable to …'

A Yes, but that's not an imposition … we aren't dictating these things as gospel.

P I can't quite see how not.

A Well, it's an important point because we are a large organization with thousands of employees, and all we do is to try and maintain a certain consistency. Now within our organization we have every right to set standards – whether they're to do with dress or time-keeping or holiday pay or whatever, or language, it's the same thing – it's a bit like part of our corporate image. Now, if people from outside ring up, and of course they do, all the time, what we do is simply tell them what we consider to be right or wrong, and they're free to accept it or not, as they please …

P So you are … you are being prescriptive …

A But not dictatorial … and we try and steer a middle

line between the 'anything goes' school and the dyed-in-the-wool traditionalists … because at the end of the day we fulfil a need, and there are people who want to know what is right and what is wrong and they just want someone to tell them … and the problem is where can they go? The dictionaries aren't any good for that kind of thing, and they don't have … I mean certainly most people don't have a grammar book of any kind, so they come to us.

P Well, thank you very much. Now if you have any queries on English grammar or usage, you can contact Amanda at *Wordwatch*, and the number is 081 … 223 …

● *listening 2 p111*

Word games.

K 1 D 2 B 3 B 4 B

After the listening passage, invite selected students to describe a word game (eg 'Call my bluff,' 'charades') that they know well and to explain the rules to the rest of the class.

Tapescript

(**O** = Oliver, **E** = Emily, **J** = Janet)

O I think it's changed really …

E No, it hasn't … I mean all the basic things are still the same – the family all together, you know, lunch, giving presents and all that …

J … and the films on TV are so good at Christmas … *My Fair Lady* for the nth time.

O No, no, that's just what I mean about it not being the same, because after lunch what we used to do was we played all sorts of word games, there was no TV – well there was but it was all in Arabic so we couldn't understand it, and anyway they didn't exactly go in for Christmas in a big way – and we used to do things like charades …

E But Oliver it still goes on.

O Maybe, but not so much and the atmosphere is different with all that, that's all I'm saying.

E But we did – we did do that the other day at New Year with Katie.

O Oh, that picture game you mean?

J What's that, then?

E Well, it wasn't charades exactly – but what you did was you – well, there were two teams, so everyone split up into two teams, and then each team thought up – let's say there were three people in each team – each team thought up three words, or idioms or names of films, books or plays – OK? And then you write them down on separate pieces of paper, and then you start, and you give a member of the opposite team one piece of paper, and he has to draw what is there and you're not allowed to say anything at all – so let's say, for example, you had the word 'football match,' you could just draw a football and then a match – like a box of matches – and the people in your team have to guess the word or phrase and you have two minutes – and if they get it then you get a point – but it's, it's quite fun.

J So it's a bit like charades?

E Yeah – same sort of idea – but with pictures.

O I wouldn't've thought I'd've been much good at that with all my artistic talents.

E Oh, you don't need to be good at all – I mean a lot of it is just guessing, and when someone gets the right word you can leap up and down, and, you know …

O You know it reminds me a bit of some of those techniques they use on those memory training exercises – you know the ones where they say you can develop a super-power memory.

E Yes, if you're learning Spanish or something, it's a brilliant way to remember vocabulary – with all sorts of strange pictures – I used to do it a lot.

J We ought to give that a go … but what I really like are car games, you know, things that you can play just in your head. Like 'I like'.

O Like what?

J Like 'I like' – you must know it.

O No, don't think so.

J It's very simple – you just have to say 'I like blah blah blah but I don't like blah blah blah' and the other people have to find the connection between all your sentences.

O I'm afraid you've lost me.

J To give you an easy example, I say 'I like cream but I don't like butter,' and then, 'I like cows but I don't like sheep.'

E So it's 'c's.

J Yes – all the things I say I like begin with the letter 'c' – and that's the connection – but that's a silly example because it's much too easy; and you have to remember that the connection can be anything at all – it might be spelling, or something to do with grammar or something to do with what colour they are or whatever …

O Do another one.

J OK, let's see, er … OK. You ready? I like butter but I don't like milk. I like, um, cheese but I don't like yoghurt.

E I think you've got food on the brain …

J I like sleeping but I don't like dozing.

O Doubles, double letters, isn't it – butter – double 't', cheese – double 'e', sleeping – double 'e'.

J That's it.

O I know one you might like – we used to do it on long journeys, um, all you have to do is have two people – or more – and you start with a letter say 'e' and you have to be prepared to say what word you're thinking of – so you might start with 'e' so that could be – I don't know, um, 'hen' for example, and the other person adds a letter – say 's', so you have 'es' – and he could be thinking of 'essay' – then back and you add 'r' for 'res' could be 'rest', um, the next person could add 't' because he's thinking of, er, 'arrested', um, then maybe 'f' at the end so you have 'restf' because you're thinking of 'restful' – then maybe, um, 'a' so you have 'restfa' – now let's say the other person doesn't think you can have a word with those letters he can challenge you – and if you've just been trying to pull the wool over his eyes and you can't think of a word with those letters, you lose a point, but let's say you were thinking of something like 'crestfallen', which has all the letters in the right order, then you win – it's good.

E And can you put letters in the middle?

O No, no, you add letters just to the beginning or the end – and sometimes it just happens that you're both thinking of the same word and if that happens you just carry on until the last person ends up with the complete word and gets a point.

E Well, let's have a go.

● *picture charades p111*

A **Introduction.** Ask students to look at the pictures on page 111. Although this is presented as a game, the technique used here can be a very useful aid to learning and retaining vocabulary. Work through the examples so that students fully understand the activity, which is to draw images that provide clues to expressions or idioms.

K **1** a brainstorm **2** a hairy chest **3** a blank stare
4 the background **5** a French window
6 a beauty spot

B **Game.** Divide the class up into two teams. Ask students whether they want to search for expressions themselves or whether they want your suggestions. If they choose the latter, here are some examples.

Give Team A the following expressions:
a couch potato / a slipped disc / a storm in a teacup / mother tongue / a time bomb

Give Team B the following expressions:
a skeleton key / to kill time / a fairy tale / to look like a drowned rat / a stuffed shirt

Explain the rules once again

1 Each team should write the expressions onto five separate pieces of paper.
2 Team A should give one piece of paper to a member of Team B. This person should not speak at all. He or she can signal how many words there are, and must draw the idea, preferably on the board. His or her team mates (from Team B) can shout out suggestions, to which he or she can react with a nod or shake of the head, but cannot speak. If the team get the answer within two minutes, Team B gets a point; otherwise, Team A gets a point. When the first person has finished, it is Team A's turn to try a drawing.

During the activity monitor both the time and the score.

WRITING

Topic-based Composition

● *introduction p112*

This is the second unit dealing with ways of approaching the discursive composition. Make sure that students understand what is meant by a topic-based structure. If they are uncertain, remind them of the way the discursive argument was approached in Unit 1. Write the following plan on the board.

Introduction
Points in favour of genetic engineering
Points against genetic engineering
Conclusion

Explain that a topic-based structure would tackle the question differently, and each paragraph would deal with slightly more abstract topics. Copy out the following plan, which is a possible way of approaching the same question using a topic-based structure, so that students can compare the two.

Introduction
Advantages and dangers in relation to conception
Benefits and dangers in relation to treatment of diseases
General moral issues now and in the future
Conclusion

● *sample composition p112*

This first model is an example of what, unfortunately, happens all too often; it is a composition without a plan and reads like a 'stream of consciousness' novel. Ask students to have a look at it and say what faults they can find with it. (You may like to point out, however, that there are no grammatical errors.)

K Ask students for their reactions. Establish that the main problems are:

1 lack of organization
2 far too many rhetorical questions
3 too many very short sentences.

Refer students to the exam tip on page 113, which warns of the overuse of direct questions.

● *link words p112*

A Allow students to look at the topic-based paragraph headings, and to match these with the second composition. The paragraphs are as follows:

K **1** d **2** a **3** e **4** c **5** b

Tell students that it is not necessary to include every idea from a brainstorming session in the final composition. On the contrary, the filtering process is a key element of this stage of planning, and it is important to reject ideas that are irrelevant or which do not contribute to the flow of the argument.

B Point out the additional importance of link words in a more complex composition like this, and check that students have filled in the blanks correctly.

K **1** At first glance **2** Unlike **3** while / whereas **4** also **5** because **6** therefore **7** however **8** whereas / while **9** just as **10** Despite

● *writing p113*

This can be set as homework. It is a fairly difficult topic, and you may like to discuss it first with the class. You could give them the following paragraph outline if you feel they need it.

1 Introduction
2 The purpose of literature and why it is relevant – develops the intellect, broadens experience, entertains, etc.
3 The purposes of literature that have been largely taken over by television – passing the time and entertainment.
4 The purposes of literature that have not been taken over by television – the *active* development of intellect and imagination. TV is passive.
5 Conclusion – literature has largely been taken over by TV, but is not irrelevant.

An alternative composition might be:

Everyone, whatever their first language, ought to learn a foreign language. Do you agree?

OVERVIEW 8

● *vocabulary p114*

K **1** C **2** B **3** C **4** A **5** D **6** B **7** A **8** C **9** C **10** A **11** C **12** A **13** A **14** C **15** B

● *blank-filling p114*

K **1** read between the
2 wonder he is
3 he was as / had been as
4 up with
5 far and
6 matter how
7 was as
8 did was
9 take it as
10 far as I

● *transformations p115*

K **1** It was Mrs Thatcher who was known as the 'Iron Lady'.
2 It was on Monday that the letter arrived. / It was Monday when the letter arrived.
3 Many school leavers do not have an adequate command of English.
4 Contrary to what the papers claim, they are not going to get divorced.
5 The older he got, the more his memory failed him.
6 There is no connection between vitamin intake and intelligence.
7 As a result of the fire, a public enquiry was set up.
8 Whether the car is repaired or not, you will still have to pay the mechanic.
9 What I found surprising was his lack of confidence.
10 It was his behaviour that spoilt the party / prevented us from having a nice party.

UNIT 9

THE CALL OF THE WILD

READING

Wild Men and Beasts

● *talking points p116*

Ask students to look at the picture on page 116.

GROUP WORK Allow students three to four minutes to discuss the questions in their books, then, if necessary, give them the following information.

These are pictures of cave paintings. The people who painted them lived in or near the caves, had mastered the art of painting in colour, and depended on the animals for food and clothing, etc.

● *reading p116*

Notes
Fernand Braudel, born in Lorraine in 1902, began writing when he was a prisoner of war in Germany. He pioneered the *pointilliste* technique described in the Student's Book.

A

K Examples of detailed descriptions, ie specific situations and references

Chinese windmills
Scissors and spoons from Istanbul
Japanese and Chinese anvils
Boats on the Red Sea and Persian Gulf
One seventeenth-century account …
One man went out of his hut … near Canton …
A fourteenth-century Chinese painting …
Wild dogs howling in the mountains … kept Gemelli Careri awake.

References to geographical areas
Siam, Ethiopia, The Philippines, Peking, the whole of Europe, etc.

Quotes
'the fields of rice, millet, and other vegetables'
'One sometimes sees troupes of three or four hundred at a time'
'who lived more like beasts than human beings'

B Reference devices.

K
1 the civilizations
2 culture
3 the empty, echoing wastelands
4 the fact that man was threatened by wild animals
5 the two or three towns, including the capital
6 Europe's
7 the wolves

C Comprehension.

K Suggested answers

1 The author criticizes the short-sightedness of those unable to look beyond our civilization. Outside our civilization exists a different world of beauty and life, which we can easily ignore or miss.
2 Town dwellers might idealize the simple country life in contrast to the harsh realities of the life they themselves lead, while ignoring the hardships that peasant life entails.
3 An unnerving atmosphere of fear and either kill or be killed.
4 Both hunter and hunted fled at the terrifying sight of three or four hundred animals on the rampage at the same time, for fear of being crushed and trampled.
5 The presence of more wolves indicated that the local inhabitants had not put enough effort into keeping the wolves at bay, either because they could not afford the time or resources, or because severe weather conditions had prevented them.
6 The *pointilliste* technique is successful in that the specific examples take the reader back into the past by recreating the world as it was and making it more 'alive'.

● *vocabulary p116*

A More detailed explanations can be found in the *Concise Oxford Dictionary*.

K
a *expended* – spent, used up (money, time, etc.)
expanded – increased in size, bulk or importance
b *invading* – entering a country (under arms) to control or subdue it, encroaching upon (a person's rights)
pervading – spreading through, permeating
c *lurked* – lingered furtively
larked (about) – played tricks on
d *flanked* – (often in the passive) to be situated at both sides of something
franked – stamped with an official mark
e *domain* – area under one rule, sphere of influence
dominion – sovereignty, control, or the territory of
f *roamed* – rambled or wandered
combed – searched systematically
g *aroused* – awakened (transitive)
arose – happened, occurred, got up (intransitive)
h *lapse* – a slight error, a slip of memory, to fail to maintain a position
collapse – fall away, break down

1 expanded
2 invading
3 lurked
4 flanked
5 domain
6 combed
7 arose
8 collapse

B

Natural, geographic features: 3, 4, 5, 6, 10, 11, 12, 13, 14
Man-made features: 1, 2, 7, 8, 9

Encourage students to look up words they do not know in a dictionary.

C

1 and **2** a, b, c, d, e, f, g, h, j, k
3 a
4 a
5 i
6 j

NB *game* refers to wild animals hunted for sport or food.

'Modern' concepts
1 all except possibly g, h, i
2 a, d, e, k
3 a, d, e, k
4 probably none
5 possibly a (for skins); b (for ivory); f (for food)
6 j

D Expressions.

1 e **2** b **3** g **4** f **5** d **6** a **7** h **8** c

E

1 play along with
2 foul play
3 play it by ear
4 played havoc with
5 child's play
6 playing with fire
7 playing cat and mouse with
8 played down

STRUCTURE

The Struggle for Survival

• *cloze development p118*

Ask students to look at the diagram on page 118.

A

hatch – **1** and **7** breed – **5** laid – **6** feed – **2**
carnivorous – **3** herbivorous – **4**

B

Corrected words in order of appearance
Unlike, exported, are, estimated, per, because, reach, stage, carry, banned, however, ancient, over, themselves, have / possess, have, while, more, released, survive

• *vocabulary p119*

A Adjectives.

1 common
2 modern
3 non-native
4 mature
5 general
6 wanted
7 sparse

Opposites
1 rare
2 ancient
3 native
4 young
5 specialized
6 unwanted
7 prolific

B Expressions.

Ask students to look at the illustration and match it with one of the expressions.

1 f **2** c **3** d **4** b **5** a **6** e

C

1 plenty more fish in the sea
2 a big fish in a small pond
3 other fish to fry
4 has taken to it like a duck to water
5 a fish out of water
6 (like) water off a duck's back

• *conditional variants p120*

A

an impossible present situation: **2b** (the second conditional: hypothetical)
an imaginary past situation: **3** (the third conditional)
a universal truth: **4** (the zero conditional)
a possible situation: **1** (the first conditional)
a theoretically possible but highly unlikely situation: **2a** (the second conditional)

B

1 A combination of the first (a possible situation) and second (here used to give advice) conditionals.
2 A combination of the second (a highly unlikely situation) and third (an imaginary past) conditionals.
3 A combination of the third (an imaginary past) and second (a highly unlikely situation) conditionals.
4 A combination of the third (an imaginary past) and second (a theoretically possible situation) conditionals.
5 The first conditional with the present perfect, instead of the present simple or progressive, and *should* instead of *would* (a possible situation).

Tell students that these forms are very common in English when we want to mix time references and meanings, but warn students that they will only be able to produce sentences like these correctly if they have a thorough knowledge of the standard forms of the conditional.

C

1 **a** *Should* can be used to mean 'in the (unlikely) event of' or 'if' and can be used in place of or in addition to *if*.
b *Should* you require help urgently, dial 999.
If you should require help urgently, dial 999.
2 **a** *were to give* emphasizes the fact that this is unlikely to happen and could be substituted by *gave*, which suggests a less hypothetical meaning.
b If I were to disappear tomorrow, what would you think?

3 **a** The omission of *If* and the inversion of *I had* makes the sentence more emphatic / dramatic.
b Had I realized how widespread rabies was in that country, I would have had an injection against it.

4 **a** These are used when we want to emphasize the only factor which prevented something good or bad from happening, often contrary to our wishes.
b If it hadn't been for the fact that the traffic was terrible, I wouldn't have been late.
Were it not for the fact that he is partially deaf, he would find it easier to communicate on the telephone.

D Other uses of *if*.

K 1 **a** only
b If only I had been more patient with my old dog when he was ill.

2 **a** Even
b Even if I try to please him, he still shouts at me.

3 **a** It is different as *would* is used to describe a past habit. *If* means 'when', 'whenever' or 'every time that' in these sentences.

EXAMPLE

If (Every time) the roof leaked, he would go / (always) went up into the loft with a mop and a bucket.

Point out the use of *would go*, etc. instead of *would have gone* and *leaked* instead of *had leaked*.

b If it was exam time, he would revise all night.

4 **a** *Would* is not normally found in the *if* clause but it can occur, like *could*, if the sentence is a polite request.
Will / *would* may occur, meaning 'to be willing to' / 'to want to', eg *If Ivan won't come to town with me, I'll go on my own.*
b I should be (most) grateful if you would / could send me a copy of your brochure.

5 **a** Unless ...
b Supposing (that) ...
c Provided (that) / As long as

6 If he were at home, he would have phoned.

E

K 1 If it hadn't been for the fact that the weather was so bad last week, we could have gone camping.

2 If the dog / it barked at passers-by, the owner would assure them that it / the dog was harmless.

3 Had you told me about the party, I would have gone / come.

4 If only we had gone by air, we would have saved (so much) time!

5 I should be (most) grateful if you would / could send us a copy of your directory.

6 Provided that your interview is successful, you will be offered the job.
Unless your interview is successful, you won't be offered the job.

7 If he were a policeman, I would have seen him wearing a uniform.

SUMMARY SKILLS

The Law of Nature

● *talking points p122*

Ask students to look at the pictures on page 122.

GROUP WORK Allow four to five minutes for students to prepare their descriptions and answer the questions, then invite one member from each group to tell the rest of the class what the group decided.

● *summary 1 p123*

A

K Suggested summary

1 Although we realize the limits of our own freedom, we are reluctant to believe that total freedom does not exist in the animal kingdom.
2 City-dwellers believe in their narrow media-vision of life in the wild.
3 In reality, life in the wild is a violent and precarious existence.
4 Our assumptions about animals in captivity are mistaken.
5 There are benefits for animals in zoos.
6 A large number of people visit zoos.
7 Zoos have a significant part to play in modern life.

B Paragraphs **1**, **2** and **4** put forward differing points of view.

● *comprehension p123*

K Suggested expressions

Paragraph 1
1 *this dictum*

Paragraph 2
2 *indulges in infanticide*
3 *the censored electronic imagery of television*

Paragraph 3
4 *a ludicrous perversion*
5 *is profligate beyond common belief*

Paragraph 4
6 *predator avoidance*
7 *pecking orders*
8 *it only consorts with its own species*

Paragraph 5
9 *without broadscale bioliteracy*
10 *for less per capita expenditure*

Paragraph 6
11 *The allure of the animal world is indubitable.*

Paragraph 7
12 *the careful husbandry*
13 *a recipe for dealing with shrinking wild populations*
14 *Victorian in their flowering*

Ask students how their chosen expressions compared with the ones above.

summary 2 p124

A Arguments for and against.

Arguments against zoos	Refutation
Animals helplessly locked away.	Animals not free to begin with.
Animals are by nature creatures of freedom enjoying a life without problems.	Life in the wild is a constant struggle for survival. Many creatures die a violent death when very young. Animals will kill to defend their territory or position.
Animals lead an unnaturally solitary life in confined spaces.	Many animals lead an even more solitary life in the wild.
Modern zoos are grim prisons.	Zoo staff spend more time with animals and look after them more effectively than people with pets. Zoos help people become more aware of animals and their importance.
Early zoos were harsh, ill-equipped places.	Modern zoos are a vital part of our education and the survival of the animal kingdom, because they breed animals and educate people about them.

B Linking information. Check students' answers for **A** before asking them to link the information using the expressions in their books.

C Summarizing part of a passage.

Points to include
The points listed in the 'Arguments against' column in **A**.

Optional summary
Students could write a summary of between 80 and 100 words on the justification for zoos. They may find this useful to refer back to when they do the writing task on page 128.

Points are contained in the 'Refutation' column in **A** and include

1 Zoos help to preserve some species of animals which may not survive in the wild.
2 Zoos try to provide similar habitats to those the animals would normally be found in.
3 Animals are well cared for and looked after in zoos.
4 Zoos educate people in the necessity of preserving the animal world.
5 Compared to other public institutions, zoos are an economical form of education.
6 Many people find animals fascinating.
7 Zoos help to preserve natural habitats elsewhere for animals.

LISTENING AND SPEAKING

Back to Nature

talking points p124

Ask students to look at the picture on page 124.

PAIR WORK Tell students to ask and answer the questions in turn, then compare their answers with another pair.

listening p125

A

1 see everything
2 live in comfort
3 15 days
4 £1,183
5 Crater
6 sheer spectacle
7 to see the black rhino
8 £2,095
9 National Park
10 to see game
11 Twicker's World
12 to see small groups of animals in close-up
13 £265 a night

B

1 wildlife TV programmes
2 the game is disappearing
3 quiet, calming and comfortable
4 lodges / on the rim of the crater
5 of reports of drought
6 foot
7 it has open plains not bush country
8 VIPs (very important persons)

Tapescript
(**P** = Presenter, **M** = Michael, **J** = Jane)

P Good evening and welcome to *Off the Beaten Track*, which tonight looks at safari holidays. If wildlife television programmes have produced any tangible result, it must be that many people now wish to experience a modern African safari for themselves. Films about animals have traditionally concentrated on Kenya, with its speeding cheetahs and roaming wildebeest. The result has been the growth of a major tourist industry, with all kinds of holidays on sale at prices from £699 running to several thousands. We sent two of our reporters to find out what was on offer. Jane reports on Kenya.

J With one and a half million wildebeest and 250,000 zebras on the move, the annual migration from Tanzania's Serengeti plains northward into the Masai Mara reserve in Kenya is one of the world's greatest wildlife spectacles. Despite what the doom-mongers say, the game is still present here in the spectacular numbers described by the first white settlers at the turn of the century. If you have the opportunity to make one brief visit to Africa and you want to see everything – and live in some comfort – the Masai Mara is the best place to go. The wildlife watcher's Big Five (that's the elephant, rhino, hippo, lion and buffalo) can sometimes be seen in a single sweep of the binoculars, although your memories are just as likely to be of elegant giraffes or baby monkeys. The Windsor Safari includes three nights at the delightful

Kichwa Tembo Camp in the Masai Mara, and five nights on the Indian Ocean coast as part of a fifteen day itinerary for £1,183. The best season is December to March.

If you fancy something rather more adventurous, you can experience the old Africa on an ox-wagon safari along the shores of Lake Naivasha, in Kenya's rift valley, either as a day trip from Nairobi or staying in five-star camps for two nights. Or you can penetrate the remote semi-desert areas of Samburu country on a camel safari – a highly recommended way to see northern Kenya: quiet, calming and remarkably comfortable. Both these cost around £50 a day and can easily be added on to your holiday if you are in Nairobi.

P Thank you, Jane. And now Michael reporting on Tanzania, Zambia and South Africa.

M Without doubt, Ngorongoro Crater in Tanzania is the top destination for those who want sheer spectacle. It's a nine-mile wide crater, is 2,000 feet deep and boasts 30,000 head of game. It's one of the best places for seeing the black rhino, which has become extremely rare. There are fine lodges on the rim of the crater and daily tours in four-wheel-drive vehicles in the crater itself. Bales Tours have a fourteen-day escorted journey for £2,095.

Alarming descriptions of drought in neighbouring Zimbabwe have hit tourist bookings in Zambia and led to cuts in prices, too. Game viewing areas in Zambia, however, are not affected by the drought. A tough but fascinating, and highly recommended way to see game is on a walking safari in the South Luangwa National Park – fifteen days with Twicker's World from July to September will cost you £2,341. Lions come close to the camp and you can meet giraffes, elephants, impalas and other species on level terms in the bush!

And now South Africa, where game viewing, notably in the famous Kruger Park, is different from the same type of activity in, for example, Kenya. South African bush country – as opposed to the open plains of Kenya – means that animals tend to be found in small groups, in close-up, but the number of species seen is just as large. Private reserves on the edge of the Kruger, such as luxurious Mala Mala, have VIP-filled visitors' books and top class service. Game drives are in open Land-Rovers. The cost is £265 a night as part of a tailor-made holiday with Southern Africa Travel.

P And finally, the top-selling safari for those who want everything! This is Thomson's *The Best of Kenya*, which links Treetops, Samburu, Lake Naivasha and the Masai Mara with a beach stay for the very competitive price of £969. It's a fourteen-night holiday and operates in April and it is available from your travel agent now.

Should you require any further information please telephone 031–655–433 and we will be happy to deal with any inquiries.

C **What a difference a letter makes.** Ask students to look at the picture on page 125 and to read the caption below it. See if students can identify the missing letter (the 'd' is missing from *crowd*).

Word sounds

(Students can look up the meaning of the words in a dictionary if necessary.)

K

1	track	/træk/	tack	/tæk/
2	kinds	/kaɪndz/	kids	/kɪdz/
3	world	/wɜːld/	word	/wɜːd/
4	first	/fɜːst/	fist	/fɪst/
5	baby	/ˈbeɪbɪ/	bay	/beɪ/
6	three	/θriː/	tree	/trɪː/
7	coast	/kəʊst/	cast	/kɑːst/
8	part	/pɑːt/	pat	/pæt/
9	shores	/ʃɔː(r)z/	sores	/sɔː(r)z/
10	camps	/kæmps/	caps	/kæps/
11	quiet	/ˈkwaɪət/	quit	/kwɪt/
12	boasts	/bəʊsts/	boats	/bəʊts/
13	fine	/faɪn/	fin	/fɪn/
14	plains	/pleɪnz/	plans	/plænz/
15	made	/meɪd/	mad	/mæd/

● *speaking p126*

Expressing preferences. Refer students to the exam tip on 'thinking aloud', before completing the speaking activity. Encourage students to discuss issues from both points of view, even if their own opinions are fixed.

WRITING

Describing an Ideal

● *introduction p126*

Underline the point made in the introduction about the apparent differences between questions. There are often very simple questions which could just as easily appear in a First Certificate paper. Stress, however, that the quality of students' answers is what is important, and that they have to demonstrate that they are capable of writing well.

● *stage 1 general approach p126*

Ask students to select the best outline for the composition.

K **Outline 1** – might be interesting, but would be quite irrelevant; the question asks about a general topic, not a personal experience.

Outline 2 – would lead to a rambling and inconsequential composition which would score very poorly.

Outline 3 – is the most promising, and is the one on which the sample composition is based.

stage 2 brainstorming p126

Ask students to write down ten of their ideas and to keep these until they have read the composition. Ask selected students for one or two suggestions.

stage 3 organization p126

The headings to the paragraph notes are as follows.

K
a Paragraph 2
b Introduction
c Paragraph 3
d Conclusion
e Paragraph 1

sample composition p127

A Ask students to read the composition and to comment on the underlined sections, which contain short sentences which should be combined to form longer ones.

B **Sentence synthesis.** Tell students to eliminate repetitive phrases, use relative clauses (refer to Unit 1), and use link words (refer to Unit 8).

K Possible answers are as follows.

2 This would rule out certain breeds of dog, such as pit-bull terriers, which are unpredictable and capable of aggression.
3 The pet would need to be manageable, which would rule out certain breeds of large dog, which, while they might be delightful as puppies, soon become too boisterous and unmanageable.
4 Much too would depend on the parents, whose preferences would need to be taken into consideration, because they would inevitably do a great deal of the caring, and would assume ultimate responsibility for the well-being of the animal.

C **Conditionals.** Repeated use of conditionals is common in this kind of composition. Allow students to read through the examples and establish that
- the conditional is used to talk about a hypothetical situation
- the present is used to talk about things that are always true.

There may on occasion be some overlap between these two areas, in which case either tense could be used, depending on the exact shade of meaning the writer wishes to achieve.

Ask students to work through the exercise and to choose the most appropriate tenses. These are

K
1 would be
2 would have to be
3 are
4 would love
5 could grow
6 could play
7 would be
8 have
9 are
10 would have
11 would make

writing task p128

The writing task can be set as homework. When marking the compositions, pay particular attention to the use of conditionals and to sentence construction.

OVERVIEW 9

vocabulary p129

K **1** D **2** C **3** D **4** A **5** C **6** B **7** D **8** A **9** C **10** D

transformations p129

K
1 If the TV hadn't packed up, we could watch the football.
2 If I could speak French, I wouldn't have had to find an interpreter.
3 Unless you leave a forwarding address, we will not be able to contact you.
4 Provided that you save some money, you will be able to buy a car.
5 Should terrapins survive their first year, they may live to be twenty.
6 If he were to tell you he loved you, what would you say?
7 Supposing that you failed your driving test, would you take it again?
8 If he had remembered my birthday, he would have given me a present.
9 If he felt depressed, he would go for a long walk across the hills.
10 Even if I had tried to telephone him, he wouldn't answer the phone after midnight.

blank-filling p130

K
1 banned
2 threatened
3 hatched
4 released
5 we don't do something to protect it
6 to ask you to
7 known you were coming
8 Unlike
9 regarded as
10 struggle for

rewriting p130

K
1 Many species are on the verge of extinction.
Many species are in danger of extinction.

2 Provided that pandas have a special diet, they survive.
Unless pandas have a special diet, they perish.

3 He took to the new job like a duck to water.
He was at ease in his new job.

4 She felt like a fish out of water in the huge hotel.
She felt out of place in the huge hotel.

5 We should / would be (most) grateful if you would / could send us a copy of your new prospectus.
Would you be so kind as to send us a copy of your new prospectus?

6 It's not worth trying to save endangered species.
It's a waste of time trying to save endangered species.

7 There is a ban on smoking on the underground.
They do not permit smoking on the underground.

8 At a guess, some turtles lay 28,000 eggs a year.
On average, some turtles lay 28,000 eggs a year.

9 If only I hadn't shouted at him.
I wish I hadn't shouted at him.

10 The customs of the people were now familiar (to me).
I got / became used to the customs of the people.

UNIT 10

THE TIES THAT BIND

READING

Family Values

● *talking points p131*

This activity may be a sensitive topic with certain students; it is a good idea to allow more forthcoming students to do most of the talking, and not to press anyone who does not wish to contribute.

GROUP WORK Ask students in pairs to read through the situation and to put the points on the list in order of importance. Then divide the class into two groups, and ask each group to come up with a final list. When they are ready, ask selected members of each group to present their list and to explain how they came to their decisions.

Ask students to say whether they think that the lists they have come up with reflect their own parents or reflect what they themselves would want to be like as parents.

Ask them whether they think there are any groups of people who should be prevented or discouraged from having children (and how this could be achieved), or whether they think that having children is an inalienable human right that cannot be interfered with.

● *reading p131*

A The reading passage is a report from *Time Magazine*. The American spellings and vocabulary of the original have been retained, and are looked at in detail after the multiple-choice and comprehension questions.

Notes

The Bronx, *Queens* – districts in New York City

bail – sum of money deposited with the court to ensure that an accused person appears for trial

crack – a highly addictive drug that is a derivative of cocaine

ghetto – a part of a city inhabited almost exclusively by a socially disadvantaged group

beguiling – deceptively attractive

sixth grade – a stage in the American education system normally reached at the age of eleven or twelve

gun-toting – carrying a gun

pajama party – a party held by a young girl (eight years and above) who has invited a group of girlfriends to her house overnight

Ask students to skim read the passage and answer the first three questions.

K Suggested answers

1 They were arrested for unlawful imprisonment and endangering the welfare of a child.
2 They behaved in this way as they could think of no other method of keeping their daughter safe.
3 Linda's attitude is that she would rather be with her parents under these conditions than dead.

B Multiple-choice questions.

K 1 B 2 C 3 C 4 B

C Comprehension questions.

K
1 They believed that Mr and Mrs Marrero were maltreating their daughter and putting her in danger.
2 They were mainly trying to prevent her from going out to get drugs.
3 The word *local* suggests that the crack houses are so widespread they are like a neighbourhood store, never more than a short distance away.
4 The writer, who seems quite shocked, implies that the parents are in an extreme situation, and are facing a discipline problem of major proportions.
5 The writer is implying that Linda was lying, by saying sarcastically that you do not go to a crack house for something as innocent as a pyjama party.

● *British and American spelling p133*

The main differences in spelling are shown by examples in the text. These are

K
1 paragraph 1 – center
Point out that this rule does not apply the other way round. A large number of words in American English that end in *-ter* also end in *-ter* in British English (matter, bitter, foster, etc.)
2 paragraph 3 – leveled
3 paragraph 4 – neighbors
4 paragraph 6 – specializes

Ask students if they can find any other individual words that have different spellings in American English. Two such examples are US *meager*, UK *meagre*, US *pajama*, UK *pyjama*. In British English, the word *program* refers to computer programs, and otherwise is spelled *programme*.

There are also a number of expressions that indicate that the writer is American. Ask students if they can find any examples of this.

Suggested answers

US	**UK**
figuring	assuming
hardware store	ironmonger's
superintendent	supervisor
fall through the cracks	fall through the net
doing drugs	taking drugs

Refer students to the exam tip.

STRUCTURE

Social Change

● *listening p133*

A **Social change.** The listening passage introduces both the grammatical focus on the perfect and also the subject of social change.

Ask students to predict the answers to the true / false questions before they listen to the tape.

K 1 F 2 F 3 F 4 T 5 F 6 F 7 T 8 F

Ask students how the information compares with the situation in their own countries. Ask whether they agree with the journalist that the decline of the nuclear family is a good thing, and why.

B If necessary, play the tape again so that the students can concentrate on the words and phrases in context.

K
1 *a traditional nuclear family* – a father who works and a mother who stays at home to look after the children
2 *Mr and Mrs Average* – a typical (average) married couple
3 *2·4 children* – the average number of children per couple
4 *soaps* – soap operas, in other words, TV shows (*Neighbours, Home and Away*, etc.) that concentrate on a group of individuals and families, and follow them through their daily lives
5 *Kellogg's Cornflakes families* – a reference to the advertisements for Kellogg's cornflakes, the breakfast cereal, which tend to show happy nuclear families of mother, father and children happily eating their breakfast in the kitchen every morning
6 *wall-to-wall cornflakes* – here the journalist (who sounds a little bitter) means that the soap operas portray nothing but nuclear families. The expression *wall-to-wall* normally refers to a carpet that covers the entire floor.
7 *single room supplements* – many package holiday prices are based on two people sharing a room, and if a single person goes, they have to pay extra (a supplement).

Tapescript

(**I** = Interviewer, **KN** = Katie Nyall)

I … Thank you, Elaine Gilbert. And next on *Family Hour* today we have in the studio Katie Nyall, who will be giving us her reactions to the latest report on family life in Britain. Perhaps the most surprising figure that has come to light is that only seven per cent of all households comprise a traditional nuclear family – that is to say, a working father, and a mother who stays at home to look after the children. Katie, could you tell us how … what your reaction is to these figures … particularly the one that there seem to be so few what you might call 'average' families?

KN I'm rather gratified in a way in that I've always known that Mr and Mrs Average and their 2·4 kids were something of a myth, and now at long last there is some actual concrete evidence of it.

I What has happened to bring these figures about – it seems quite extraordinary?

KN Well, there are many more divorces for a start, so there are a lot more single-parent families and single-person households; people are living longer, and the majority of old people in this country still live alone in their own homes rather than going into institutions; and then of course there are vast numbers of married women with children, who work full-time.

I Why do you suppose, then, that we still have this image of the typical family if in fact it is so far from that?

KN I think it's partly because the opposition to the idea of the family – if you can call it that – has always come from rather unfashionable sources. Firstly, Marx and Engels were very unenthusiastic about it and saw it as an institution that typified the bourgeoisie …

I And we know what they thought of them.

KN Yeah, and then later, the feminist movement wasn't very sympathetic to the nuclear family either, because they felt it embodied all sorts of very conservative and traditional values and roles. So, because the opponents of the family have been fairly left-wing or feminist, the things they've been saying have been largely ignored, and we find ourselves in the middle really of an enormous social upheaval, and everyone is behaving as if nothing has changed at all.

I What is it then that keeps all this self-delusion going – is it television?

KN Partly, yes. Though there are some soaps that rather pointedly don't have any Kellogg's Cornflakes families at all, there are plenty of others that are wall-to-wall cornflakes.

I So you wouldn't blame the media entirely?

KN No, the worst culprit by far is the advertising industry, who are so far behind the times it's almost unbelievable, and they are constantly projecting Mr and Mrs Average in what they are trying to sell. And even if you do see Dad in the kitchen you can be sure that he's about to make some hideous mistake, and the message is of course that he shouldn't be messing about in strange places.

I Do you think they'll change?

KN What … the advertisers?

I Yes.

KN In the end they'll have to. But first they'll have to overcome their innate conservatism, because they don't want to mess about with a formula that seems to work, well at least for the moment.

I And do you think that if they do change there will be any kind of knock-on benefit?

KN Oh, absolutely … and the sooner people become aware of the way people really do live the better. For a start, the ninety-three per cent of us who don't live in a cosy nuclear family will stop feeling in some way deviant, which would be no bad thing. And secondly, we would almost certainly see some more provision for the needs of the majority, such as help for working mothers, really good take aways, holidays with no single room supplements, more housing aimed at single people and so on.

I On the whole then, do you think these changes are a good thing?

KN Whether or not they are good is neither here nor there, the fact of the matter is that society is changing, and it's much more worthwhile to embrace that change and the excitement of it rather than simply try to pretend that it isn't happening.

• *cloze development p134*

The words and phrases that have been corrected are in bold.

K GET THAT RIDICULOUS FAMILY OUT OF HERE!

Lies, damned lies and awkward statistics temper the mood of the week as we see the latest snapshot of the country with the publication of *Social Trends 22*. For as their statistics chronicle **what** are probably the most rapid social changes **in** British history, we are surrounded by forces who will say **black** is white, if necessary, in order to deny the evidence **of** the figures.

Basically what the survey tells us is **this**: marriage is in steep **decline**, divorce the highest **in** Europe, remarriage declining further **still**. Single persons living alone now account **for** more than a quarter of all households, lone-parent households are **on** the rise, and although the majority of parents **are** still married, an astonishing 28% of babies are now born **outside** wedlock.

Put all these **together** and you may be shaken, if not stirred. But then consider the **most** extraordinary figure of all. The percentage of households now living Kellogg's Cornflakes style, with a **working** husband and stay-at-home-with-the-kids wife, is actually **just** a fraction over seven per cent, **or** around 1·4m of our 19·5m households.

In 1979, when the first statistics became available, the figure stood at nearly 12%, and since then there has been a persistent **downward** trend. It means, in other words, the dear little nuclear **family**, which was born of – and for – the industrial revolution, **has** gone. It did not even last 200 years. RIP.

Notes

There are a number of expressions and ideas that may not be familiar to the students. Ask students to comment on the items below and establish the following.

lies, damned lies and awkward statistics – there is a common expression that 'there are lies, damned lies and statistics', which essentially means that statistics can be manipulated (particularly by politicians) to substantiate almost any point of view. Here the word *awkward* is used, indicating that the writer believes the statistics are true but thinks that people will want to ignore them.

shaken if not stirred – the expression *shaken, but not stirred* refers to a way of preparing a cocktail and was popularized in the James Bond films. Here the words are used with a different meaning: *shaken* means 'shocked', and *stirred* means 'roused to action'.

RIP – an abbreviation found on gravestones meaning 'Rest in Peace'.

• *present perfect simple and simple past p134*

A Ask students to comment on the extracts from the listening passage and cloze test.

K **1** *has come to light …* The present perfect is used here because it is a recent event, the results of which are still evident. In addition, there is no time reference as to when this information came to light.
Give students some other examples of this aspect of the present perfect, and ask them to give you a sentence in the present tense that relates to each of the statements.

present perfect	possible comment
Jack has broken his leg.	(He can't walk)
My parents have gone to America	(They are in America now)
I've sent you a cheque.	(It's in the post)
We've run out of petrol.	(The tank is empty).

2 *I've always known* Here the present perfect is used to refer to a state that has existed continuously from the past up to the present.

3 *were* Here the simple past is used as the activity is completed. The thinking is in the past and is no longer going on.

4 *stood, has been* The verb *stood* is in the simple past because it has a definite time reference (in 1979); *has been* is in the present perfect because of the time adverbial *since* and because the trend is still continuing.

B **Right or wrong.**

K **1** Right. Here the word *since* means 'because', and therefore the present perfect isn't necessary.

2 Wrong. Here the word *since* relates to a period of time, so the verb should be in the present perfect, ie *has been.*

3 Right. The word *when* almost always indicates the need for the simple past rather than the present perfect. This particular structure, *When have you ever …* is used to indicate a certain amount of disbelief on the part of the speaker. *When* also has a plural meaning (ie 'on what occasions').

4 Right. In American English (cf *Gee*), the simple past is acceptable with the time word *just.* In British English you would need to use the present perfect.

5 Right. In this sentence, the speaker's parents went to America some time / a few days ago and are still there.

6 Right. This is correct, because although the subject is dead, the sentence really refers to Shakespeare's works and the influence they have continued to have up to the present time, so it has a past and present reference.

7 Wrong. In this sentence, which refers to the immediate future, we use the present tense. However, with *This is the first / last / best / worst time*, etc, we use a perfect tense.

8 Right. Unspecified time expressions such as *recently*, *lately*, *before*, *yet* are commonly used with the present perfect.

9 Right. Neither of the periods of time are seen as being completed yet; the speaker may live abroad again and, if not, will by definition continue to live in England.

10 Wrong. This is perhaps the most common error, from Lower Intermediate level upwards, and yet breaks the simplest rule to understand. The present perfect is not used to talk about finished actions in the past where there is a specific past time expression such as *a few days ago*.

● *perfect tenses p134*

A

K 1 will have closed (*will be closed* is also possible, but the rubric asks for a perfect tense)
2 have ever met
3 will have known
4 had changed
5 has been taken away
6 will only just have got back / will have only just got back
7 had been ransacked
8 had never had
9 haven't done
10 I had never found

B Discussion.

The purpose of this activity is to allow the students to have a partly directed discussion. The questions are framed so that students can use the past, simple present and present perfect to describe changes that have taken place. For example, a full reply to the fourth point might be:

Twenty or thirty years ago people **did** a lot of routine manual tasks in offices, but the use of computers **has become** much more widespread, and nowadays there are hardly any businesses that **don't use** them.

Monitor what is said and focus particularly on the use of tenses.

● *present perfect simple and progressive p135*

The use of the present perfect progressive with *for* and *since* should be familiar to students. The use of the present perfect progressive without a time adverbial is more problematic; sometimes it is used to indicate that an activity is still going on, and at other times its use indicates that the activity has finished.

A Ask students to look through the examples.

K 1 *I've been playing squash with Jim* might be said about a finished activity by someone who was very hot and tired, and still dressed in shorts and a sports shirt. The present perfect progressive is often used to talk about an activity that has only recently finished, and where the speaker is still hot, cold, dirty, tired, etc. *I've played squash with Jim* indicates that the speaker has had a game with Jim at an unspecified time in the past which is recent.

Invite students to finish the following sentences.

I've been painting the ceiling in the dining room; that's why …
I've painted the ceiling in the dining room, so …

2 *Jess has been writing her thesis.* Here the probable context would suggest that this activity has not yet finished. The present perfect simple *has written* suggests that the thesis is complete.

Ask students to finish the following sentences.

I've been reading *The Final Mystery of Sherlock Holmes* …
I've read *The Final Mystery of Sherlock Holmes* …

3 *I've been phoning her, but I think she must be out.* The present perfect progressive is being used because the action has been repeated an unspecified number of times. The use of the progressive implies that the activity will continue.

I've phoned her, but I think she must be out. Here the present perfect simple is used because the activity is seen as finished; the present perfect simple is also used in this way if the number of times that the action has taken place is stated. You would therefore say: *I've phoned her five times, but I think she must be out.*

Ask students to finish the following sentences.

Jane has been having terrible rows with Peter …
Jane has had a terrible row with Peter …

4 Remind students that the progressive tenses can suggest that an activity or situation is temporary rather than permanent.

Jack has been living with us since he came to England suggests that this is only a short-term arrangement.
Jack has lived with us since he came to England suggests that Jack is now seen as a member of the household.

Ask students to finish the following two sentences.

He's been working for British Telecom …
He's worked for British Telecom for years …

5 Rules 1 to 4 describe the most common uses of the present perfect progressive. Ask students to look at the next two sentences.

He doesn't want to come with us because he's already been skiing twice this year appears to contradict rule 3 in that you cannot use the present perfect progressive when you state the number of times an action has been completed. Remind students that you would say *I've phoned her twice*, *I've written to him three times*, etc. The real explanation of this usage is that it is in fact the present perfect simple of the verb *to go skiing*. Remind students that there is a difference between *He's gone to the shops* and *He's been to the shops*, and the latter suggests that he has returned. Therefore, *he's been skiing twice* means that he has gone and come back twice.

He's exhausted because he's been skiing all day follows the usage as described in **1**.

6 Explain that these two sentences are exceptions; while they are common, they do not represent a pattern that all stative verbs can follow.

B

K 1 have you been doing
2 have had
3 have been working
4 has changed, has checked, hasn't completed
5 have been learning
6 have been sitting
7 have been meaning, have known
8 has been getting

● *British and American English p136*

A **Grammar and vocabulary.** This is intended as a relatively light-hearted activity after the grammar section.

K 1 American. In British English one would say *write to me*.
2 American. The British equivalent would be *The prime minister, Mr Major …* . In addition, British English would not use the preposition *with* after *met*.
3 American. The British equivalent of *diaper* is *nappy*. In addition, British English would use the present perfect *I have just changed it*.
4 British. In American English you would use the expression *collect call*.
5 British. The American equivalent would be *He works at the liquor store Monday through Friday and as a mailman at the weekends*.
6 American. The British equivalent would be *My sister was really angry when her jewellery was stolen and she's never got over it*.
7 American. This sounds very strange to British ears, and the British equivalent would be *The policemen were told to look out for a man wearing black braces and blue trousers*.
8 British. The equivalent car parts in American English are: *hood* instead of *bonnet; trunk* instead of *boot*; and *fender* instead of *bumper*.
9 British. The context points to the fact that gas refers to natural gas, the domestic heating fuel. In American English, *gas* means *petrol*, which would not make sense in this sentence.
10 American. In British English the words *alumni* and *anyplace* would be *graduates* and *anywhere*. However, *graduates* applies to universities only (not schools) in British English. The word *school* in American English can refer to a school, college or university.

The completed lists should look as follows, with the British English equivalents first.

a differences in vocabulary – nappy / diaper, reverse charge call / collect call, off-licence / liquor store, postman / mailman, angry / mad, policemen / patrolmen, braces / suspenders, trousers / pants, boot / trunk, bonnet / hood, bumper / fender, petrol / gas, graduates / alumni, college / school, anywhere / anyplace
b differences in the use of prepositions – write to me / write me, meet someone / meet with someone, Monday to Friday / Monday through Friday
c differences in tenses and verb forms – I have just changed it / I just changed it, got / gotten
d differences in spelling – jewellery / jewelry
e differences in the use of adverbs – really / real, anywhere / anyplace

B **Discussion.** It is worth pointing out to the students that the differences between British and American English are in fact relatively slight, and are less significant than the differences between standard English and varieties spoken in Wales, Scotland and Ireland. Above all, do not give students the impression that they will have to re-learn English if they want to communicate with Americans.

SUMMARY SKILLS

Telecommunication

● *talking points p137*

GROUP WORK Ask students to discuss the contribution each item on the list has made to communications and decide which has made the most / least impact. Ask students if they can think of any other items to add to the list.

● *reading p137*

Explain that the saying 'Don't call us, we'll call you' is regarded as a sort of amusing 'catch-phrase', as it was a standard reply to someone who had gone for an audition or interview. The explicit meaning was that if the prospective employers were interested, they would contact you, so it would be useless to enquire further about the outcome. The implicit meaning was that you would probably never hear from them again as they were not interested in you or what you had to offer. The title of the passage is a variation on the saying in that it states explicitly that there will be no further contact between the people involved. The passage is fictional.

PAIR WORK Allow three to four minutes for students to read the passage and decide whether the statements are true or false. As they do so, ask them to correct the sentences which are false.

K **1** F **2** F **3** T **4** T **5** T **6** F **7** T **8** F **9** F **10** F

● *comprehension p138*

K Suggested explanations

1. to free myself from the magical fascination (for telephoning)
2. my wild excitement when using the telephone
3. (slang) a dose / an injection of a drug which will have an immediate effect
4. no feelings of apprehension about, or resistance to, what I was doing / myself
5. not skilled at knowing how to behave in society
6. the (busiest) time when the maximum charge is made for calls
7. become bad or worse
8. the sudden bouts of feeling afraid and suspecting or mistrusting others / delusions of persecution or self importance
9. a radio device with a bleeper to inform the person wearing it that someone needs to contact them urgently, and a telephone you can carry around and use anywhere
10. sitting limply in a corner of the room, crying and clasping the 'trade' telephone directory
11. holding the phone as if it were a baby in a baby's bed (cradle)
12. disconnected me in the middle of my phone call and left me feeling stranded / suspended in mid-air (with the receiver still in my hand)

● *summary p138*

A Improving a summary.

K Suggested summary

2. He started to detest any obstacle which prevented him (from) phoning. After hearing imaginary phones, he took endless steps to ensure people phoned him.
3. When his colleagues tried to cure him, his violent reaction resulted in his losing his job.
4. He suffered physical defects in his ears and was eventually arrested for demolishing a phone box in a fit of temper.
5. After counselling he can own up to his addiction, which is now under control.

B

K Points to include

1. his feelings of false confidence when he was on the phone
2. his inability to relate to people unless on the telephone
3. his obsession for telephoning
4. his fear of not being able to make or receive calls
5. the fact that he was spending all his time at work telephoning
6. the position of his head
7. the problems with his ears

Optional summary

Students could write a summary of between 60 and 80 words on how Jim's addiction affected his friends and colleagues.

Points to include

1. they received many phone calls
2. they received messages asking them to phone Jim
3. Jim rushed to make phone calls when he visited them
4. Jim couldn't relate to them unless he was on the phone
5. he wouldn't speak to them at work
6. one colleague was attacked by Jim
7. the people he lived with refused to pay their share of the phone bills
8. his friends and family are apparently still fond of him, despite what happened.

LISTENING AND SPEAKING

Togetherness

● *talking points p139*

Ask students to look at the picture on page 139 and to comment on the relationship between the couple.

Ask students to read through the two lists and to answer K the question. The answers from men in the original survey are in Column 1 and those from women are in Column 2.

Extend the discussion by asking

- what the most significant differences between the responses are
- whether they would agree with the views expressed in the survey
- whether there are any qualities mentioned here they would not look for in a partner
- whether there are any qualities they would look for in a partner that are not listed here.

Optional activity

If there is a reasonable balance of the sexes in the class, this can be approached as a pyramid discussion. Copy the following onto the board:

consideration	*practicality*
faithfulness	*reliability*
hard-working character	*strong will*
intelligence	*sense of humour*
loving nature	*tenderness*
physical attractiveness	

Explain that these are qualities that are generally thought to be important when considering a potential marriage partner. Ask students to select ten of these and rank them in order of importance. Then ask all the male students to form one group and all the female students to form a second group. Ask each group to come to a collective decision. Then compare the groups' choices with those given in the Student's Book.

● *listening 1 p139*

This listening passage is relatively simple, but it is useful in exam training in two ways. Firstly, the questions do not follow the order of the script exactly, and you may like to point out to students that it is useful to read the questions through carefully before the passage is played. Secondly, not all the questions have equal weight; some require a simple one word answer, and some require quite a lot more. These kinds of difficulties often cause problems in the real examination, and students need to be prepared for them.

The completed notes should look as follows.

K Interview with director of a Marriage Guidance Centre

Basic set-up

There are 160 centres in the country.

Each centre is responsible for funding, number of employees and size of waiting lists.

Headquarters is at Rugby.

This centre has 38 counsellors, and does over 10,000 interviews a year. It is the busiest centre outside London.

Training

Possible candidates are sponsored locally.

Then candidates are sent to HQ for national selection.

Successful candidates then go on a residential training course.

Course funded by Home Office.

Qualifications required

Formal: none.

Other: warmth, openness, own ideas (but not too dogmatic), intelligence.

Areas of work

1 Relationship counselling (main part of centre's work).
2 Sex therapy.
3 Preventive work in schools.
4 Work for local firms.
5 Work for theological colleges.

Tapescript

(**J** = Journalist, **D** = Director of Marriage Guidance Centre)

J Could you tell me a little about the … er, well, your organization and how it works and what the set-up is?

D Basically, each centre is autonomous and er we are … we are responsible for our own funding, the number of people we employ, for keeping down our waiting lists, etcetera etcetera … and there are about 160 Relate centres in the whole of England and northern Ireland and the actual centres, the actual country, is divided into six regions and we are part of the west region and we have a centre in Rugby where the college is, where the director and all the national staff operate from and where the training's done.

J Oh, right, so the training … ?

D So, basically, the vast bulk of the training of counsellors is done in Rugby and some of it is done in the region so, depending on which region you belong to is which region you go to for your training …

J So what is the relationship between you and, er, the sort of parent organization … do they … ?

D They …

J … they select the trainees, do they?

D Er, no, we …

J … or do they do the training?

D We do our own sponsoring locally and we send them forward nationally for national selection … it's quite a procedure to get through, and if they agree that they are counsellor material at selection then they go forward to the training … the actual, um, residential training is paid for by the National Relate, ie the Home Office because they get a grant from the Home Office …

J I see and I mean, are they … are they psychologists … do they have to have a background?

D No, not necessarily … you need people with warmth. Openness. Someone who's got their own ideas but are not going to impose those on someone else. You need to have quite a lot of intelligence in order to be able to read and absorb what they're reading, but they don't have to have any formal qualifications …

J Oh, right. So how many do you have, how many counsellors do you have here?

D At the moment I've got about thirty-eight.

J Thirty-eight?

D Yes.

J Gosh, that's busy.

D Yes, it's a very busy centre. In fact we're the largest centre outside of London – well, not the largest, we certainly do more work than anyone else outside London at the moment – we're offering, er, over, over 10,000 interviews a year … not all are taken up because we do have a short rate which is quite normal in this sort of work …

J Do people normally come to you off their own bat, so to speak … or …

D Most are self-referred although we do get quite a … about a quarter of our clients come because they are referred by their doctors. I mean the self-referral is a very sound one because the motivation is there …

J And so basically what … what kind of work do you actually do here?

D Well we do what we call our core work which is relationship counselling which is the bulk of our work. We also do RST which is Relate Sex Therapy, which is a very successful part of our work, and we also do some educational work, but not a vast amount.

J Is that in … round schools?

D Yes … yes … preventative work – we don't do an enormous amount in schools, and partly because we can't afford to do that additional work without being paid for it, and there's not a lot of money around for it … and we've done work for a couple of local firms preparing people for retirement … and we do work for theological colleges studying marriage and family life, and we do two weeks, usually two-week courses at those a year …

J So you're branching out – or has that always been part of your range?

D Um … we … yes, it's always been part of our range … .

● *listening 2 p140*

You may like to point out that the second passage is with a different person from the same organization as in Listening 1.

A

K 1 T 2 F 3 F 4 F 5 F 6 F 7 F 8 F

Tapescript

(**J** = Journalist, **C** = Counsellor)

J What are the factors that you would say … that you would describe as being really important in a relationship? … I mean because obviously you tend to see people … by virtue of what you do … basically see them when things have gone wrong …

C Yes, well, that's difficult … a very difficult question to answer …

J Well, if you take a couple say – and they're madly in love and have been for three months or so or whatever, what should they do to keep those feelings going?

C I think it's important to realize that a relationship is a dynamic entity or concept, and it's something that changes, and what you're talking about is really just a first flush … and it's something that has to fade.

J Isn't that rather … well, a rather cynical attitude?

C No, not at all … that phase of what people think … what people call being in love is very real … all that dizzy passion and excitement … but it's a myth that that … romantic state is true love … and it's very damaging because people think that it can last or that it should … and it's terribly important to realize that it's just a phase.

J So what happens after it?

C Well, it's what we call the 'hangover' phase and it's often a sense of disillusionment when people go off each other … but it's like you're not just seeing someone warts and all, you're just seeing all warts …

J And that's when people tend to break up, is it?

C Well it can be and sometimes that may be the best thing, because after all we … not everyone is suited to each other … but ideally what should happen is that when the hangover has passed, you can get through the sense of disillusionment and start to construct a more fundamental kind of love.

J What pointers could you give someone, then who, say, wanted to get married … is there, for example, an ideal age?

C For getting married?

J Yes, or deciding to give things a go, from the point of view of statistics.

C Well, statistically speaking, it has to be said that couples who marry in their late twenties, in this country anyway, have a better chance of making a go at it than, say, people who get married in their teens … but I mean …

J Why? Why should that be … ?

C Er … I think it's basically because on the whole people are changing at that age and still developing, and by the time a couple are thirty, if they've been together for ten years, they might have turned into two completely different people.

J Oh, right …

C … but these are just statistics … and there's no right or wrong age, and you can't say that a young marriage is bound go to wrong any more than an older one is bound to go right …

J And what do you think of people, say, coming from similar backgrounds and having similar interests, and so on? I mean, does that help or do opposites attract?

C Well, I think of course that things like that can give you, a head start in terms of compatibility, and a lot of people, but by no means all – go for people who are fairly similar.

J So, on the whole it's a good thing?

C Yes, but there's also something rather more important and less obvious than those what you might call surface similarities, like education and background and so on … and that's the deeper self, you know, the values and ideas you've developed about love and life and relationships, and what sort of behaviour is OK and what simply isn't on …

J Uh huh.

C Now most of these are developed in childhood – and people sometimes aren't aware of them, because of the way they were brought up and the way their parents behaved and so on. They have very deep-rooted ideas about what's right and wrong in a relationship, and what the roles should be …

J I see … so your sort of programming has to be compatible.

C Exactly … there are lots of other qualities that help, like liking your partner for a start, respecting them, making an effort, er, generosity, sense of humour …

J It's said a lot, that – I find it a bit odd – why is it so important?

C Well, by sense of humour I don't mean that you have to spend most of your life rolling in the aisles, but it's important in that when you come across problems, you can keep a sense of proportion – don't make a mountain out of a molehill.

J Oh, I see.

C And there's one more area that is vital – perhaps more so than anything – clearly, the more a couple are able to communicate, in every sense, both verbally and physically, the easier it is for them. Because in the end there are bound to be stresses and strains in a long relationship and they can be … whether they are from factors inside a relationship or things outside, like the loss of a job or coping with bereavement and so on … and it's important that people don't bottle things up and learn to express their feelings, because that's when things can break down … and listen … and I don't just mean hear what someone is saying … but actually listen to what the other person is getting at, too.

B **Vocabulary.** Ask students to give brief explanations of the words and phrases used in the passage.

K Possible definitions arc
1 a first very exciting phase
2 intoxicating love and excitement
3 the sense of deep disappointment after the first phase
4 seeing someone with their faults
5 pieces of advice
6 according to the statistics
7 firmly-set ideas
8 exaggerate the importance of a problem or difficulty
9 getting over the death of a loved one
10 keep feelings inside.

● *reading p140*

Ask students to look at the picture of Shakespeare and sonnet 116 on page 140. This sonnet has been included to counterbalance some of the attitudes towards love expressed in the listening passages. Ask students to read through the passage to get a general idea of the meaning and then to answer the questions that follow.

K Suggested answers
1 The main message is that true love is real and lasts for ever.
2 This means that true love remains constant, even if the other person's love changes or fades.
3 In line 5 Shakespeare gives his definition of true love. He compares love's constancy to a *mark* or lighthouse, which is always in a fixed position and stands firm against storms or *tempests*. He develops this nautical image by comparing the soul with a *bark* or ship, with love as its guiding *star*. In line 8 *although his height be taken* refers to the use of a sextant, which was an early navigational instrument.
4 None, although attractiveness and physical features are affected by time.
5 The last two lines make it clear that Shakespeare is completely convinced that he is right.
6 Ask selected students for their responses to this question.

WRITING

Steps and Measures

● *introduction p141*

Allow students to read through the introductory section. If necessary, give them some additional examples of composition titles, and ask them whether the following can be classified as 'true or false' or as 'steps and measures' questions.

1 Stricter punishments reduce the level of crime. Discuss.
2 The industrialized countries are doing irreparable damage to the environment. What can be done to improve the situation?
3 Marriage is an outdated institution. Do you agree?
4 Briefly describe the education system in your country and outline ways in which it could be improved.

1 and **3** are the 'true or false' questions; **2** and **4** are 'steps and measures' questions.

● *question interpretation p141*

K Suggested answers
a It takes for granted the fact that juvenile crime is at record levels.
b You could give examples of a recent case, and perhaps compare the present with the past.
c If you decided to disagree with the opening statement, you would have to support your arguments with statistics which you would probably not know; you might end up not answering the question.
d It would not be relevant in the least; the question is about juvenile crime.
e You need to analyse what the causes of the problems are.
f You could summarize your recommendations and make a comment as to how effective they would be.

● *sample composition p141*

K The correct order is
a paragraph 2 **c** paragraph 3
b paragraph 4 **d** paragraph 1.

Ask students to find out what links there are between paragraphs 2 and 3. They should see that the two paragraphs follow the same pattern, which is

Paragraph 2
A comments about the social environment
B comments about education
C comments about the role of the family

Paragraph 3
A ways of improving the social environment
B importance of improving education
C difficulties of solving the problems related to family life

● *timed writing task p142*

Ask students to look at the picture on page 142 and to note down any ideas it may suggest to them.

Refer students to the exam tip on style in a formal argument. At some stage it is important to ask students to write compositions within a specified time limit. If you feel confident that students will do this on their own at home, it can be set as homework; if not, it is worth doing it in the class, and you can also ensure that they do not use dictionaries, which they will not be allowed to do during the exam.

Here the rubric allows one hour for the writing itself, because it is the first time the students have been asked to do this. In the examination they will have less time than this because they will have to plan the composition as well. You may wish to allow 15 minutes for Stages 1 to 3 and to reduce the time limit for the actual writing to 45 minutes.

OVERVIEW 10

● *vocabulary p143*

Refer students to the exam tip before doing the vocabulary exercise.

K **1** C **2** B **3** D **4** D **5** B **6** A **7** D **8** D **9** A **10** A

● *blank-filling p143*

K **1** has been away
2 have shrunk
3 of the best programmes / games / (TV) films
4 you have done / finished the work
5 earth have you been doing
6 will have had

● *transformations p143*

K **1** Basically, the more a couple can communicate, the happier they are / will be.
2 I'm trying to cut down on fatty foods.
3 I have never heard such a shocking story.
4 This is the first time that my brother has flown solo in a glider.
5 This will be the last time we see each other before I go.
6 By the time I got to the station, the train had left.
7 It is ten years since the school was founded.
8 The house looks better now that it has been repainted.

● *rewriting p144*

The purpose of this exercise is to alert students to the fact that phrasal verbs can have more than one meaning.

K **1** **a** is (just) not on
b is (still) on
2 **a** getting at
b getting at
3 **a** go for
b went for
4 **a** has broken down
b have broken down
5 **a** had gone off
b had gone off

UNIT 11
THE HARD SELL

READING

Supply and Demand

● *talking points p145*

Draw students' attention to the exam tip.

GROUP WORK Allow three to four minutes for students to make their choice and add two or three suggestions of their own to the list, then invite each group to tell the rest of the class what they decided.

● *reading p145*

A

Notes
Dr Mackay (1814 – 1889) – Scottish writer, educated in London and Brussels. The article is based on his book *Memoirs of Popular Delusions and the Madness of Crowds* (1841).

B Multiple-choice questions.

K **1** D **2** C **3** D **4** B **5** B **6** B **7** B

● *vocabulary p146*

A

K
1 merchant
2 a rare commodity
3 exchanges / stock markets
4 speculators
5 stock-jobbers
6 judicious trading
7 defaulters
8 beggary
9 purchaser
10 vendor

B

K
1 went for
2 crashed
3 spread
4 fluctuates / fluctuated
5 traded
6 dabbles
7 made
8 ruined

C Expressions. Pick up means 'find, buy or acquire'

K
1 chosen / singled out
2 blaming / victimizing
3 learned
4 collect
5 become infected by
6 eats very little and without enthusiasm
7 select
8 start a fight
9 moved slowly and awkwardly
10 start again with what is left

D

K
1 pick up
2 picking on
3 pick up the pieces
4 pick up
5 picked their way
6 pick a quarrel
7 picking at
8 picked out

STRUCTURE

Selling your Wares

● *talking points p147*

Ask students to look at the pictures on page 147 and compare them.

A PAIR WORK Allow two to three minutes for students to decide on their reasons for (not) buying from the people mentioned on the list, then ask them to compare their decisions with another pair.

B GROUP WORK Allow four to five minutes for this activity.

K Suggested explanations

a charity shop – a shop selling donated goods to raise money for worthy causes

a jumble sale – an event organized by volunteers when people bring unwanted goods, clothes, etc. to raise money for a specific cause

a car boot sale – an event when people fill the luggage space in the back of their car with goods and sell them from the 'boot' or back of the car

a pawnbroker – a person who lends money at interest on the security of personal property deposited

hire purchase – buying in instalments with added interest and paying back over a specific period of time

interest free credit – money lent without accruing any added interest

plastic money – credit cards, eg Visa, American Express, Access

discount prices – prices lower than they would be normally, eg 20% cheaper, a 20% discount

Encourage students to think about the implications of the items mentioned, eg helping people, getting even further into debt, dangers of losing credit cards or having them stolen, being persuaded to spend more than you have, saving money.

● *cloze development p148*

A Draw students' attention to the exam tip.

K I sold funeral insurance to North Carolina black people. I myself am not black. Like everybody **1** who was alive fifty-nine years ago, I was young then, you know? I still feel **2** bad about what went on. My wife says: Telling **3** might help. Lately, worrying over this takes a percentage of my sleep right off the top. So I'm telling you. OK?

I **4** did it to put myself through college. I knew it wasn't right. But my parents worked at the cotton mill. I went **5** everything they earned before they earned it. I grew **6** in one of those employee row-houses. Our place stood near the cotton loading-ramp. Our shrubs were always tagged with fluff blown off stacked bales. Mornings, the view might show six white, wind-blown hunks, as big as cakes. You didn't understand you'd steadily breathed **7** fibres – not till, like Dad, you started coughing at age forty and died at fifty-one. I **8** to earn everything myself. First, I tried peddling the *Book of Knowledge*. Seemed like a good thing to sell.

I attended every training **9**. The sharp salesman showed us how to let the 'T' volume fall open at the Taj Mahal. Our company had spent **10** little extra on that full-page picture. In a living-room the size **11** a shipping crate, I stood before my seated parents. I practised. They nodded. I still remember, 'One **12** of the finger takes us from "Rome" to … "Rockets"!' Before I hiked off with my wares, Mom **13** pack a bag-lunch, then wave from our fuzzy porch, 'Jerry? Say "Please" and "Thank you very much." They like that.'

Other sales kids owned cars. I had to walk from house to house **14** my sample kit; twenty-six letters' worth of knowledge gets heavy pretty fast. My arms and back grew stronger but my spirits sort of **15** in. Our sales manager assigned me to the Mill district – he claimed I had inside ties. The only thing **16** than facing strangers door-to-door is finding people you know there.

Grinning, they'd ask me in. Mill employees opened their ice-boxes, brought me good things. I chattered my whole memorized **17**. Neighbours acted proud of me. But I felt like a circus dog and stuffy teacher, mixed. Like a crook. When I finished, my hosts **18**, said this book-set sure sounded great. Then they admitted what we'd known **19** along – they just couldn't afford it. I'd spent forty minutes ignoring this. They looked troubled as I backed out, smiling. 'Hey,' I called. 'You'll save for the down payment. You'll get "Knowledge" in time – it'll mean more to you.' Then I knocked at the next door. I stood **20** for an empty house.

B Passage interpretation.

K Points to include

1 He feels bad about it / it wasn't right.
2 He hated having to carry the heavy books / He had no car.
3 The more he tried to sell the book, the more depressed he became.
4 He felt like an actor / boring instructor, academic / a criminal.
5 He hated the job, trying to sell to (friendly) people he knew.
6 He knew the people couldn't afford to buy the book.

● *direct / reported speech p149*

A

K Pronouns: *I* to *you*, *they* to *we*
Tenses: *had* to *have*, *sounded* to *sounds*, *couldn't* to *can't*
Add speech marks, inverted commas

B

K The speaker might have said 'Please / Do come in.'
Reported questions.
He / She / They asked me if / whether I had ever sold books before.
He / She / They asked me how many books I had sold.
Ask students to identify the changes made, ie pronouns, tenses, word order, insertion of *if / whether*.

C

K 1 Paul explained that (in order) to mend the fuse, you first unscrewed / had to unscrew a particular part.
2 Sally whispered that her father had just won a lot of money.
3 The thief confessed that he had done it.
4 Rebecca announced that she wasn't going to marry him.

D

K The tenses do not change.
1 The President says that they are negotiating terms at the moment.
2 She said she might pop round this evening.
3 He says (that) if he were younger, he would learn how to use a computer.
4 The teacher asked the students if they would mind not smoking in the library.

E

K The phrases are not correct.
Suggest should be followed by *-ing* when the speaker is included in the suggestion.
Suggest should be followed by *that*, etc. either when the speaker is included, or (more usually) when the speaker is not included in the suggestion.
1 The students suggested having a barbecue.
2 Tim suggested that his mother had / should have a barbecue.
3 Bill suggested trying that new place for dinner.
4 The teacher suggested (to the student) that (s)he did / should do that essay again.

F

K 1 on doing
2 to having / having had
3 not to cross
4 about taking
5 for not complying / having complied
6 making / having made
7 to sue
8 about having / having had
9 to be set
10 to vote

Suggested answers
1 No, I'm going to do the job myself.
2 I don't see why I should write the report again.
3 Now, remember, don't cross the road by yourselves.
4 Could you give us some information about your English courses?
5 It's a disgrace! The management has ignored the new safety regulations.

6 Yes, I'm afraid I did make a mistake with the prescription.
7 I warn you, I'm going to sue the company for neglecting safety precautions.
8 I really hate and detest having to get up so early in the morning.
9 Please, please let me out.
10 I urge you all to vote against the unpopular tax bill.

G

K that day, the day before / the previous day, the day after / the next day, at that time / then, that / those, there and then, the week after / the next week, the week before / the previous week, the year before / the previous year

NB Emphasize that words relating to the present change only when circumstances change.

eg *We're having a sale here tomorrow.*

She said they were having a sale here tomorrow.
(Overheard in a department store today, and reported later in that store.)

She said they were having a sale there the next day / the day after.
(Overheard in a department store, eg last week, and reported later elsewhere.)

● *reporting verbs and accompanying adverbs p151*

A

K 1 He conceded that he might not have put as much effort into the job as he could have done.
2 He denied stealing / having stolen / protested that he had not stolen the money.
3 She announced that she was going to have a baby.
4 The student protested that he really had done the homework himself. / denied copying / denied having copied the homework from anyone else.
5 The gymnast boasted that (s)he was the greatest gymnast ever.
6 The little boy muttered (under his breath) that he needed to go to the bathroom.

B

K 1 grudgingly
2 defiantly / angrily
3 proudly / discreetly
4 defiantly / proudly
5 pompously / proudly
6 discreetly

Ask students to read out one sentence each to try to convey the mood suggested.

SUMMARY SKILLS

After-Sales Disservice!

● *talking points p151*

Ask students to look at the illustration on page 151.

A If necessary, explain that the 'in-tray' for paperwork, etc. contains items which need to be dealt with (often urgently). The use of the contents of the in-tray as a desk leg indicates how unimportant the person behind the desk thinks they are, ie he is not interested in dealing with them at all!

B **Simulation.** Draw students' attention to the exam tip before going on to the simulation activity. Allow three to four minutes for this activity. Encourage students to discuss each item on the list, saying why it would / wouldn't be useful. Compare decisions when students have finished.

● *reading p152*

Asking questions to focus on information. Tell students to avoid writing simply *What happened next?*, and questions eliciting yes / no answers, and focus on the most important details.

K Suggested questions

3 Why was this not a serious problem?
What was wrong with the gadget?
What annoyed the writer?
4 How could the computer journalist have solved the problem?
Why did she choose not to solve the problem quickly and easily?
What did the journalist decide to do?
5 What explanation did the company offer for the defective item?
How did the journalist react to the company's explanation?
Why was she so angry?
6 How did the company react to her reply?
Why was it so difficult to get hold of the manager?
Why was the 'official' surprised?
7 Why was the journalist impressed?
Why was the employee unable to bring the reply to his screen?
What promise did the employee make?
8 What was the journalist tempted to do?
What prompted the second letter to the 'invisible' managing director?
What did the letter say?
9 Why did the company's public relations firm telephone the journalist?
Why did she decide to 'reveal all'?
What effect did this revelation have?

GROUP WORK After comparing questions, students could divide into groups of three or four and ask each other some of their questions. Ask them if the answers were what they expected.

Optional exam tip
Encourage students to ask themselves questions while they are reading, to focus on what the passage is about.

● *comprehension p153*

A

K Suggested answers

1. A never-ending story relating all the problems, implying there will be a long list of things which go wrong.
2. End up not being reliable after being pushed to and fro through the postal system. *Shunted* implies that things are handled roughly.
3. Heaping scornful abuse on previous damage already done. She felt it was the manufacturer's responsibility to arrange for equipment to be replaced, and not hers.
4. He would never come out of this meeting because (a) he was not in one or (b) he did not want to talk to the caller or (c) this was the standard excuse made when he did not want to be disturbed, or all three.
5. The alleged reply had never actually been sent (so it could not possibly be read out). The implication is the official is lying.
6. The weeks came and went as they do normally (this stresses the wait for the non-existent response). *Duly* implies that she was not surprised about this in the light of the company's lack of concern.
7. Silence was once again predominant, ie nobody contacted her.
8. My firm decision was no longer as strong (because of all the problems).
9. I told the public relations firm everything that had happened, including (presumably) what her job was, and the bad publicity the company was likely to receive.
10. Instead of / in place of (French). She implies this was not proper compensation.

B

K
1. the guilty parties
2. this sorry saga
3. fell victim to
4. took the management's eye off the ball
5. a fatal error
6. short-changed
7. to drag on indefinitely
8. sluggish

● *summary p153*

K Points to include

1. They stated on the phone that customers would not worry about the missing features, but could return the item for a replacement.
2. No reply sent to first letter of complaint.
3. An employee stated on the phone that a reply had been sent on 28 December, but couldn't confirm this when asked to.
4. Replacement promised.
5. Replacement not sent.
6. No reply sent to the second letter of complaint.
7. Public relations phone to see if customer is interested in another product, hears writer's complaint.
8. Equipment arrives next morning.
9. Letter of apology arrives the next week, plus software to appease customer.

Optional summary (up to 50 words)
Students could summarize what the writer feels the company should have concentrated on, and the advice she gives should this happen to you.

Points to include
The company should have concentrated on:
- its service to customers
- the standard of its products
- replacing goods or refunding money immediately.

Should this happen to you:
- do not become involved in lengthy correspondence
- report it to a local Trading Standards Office, which will ensure rapid results.

LISTENING AND SPEAKING

A Foot in the Door

● *talking points p153*

Try your hand.

1. PAIR WORK allow three to four minutes for this activity.
2. Allow four to five minutes for class feedback.

● *listening p154*

A The ten-point plan, part 1.

K
1. one hour.
2. the whole business.
3. can guarantee a sale in an hour.
4. **a** your customer
   b paperwork
5. smart but casual clothes.
6. all the equipment you need.
7. enthusiastic / smiling.

Tapescript
(**S** = Sales manager, **R** = Recruit)

S Let me explain the 10–point plan which operates on a scale of one hour.

R A plan for selling, you mean?

S Well, it's more than that. It's a complete strategic approach to the whole business really. If you follow all the points in the plan you can almost always guarantee a sale in an hour. The important thing is preparation. First, identify your customer and make sure you prepare all the necessary paperwork. You can't make any kind of successful sale without it. Find out exactly where the customer lives – and before you go, check your appearance.

R Sort of smart but casual?

S Exactly! No way-out, scruffy clothes but not too prosperous either, if you see what I mean! Then the kit – you must take all the equipment you need for the water test … and you must look enthusiastic and smile! The right attitude is vital.

B **The ten-point plan, part 2.**

Ask students to look at the ten-point plan on page 154. There are thirteen spaces.

K
1 Greeting
2 prejudge people
3 Make friends
4 Start selling
5 Are you the sole owner of the property?
6 Scene setting
7 for barriers
8 Go through demonstration
9 tonight
10 Trial
11 Handle any remaining objections
12 Consolidate
13 Thank for hospitality

Tapescript
(**S** = Sales manager, **R** = Recruit)

S Spend the first two minutes greeting the occupants of the house. This greeting stage is vital. Better to see a husband and wife together, ideally, and *don't* prejudge what kind of people they might be. You'd probably be wrong! You'll hear the usual objections at the door but introduce yourself politely and keep smiling!

R What does this 'ice' section refer to?

S That's your opportunity to break the ice. The first thing you do is make friends, then identify any problems your new 'friends' may have and find out what they need and really want. Once you've done this, you'll find it easy to start selling. You need to qualify the company really. Now comes the time to ask questions.

R What kind of questions?

S Oh, things like 'How long have you lived here?' – you can probably use the answer later! Do you work locally? And a very important one: 'Are you the sole owner of the property?'

R The sole owner? Oh, yes, of course. If there are several people sharing the premises, it's more difficult for one alone to make a decision.

S It's impossible! The next stage is scene setting. In fifteen minutes you should have set the scene for your sales pitch. At this particular stage you should watch for any barriers, such as finding the necessary money, deposit, etc. In the first half-hour you should have gone through your demonstration.

R The demonstration – that's the …

S The water test … never fails to convince! The next five minutes you should spend qualifying the product and gently insisting that you need a decision that night.

R And when do you mention the price?

S Only at the thirty to forty minute stage – when you approach the trial closing. You're still selling the product but on your way to closing the deal.

R So the trial closing is a kind of practice run?

S In a way, yes. The actual closing gives you a final opportunity to handle any remaining objections.

R What kind of objections might there be at this closing stage? I would have thought that by this point …

S No, no. Never assume anything. The reluctant customer will always keep one or two remaining objections up his sleeve to try and squeeze out at the last minute but you can deal with this by using as many closes as you need.

R And what about the final stage?

S Well, this is what we term 'consolidate'. You check the order form and the customer copy, be reassuring, and, most importantly, tell them what happens next. They'll be eager for further details. When you've gone through what the next step is, talk about something completely different, then thank them for their hospitality and tell them that you'll see them when the product is installed. Any questions?

R Er … dozens but I can't quite pin them down at the moment …

S Well, good luck and remember – your first sale is always the best!

R Yes, if you ever make one!

● *vocabulary p155*

A **Homonyms.**

K Suggested answers (other explanations can be found in the *Concise Oxford Dictionary*). The first meaning given in each set refers to its use on the tape.

1 well-groomed, clever, in good repair, stylish, to feel acute pain or distress
2 to shatter, interval, opportunity, to make or become inoperative
3 one and only, undersurface of the foot, flatfish
4 to establish, a number of things or people belonging together, setting for a play or film, styling of the hair, to put, lay or harden
5 a place in which events in real life, drama or fiction occur, a piece of a play, a landscape or a view

6 area of play in a field game, the highness or lowness of a (musical) tone, to erect and fix (tent), throw and fling
7 a point or period in a process, the theatrical profession, a point or stopping place on a route, to present a play
8 the exhibiting or explaining of specimens or experiments, outward showing of feeling, a public meeting
9 a trying or experimenting, a judicial examination, a sports match to test ability
10 a business arrangement, a large amount, a specified form of treatment, to distribute cards, to trade in, to take measures concerning

B Expressions.

K 1 a a good buy
b a bad buy
2 to shop around
3 to break even
4 to buy in bulk
5 out of stock
6 a it goes bankrupt
b it goes to the wall
7 to buy on credit

● *speaking p155*

Ask students to look at the pictures on page 155.

A PAIR WORK The picture on the left is of a cigarette advertisement in Egypt. The picture on the right is of a soap advertisement in India.

B GROUP WORK Give students five minutes to discuss the statements in groups of three or four. Ask selected groups for their conclusions.

WRITING

Task-based Composition

● *introduction p156*

Directed writing. Remind students of the previous task-based compositions they have tackled – the newspaper report on the flood in Unit 3 and the formal and informal letters in Unit 6. The question here is similar to one they might get in an exam, although the prompts are more contextualized.

● *stage 1 general approach p156*

The title. Establish that the question asks for a report and that the style needs to be fairly formal and business-like. Ask students to expand on this, and to suggest what kinds of language items you would expect to see in a report and what would be avoided. (This revises the differences between formal and informal language that were covered in Unit 6.)

Remind students to look carefully at the kind of composition that is specified, because if they use the wrong basic style they will get into serious trouble.

● *stage 2 brainstorming p156*

General themes. Point out to students that they will need to write a composition of 300 or 350 words. This means that the comments given are not detailed enough in themselves as a basis for the composition, and they need to speculate and make deductions about them. Go through the first example, and show how the questioning technique can lead to greater awareness and understanding of the problem.

Ask students to perform the same task with comments **b** to **f**. When they have compared their answers in pairs, ask selected students for their ideas on each of the comments.

● *stage 3 organization p156*

Paragraph planning. Expand a little on the point made here. There is a temptation in this kind of question to write a short paragraph about each specific complaint or comment, but this is not really an adequate approach for a Proficiency composition. In questions like this, complaints or comments are generally symptoms of underlying problems, and the challenge is to find out what those fundamental problems are.

Ask students to look carefully at the comments and at the sample composition and to identify the three main problem areas. In this case, there are two comments that illustrate each fundamental problem. Their completed notes should look as follows:

K Paragraph 2 Main problem area: insufficient variety of titles, mentioned in complaints b and f
Paragraph 3 Main problem area: inadequate publicity material, mentioned in complaints c and e
Paragraph 4 Main problem area: computer or administration, mentioned in complaints a and d.

● *sample composition p156*

Language focus. Students should always try and use their own words where possible, and should paraphrase comments or complaints. Ask them to find how the model composition paraphrased the words in the Language Focus section.

K *so dull* – not adequate
the choice of books – the variety and range of titles
Cattle Diseases in Botswana 1962–65 – specialist titles
blurb – information … about each title
your leaflet – catalogue / publicity material
a bill for £2,339,126.00 – grossly inaccurate invoices
sent me 25 copies – multiple deliveries

● *writing task p157*

This can be done in class or set as homework.

If you think your students may have difficulty in identifying the three basic problems that are raised by the comments, go through these in class. It is important for students to master this technique as it will give them the basis for their paragraphs. In the example here, the main problems are

1 The product range is not good enough. This is mentioned in the following comments.
'It's all just rubbish – I mean, who wants to go on buying dusters week after week?'
'There are always things we need but they never seem to have any of them.'
2 The salesmen need to be properly trained and managed. This is mentioned in the following comments.
'The fellow who came the other day was so surly and rude I asked him to leave even though I actually could have done with a couple of drying-up cloths.'
'I asked him if you could use the polish on furniture and he didn't have a clue.'
3 Potential customers are worried about security. This is mentioned in the following comments.
'You've got to be so careful these days with all these con men around.'
'They look so scruffy. I can't imagine ever letting one of them into my house.'

OVERVIEW 11

● *vocabulary p158*

K 1 B 2 C 3 C 4 C 5 D 6 D 7 B 8 C 9 C 10 B

● *transformations p158*

K
1 She suggested having a pizza. (Also: She suggested to her children that they had / should have a pizza.)
2 Sam boasted that he had passed his driving test first time.
3 Mary warned her friend not to tell anyone or (s)he'd / would be sorry.
4 The youth protested that he hadn't broken the window.
5 Anne suggested to Susie that she / that Susie should tell her parents about it. (Also: … that she told …)
6 The old man in the queue asked me if / whether I had been waiting long for a bus.
7 Julia insisted that she was going to change / on changing the wheel on the car herself.
8 The manager wanted to know if I had made up my mind about the job.
9 She accused me of stealing her gold bracelet.
10 The secretary asked me tactfully not to mention / if I would mind not mentioning the incident.

● *blank-filling p159*

K
1 accused
2 threatened
3 if (s)he had (kept)
4 spread
5 collapsed
6 pick up
7 she would never tell
8 What on
9 should have told
10 if I should

● *rewriting p159*

K
1 The business is hardly breaking even at the moment.
2 Nowadays goods are often bought on credit.
3 The father urged his son not to drink anything alcoholic if he was going to drive home.
4 We always buy in bulk in order to make more profit.
5 The old woman pleaded with the intruder not to take her money as it was all that she had.
6 He dabbled in antiques, which made him a little extra money.
He made a little extra money as / because he dabbled in antiques.
7 The new manager is always picking on me (for everything that goes wrong).
8 The car went for £1,500.
9 There is not much call for books on animal diseases in Outer Mongolia.
10 We shall discuss the recommendations in full at the next meeting.

UNIT 12

TAKING LIBERTIES

READING

The Killing Fields

● *talking points p160*

This unit looks at the concepts of liberty and justice rather than at crime and punishment, and this introductory part is designed to make students think about the first of these.

K **1** Ask students to comment on where in the world it is or has been illegal to do the things which are mentioned. There are many countries where laws against these activities exist, and the answers below are only examples.

- **a** Most totalitarian governments, both left wing and right wing, have laws against criticism.
- **b** In the USA during Prohibition, and in many Islamic countries such as Saudi Arabia.
- **c** In England during the reign of Queen Mary a number of Protestants were executed for not embracing Catholicism; many other examples of this exist throughout history.
- **d** The former Soviet Union controlled the movements of people strictly.
- **e** Saudi Arabia.
- **f** Ireland.
- **g** Cambodia under the Khmer Rouge.
- **h** Malaysia.
- **i** Iraq, apparently.
- **j** China.

PAIR WORK Ask students to discuss Questions **2**, **3** and **4**. These questions lead into the reading passage about an individual's experience under a totalitarian regime.

● *reading p160*

A Ask students if they have seen or heard of the film *The Killing Fields*; if they have, ask them to provide a brief résumé of the main points; if not, give them the background information.

Notes

The passage comes from a book written by Haing S. Ngor, a Cambodian doctor. It details his experiences during the Cambodian revolution when the country was ruled by the Khmer Rouge under the leadership of Pol Pot. The revolution led to the forced exodus of the majority of the people in the cities, and the population was sent to work in the rice fields. Many people died or were killed there, hence the name of the book *The Killing Fields*.

Ask students to explain the following words and phrases or supply them with the explanations that follow.

the front lines – refers to the front lines in a battlefield where the most intense fighting is taking place

kramas – a kind of blanket

pitiful – causing sorrow and compassion

shoulderboard – a pole carried on the shoulder to which bags can be attached for transportation

edema – a medical term for swelling

bloated – puffed up

scrawny – this adjective is often used to mean thin, but also conjures up the image of being covered in wrinkled skin, like the neck of a chicken.

trudged off – walked away laboriously

hobbled off – walked away lamely, limped

B Multiple-choice questions.

Refer students to the photograph on page 161. The photograph is of Haing S. Ngor (on the right), and Dith Pran (on the left), both survivors of the Cambodian revolution. Haing S. Ngor played Dith Pran in the film adaptation of *The Killing Fields*.

K **1** B

2 C (*new* here means 're-educated' politically so as to conform with the beliefs and values of the revolutionary government).

3 D

4 C

5 B

6 D

Ask students what they think the occupation of the writer is. ANSWER A doctor.

C Style

K **1** One example is *For all we know we were going to the moon*. There are numerous examples throughout the passage.

2 The vocabulary is fairly simple and informal, with the exception of a number of phrases in paragraphs 3 and 6.

3 There are three very short sentences:
The following morning the exodus began.
Another journey.
It was a cold morning.
The length of the sentences mirrors the feelings of the writer in that at the time he was exhausted, and these short sentences reflect that sense of weariness.

4 Paragraph 3 is descriptive; the sentences are much longer and this is well suited to the panorama being described; there is extensive use of adjectives, for example in sentence 4: *shrunken*, *haunted*, *vacant*, *thin*, *puffy*, *bloated*.

5 The passage is almost conversational.

6 The effect of this matter-of-fact and almost conversational tone is that the reader feels that the writer is simply talking and the experience sounds like a true story, which it is. A more formal style would have made the story less immediate and personal.
7 Ask students for their comments.

● *language focus p161*

A ***the use, to use, used to do*** **and** ***used to doing.*** Run through the examples of the different forms of *use*.

K 5 The forms with a /s/ sound are **1**, **3** and **4**. The form with a /z/ sound is **2**.

B

K **1** c **2** d **3** a **4** b

C

K **1**	used to	**6**	use
2	used	**7**	used to
3	use	**8**	get used to / have got used to
4	were used to	**9**	use
5	used		

Refer students to the exam tip on revision schedules.

STRUCTURE

The Scales of Justice

● *talking points p162*

PAIR WORK Ask students to run through the list of crimes and say which two words are popular rather than legal terms. ANSWERS *joyriding* (driving stolen cars), *shoplifting*.

Ask students to discuss Questions **1** to **3**.

● *cloze development p162*

The cloze test leads into the work on gerunds and infinitives by presenting a number of common uses of the gerund and infinitive. Before doing this exercise, make sure that students are aware that it is more like a contextualized 'blank-filling' exercise than a cloze, and that they will be required to write up to three words in each gap.

K **1**	to disregard	**6**	driving	**11**	to hear
2	being knocked	**7**	to ensure	**12**	to be swayed
3	reporting	**8**	to murder	**13**	to concentrate
4	to serve	**9**	shooting	**14**	coming
5	get over	**10**	to have fired	**15**	to leave

Go through the correct answers with students before moving on to the next exercise.

● *gerunds and infinitives p163*

Refer students to the exam tip.

A Examples of these uses of the gerund are:

K **1** *being knocked off.* Ask students to think of other examples of the gerund being used in the passive. Suggest they think of a sentence beginning *In spite of…* .
2 *(without) reporting.* Remind students that (as long as the verb depends on the preposition) the gerund is always used after a preposition rather than an infinitive. When the word *to* is a preposition it is followed by a gerund as in *look forward to seeing you.*
3 *(stopped) driving. Stop* is followed by either the infinitive or gerund, but its meaning changes, and this area is looked at in more detail below.
4 *(his) shooting.* Ask students to provide further examples of this use. Point out that in less formal English, the object pronoun is used rather than the possessive pronoun. For example, in informal English, one might say *Do you mind me sitting here?* rather than *Do you mind my sitting here?*
5 *Coming (to a decision was not difficult).* Ask students to provide additional examples. Point out that sentences can be rewritten as *It* + verb + adjective + infinitive. For example
Coming to a decision wasn't difficult.
It wasn't difficult to come to a decision.

Passing your driving test is easy.
It's easy to pass your driving test.

B

K **1** *(the opportunity) to disregard.* Point out that some nouns are followed by the infinitive, eg *reluctance to help*, *determination to succeed*, etc. Sometimes nouns are followed by a preposition, in which case they take the gerund, eg *no intention of leaving*, *doubts about going ahead*, etc. This is an area that is commonly tested.
2 *(was) to serve.* This example is complex because it refers to the future in the past. Ask students if they can think of other examples of the infinitive being used to refer to the future. It tends to be used in two ways that have a future element. Firstly, it can be used as an order, as in *You are not to do that again.* Also, it can have the meaning of *going to* and this use is common in newspapers: *The President is to visit Oxford next week.*
3 *(could not) get over.* Ask students what other verbs apart from modals are commonly followed by the bare infinitive. They are *make*, *let* and, depending on the context, verbs such as *see*, *hear*, *watch*, *notice*, *feel* and *help* (where *to* is optional).
4 *(wrote a letter to the Queen) to ensure.* Here the infinitive means 'in order to'.

5 *(attempted) to murder.* Ask students to provide other examples of verbs that are followed by the infinitive. Examples are *arrange*, *decide*, *plan*, *intend*, *promise*, *threaten*, etc.
6 *to have fired.* This is commonly used with passive expressions such as *He is thought / believed / known / said*, etc. when they refer to the past.
7 *(receives a phone call) to hear.* Often the word *only* is used in front of the infinitive and it generally refers to a misfortune of some kind. Other examples are *I got to the office only to find that I had left my keys behind*, or *They arrived at the airport on time only to discover that the plane had been cancelled.*
8 *(warned the jury not) to be swayed.*
9 *(advised them) to concentrate.* Ask students if they can think of other verbs followed by a direct object and infinitive. Other examples are *allow*, *encourage*, *force*, *invite*, *order*, *remind*, *teach*, *tell*. With *advise*, *allow* and *permit*, the gerund is used if the person concerned is not mentioned, eg *We don't allow smoking in the office.*
10 *(relieved) to leave.* Ask students to think of other examples.

C Transformations.

K 1 There's no point (in) appealing against your sentence.
2 He has no intention of giving up the fight to clear his name.
3 He is thought to have been staying in London at the time of the assault.
4 It came as a great shock to Elizabeth when she heard of her brother's arrest / to hear the news of her brother's arrest.
5 The complexity of the case prevented the jury from reaching a verdict.
6 Mr Jenkins was the last witness to be called.
7 I'd rather you didn't discuss details of this case in public.
8 If you are called to do jury service, it'll mean your having to take / taking time off work.
9 You were a fool to leave fingerprints behind.
10 Craig denied firing / having fired the gun.

● *changes in meaning p164*

A

K 1 **a** *I regret to say* is a way of introducing bad news, and means 'unfortunately'.
b *I regret + ing* refers to something you did in the past which you now wish you hadn't done.
2 **a** *try* + infinitive means to attempt to do something.
b *try + ing* is used when we mean 'to experiment', not necessarily successfully.
3 **a** *remembered seeing* means that he had seen Jane and remembered the fact that he saw her. The seeing came before the action of remembering.
b *remembered to send* means that she did not forget her mother's birthday. The remembering came before the action of sending.
4 **a** *went on to talk* means that he talked about the Renaissance subsequently.
b *went on talking* means that he continued talking without stopping.
5 **a** *never forget seeing* means that I saw the Taj Mahal and the memory will always be with me.
b *forgetting to lock* means that he did not lock the door because he did not remember to.
6 **a** *stop to have* implies that we are going somewhere, perhaps driving along a motorway, and need to stop driving in order to have something to eat.
b *stop going* implies that they used to go out a lot but no longer do so.
7 **a** *I dread to think* means 'I don't want to think', and is often used to talk about a reaction that is likely to be negative or hostile. Another example is *I dread to think what he will do when he finds out that you have decided to leave him.*
b *dreaded having to see* means the opposite of *look forward to.*
8 **a** *needs reorganizing.* The verb *need* has a passive meaning when it is followed by the gerund. Here it means 'needs to be reorganized', which is also possible.
b *need* + infinitive is the most common form of the verb *need* and expresses necessity.
9 **a** *meant to write* means 'intended to write'.
b *it'll mean being away* means 'it will entail / involve being away' or that 'being away will be a consequence of joining the Navy'.
10 **a** *helped to make.* Here *helped* means 'assisted'.
b *I can't help feeling* means 'I can't stop myself feeling'.

Ask students to look at the illustration on page 164 and to match it with one of the above sentences.
ANSWER **10b.**

B

K 1 learning / having learned
2 to become
3 to think
4 modernizing / to be modernized
5 living
6 to make / make

SUMMARY SKILLS

Who Dunnit?

Explain that the title of this section means 'Who has done / did it?' and is used to refer to who committed the murder / crime, usually in fiction.

● *talking points p165*

Ask the students to look at the photographs on page 165.

K Characters are (from left to right)

Batman – originally a children's comic strip character, now a cinema screen hero.

Supergirl – a cinema screen heroine.

Hercule Poirot – a Belgian detective created by Dame Agatha Christie (1890–1976). The Belgian detective first appeared in *The Mysterious Affair at Styles* (1920).

James Bond – the invention of author Ian Fleming (1908–1964). The now famous Secret Service Agent 007 (00 means 'licensed to kill') first appeared in 1953.

Choose two or three students and ask them briefly to describe why the detective story or thriller was entertaining.

● *extracting informatmon p165*

Notes
G. K. Chesterton (1874–1936) – His most famous novels are those dealing with the naïve priest / detective who first appeared in *The Innocence of Father Brown* (1911).

Allow two to three minutes for students to skim read the story, then ask them to fill in the missing words in the vocabulary exercise.

● *vocabulary p166*

K
1 dead
2 stabbed
3 testified
4 witnesses
5 confirmed
6 searched
7 trace
8 scene

● *comprehension p166*

A GROUP WORK Allow three to four minutes for students to prepare answers to Questions **1** to **6**, then ask students to supply answers and evidence from the text for their opinions.

K Suggested answers

1 Both the park and the entrance to the summer-house had been under constant observation and all the witnesses' stories correspond.
2 If anyone had stepped off the path, the delphiniums would have been damaged and, as the path of flowers ran directly to the summer-house, anyone leaving the path would have left some evidence of having done so.
3 He had been out late the previous night.
4 It was quite an unusually warm welcome.
5 To be 'courting', or going out with someone, with the intention of becoming engaged to be married.
6 He was talking to Miss Druce on the terrace.

B Crime-solving.

K 1 List of witnesses / suspects
A Patrick Floyd (secretary)
B Janet Druce (daughter of the dead man and in love with Dr Valentine?)
C Donald Druce (son of the dead man)
D Dr Valentine (in love with Janet Druce?)
E Mr Aubrey Traill (solicitor)
F, G Two nephews

2 Suggested location of crime and suspects (Letters refer to people in **1** above).

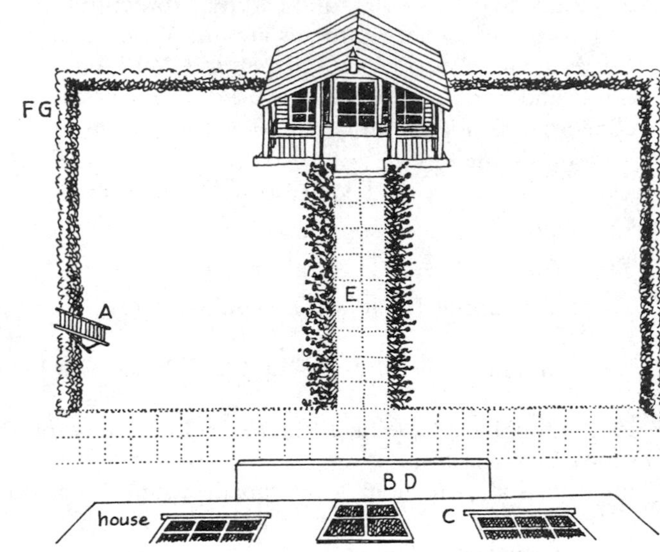

3 Timetable of events leading to the murder
1 Colonel Druce annoyed earlier in the day by his son's irregular hours.
2 Colonel very friendly when receiving his two nephews that morning.
3 Nephews were out for a walk when the murder was committed.
4 At 3.30, Janet Druce went to the summer-house to ask her father when he wanted tea.
5 Janet met Traill on her way back to the house and directed him towards the summer-house.
6 At approximately four o'clock Traill appeared at the door of the summer-house with the Colonel, who seemed very cheerful.
7 At approximately 4.10, Janet went down the garden and found her father dead.

4 Possible motives

Patrick Floyd (secretary) – maybe he didn't like his boss, he was the nearest person to the Colonel after Traill left, as far as we know.
Janet Druce (daughter) – maybe she wanted to marry Dr Valentine against her father's wishes.
Donald Druce (son) – father annoyed with him, maybe he was afraid he would be cut out of his father's will.
Dr Valentine (suitor) – not on good terms with the Colonel, maybe he wanted to marry Janet against the old man's wishes so had to get rid of him.
Mr Aubrey Traill (solicitor) – had possibly quarrelled with the Colonel, but it is unlikely.
Two nephews – possibly usually disliked by the Colonel but warmly welcomed on that day, which seemed rather suspicious – no obvious motive but their whereabouts were unknown at the time.

● *summary p166*

K Suggested insertions

That afternoon Floyd had been clipping the hedge **at the top of the step ladder and had a view of the whole garden** during the time the murder must have been committed. Consequently, he had witnessed Janet offering her father tea, **and the arrival and the departure of the solicitor**. During this time he saw no one else in the vicinity of the summer-house entrance. He was still engaged in his task when Miss Druce re-appeared **ten minutes later and found her father's body**.

● *problem-solving p166*

Ask the students to look at the picture on page 166.

Allow three to four minutes for students to arrive at a conclusion, then read out what really happened.

K **Solution**

Harry Druce, the Colonel's nephew, had lost a lot of money gambling at Monte Carlo and was in debt. He had been out walking with his brother Herbert and had stopped, supposedly to light a pipe. He had in his possession a walking stick. This walking stick was really a sword stick, which had an extra long blade, which he had pushed through the hedge, the flimsy wall of the summer-house and the chair on which Colonel Druce was sitting, into the old man's back. Harry then threw the sword stick into the sea for the dog to retrieve but, because of its weight, it had sunk without trace. He had once again been gambling; this time on the fact that his uncle (who was furious with his own son Donald at the time and had shown an unexpected friendliness towards Harry) had changed his will in his own favour. However, when Harry later learned that his uncle had left everything to his daughter Janet, and that he had committed the murder for nothing, he killed himself.

Ask students for their reactions to the original solution, eg do they think it is plausible, far-fetched, predictable?

LISTENING AND SPEAKING

Crimes and Punishments

● *speaking 1 p167*

Ask the students to look at the picture at the top of page 167.

A **Picture discussion.** Ask students to discuss the questions in pairs or small groups.

K **2** The symbolic significance of the statue is as follows: The scales represent fairness and equal treatment for all, and the sword represents punishment.

B **Weighing the evidence.** This activity can be done in small groups. When the students have finished, students from each group can present their decisions, and they should be encouraged to justify them to the rest of the class.

● *listening p167*

A

K **1** T **2** F **3** T **4** F **5** F **6** T **7** F **8** T

Tapescript

(**I** = Interviewer, **DL** = Dr Lafford)

I Today in the studio we have Dr Lafford, from the Forensic Science Service, who is here to tell us a little more about forensic science …

DL Good morning.

I Now, I think most people have a fairly good general picture of the kind of work you do – in many ways it's a development of Sherlock Holmes and his microscope, isn't it?

DL Yes, you could put it that way, although we've come a long way since then of course … but Holmes provides us with a model – a very good model in fact – of the kind of approach … psychological approach … that a forensic scientist should have. And that is that the forensic scientist is absolutely impartial.

I So you're not strictly speaking part of the police force … ?

DL No, we are quite separate.

I Could you tell us a little about your work and what it is you do?

DL Well, the basic principle behind forensic science is that every contact leaves a trace. Wherever we go, whatever we touch, there is a mutual transfer of material. The shoe that leaves a mark on the ground also picks up traces of dirt, and the hand that makes a fingerprint also carries away particles from the object that was handled … and hair or fibres are easily passed from one person to another …

I I see, so it's not just that the suspect leaves clues at the scene of the crime, the scene of the crime leaves clues on the suspect–

DL Absolutely, and that is normally the most compelling evidence – not just when you have a fingerprint for example, but also where you've found traces of, say, the carpet at the scene of a crime on the suspect's clothing, and that of course can be very hard to explain away.

I Is your work fairly straightforward – a question of seeing whether various samples match up?

DL No, no, no, not at all … forensic science is often a very painstaking task – and very time-consuming – much more so than previously in fact, because the range of tests has mushroomed … for example, we might be given some pieces of a headlight swept up after a hit-and-run accident and asked to identify the car, so we would fit the thousands of pieces together like a vast jigsaw, and might be able to identify the number embossed on the back of the glass … that would help us identify the model of the car, the make, the age, and so on, making it easier to search for the suspect … and then, once the car was located, we could tell whether the lights had been on at the time of the accident by examining the light bulb, because there would be minute pieces of molten glass on the metal filament in the bulb …

I So you need some fairly sophisticated equipment as well as patience …

DL Indeed. Now, the electron microscope is invaluable in our line of work – and it basically does two things – it gives us a fantastically detailed image, so, for example, you can tell whether a piece of hair has been broken, or cut with a pair of scissors or a knife. And it can also give you the chemical composition of a sample, so that you can take perhaps a tiny flake of paint on a suspect's clothing and match it with paint at the scene of the crime.

I Are you at the stage, then, when you could say that the evidence you provide is foolproof?

DL No, no, not foolproof. There is always room for human error and there's nothing that can be done about that … forensics is not an absolute science – I mean, let me give you an example. Now, Sherlock Holmes might have found a strand of hair at the scene of a crime, perhaps black and two inches long, that would have helped him identify the murderer on the basis that the hair matched the murderer's. Now we also examine hair … but in the example I gave you, perhaps one person in twenty has black hair two inches long, so we need to improve the analysis to narrow down the number of possible suspects. So we would analyse the strand of hair … using the electron microscope, as I was saying earlier … look at its chemical composition, whether it came from a man or a woman, see how it was cut, whether it showed traces of any particular chemicals and so on, and in that way instead of saying that one person in twenty had hair like that, it might be one person in 500,000 or a million. That would be just about as far as we could go. Now there's no such thing as a certainty … just a balance of probability, even with the most advanced techniques of genetic fingerprinting. The evidence we provide is there to be interpreted, and that's very important.

I Well, Dr Lafford, thank you very much. We'll take a break now, but stay with us and we'll be back …

B **White fingerprints.** Students may like to try this experiment out in class. If they decide to do so, and they are young students, strict supervision is necessary. The steps that Dr Lafford mentions are as follows.

K
1 C Press finger on glass slide.
2 D Place blob of superglue in glass dish.
3 E Balance slide upside down over superglue.
4 A Cover dish for two hours.
5 B A white fingerprint is developed.

Tapescript

(**I** = Interviewer, **DL** = Dr Lafford)

I Hello again. Now, if you've just joined us, today in the studio we have Dr Lafford, who's been telling us a little about his work at the Forensic Science Service … and during the break we've just been talking about white fingerprinting, which might interest our listeners because it's something they could try out at home. Over to you.

DL Thank you. Well now, what we call white fingerprinting is a technique that we have developed fairly recently, and it was developed as an alternative to dusting for fingerprints. And it's a technique that one could carry out fairly easily at home, as long as one is reasonably responsible with superglue—

I Why does it have to be superglue, by the way?

DL Well, the test relies on the interaction between the chemicals that are present in sweat and the vapour from the glue which would not be present in, say, er, epoxy resin.

I Right, so what steps do you take?

DL Well, you take a sample by pressing the index finger onto a plate of glass – make sure the surface receiving the print is clean of course, perhaps give it a quick wipe down – any piece will do, but one of those slides you use with microscopes is probably the easiest – and then you get a small glass dish and place a pool of the superglue in the bottom of the dish. Then you take the slide and put it on top of the dish so that the side with the print is facing the glue. After that you cover it up so that the vapour gets a chance to concentrate, but it's no more difficult than other, er, well, in the laboratory we can use other techniques such as using light to make the print fluorescent but this'll do the trick. Then all you have to do is wait a couple of hours, and you … well, when you take the slide out you'll see what we call a white fingerprint on the slide.

I Well, that's fascinating – I think I'll have a go myself when I get home … but to get back to the technique, presumably this means you can only do this with fairly small objects such as glasses or door-handles and things …

DL Oh no, no, no not at all, not at all – we sometimes take a whole car and seal it in a tent and expose it to the vapour, and it works very well – all you need is an adequate concentration, and the fingerprints are quite clear …

C **Expressions.** Ask students to do this exercise in pairs so they can pool their knowledge.

K
1 the letter of the law
2 lay down the law
3 above the law
4 the law of the jungle
5 take the law into his own hands
6 a law unto himself

● *speaking 2 p168*

A **Commenting on a passage.** In all there are three passages here. Do the first passage as a class activity so that students can see examples of the kinds of questions and answers that are required.

Notes
The passage was spoken by a judge at the end of a terrorist trial. It was also said that the six men would have been hanged if the death penalty had existed. Sixteen years later the men (the so-called 'Birmingham Six') were released after it was discovered that the evidence against them had been fabricated by the police.

K
1 The passage is spoken.
2 The passage is addressed to the people who have been found guilty.
3 The passage might come from a newspaper report of the trial.
4 A judge.
5 It raises the issue of what an appropriate sentence for murder might be.

B **Pair work.** One student should read Passage 1 and the other should read Passage 2. Allow students five to ten minutes to complete the task.

C **Communication activity.** Go through the first example about rioting, asking students for their reactions to and comments on the different opinions mentioned.

Ask each student to complete the five sentences without consulting each other. They should try and think of interesting or provocative opinions and be prepared to justify them.

GROUP WORK Ask students to take it in turns to read out their sentences, and to comment on and react to each others' ideas.

WRITING

True Stories

● *introduction p169*

This part looks at ways of telling anecdotes or true stories, and develops the point, made in the reading section, that a suitable style for a true story about a personal experience is a fairly informal first person narrative. Ask students to answer the first three questions.

1 Both narrators are possible, although a first person narrator will be more suitable in some circumstances; a third person narrator makes a story less personal.
2 A conversational style is more appropriate.
3 Informal vocabulary is more appropriate.

● *sample composition p169*

A Ask students to look at the objects in the picture on page 169 and then to skim read the composition. Explain that they will be asked to fill in the missing parts in a moment.

Notes
SAS – Special Air Service (of the British Army).
Make sure students understand that none of what the visitor said was true, including his claim to be a Muslim.

B **Sentence selection.** Explain that students need to choose one phrase from each pair to fill in the blanks in the composition. Point out that all of the phrases are grammatically correct, but that they should choose the phrases that best fit in with the overall style of the story.

Go through the options and ask students to say which of the phrases they chose and why. The following are the ones that are the most suitable, though if students disagree, encourage them to give their reasons.

K
1 **a** This kind of detail is an important feature of telling a personal anecdote; it provides a lot of information and personalizes the story.
2 **a** In the context of the story as a whole, this is the best option; it is a slightly formal structure, but this formality contrasts with the rest of the passage and tells the reader that the narrator wishes to stress this sentence. The reader will take particular note of the phrase ... *or so he claimed* and will realize that Gordon is not quite what he seems.
3 **b** This is the more informal of the two sentences, particularly because of the use of the emphatic *did*, the word *quite*, and the verb *wandering around*.
4 **b** This is a more dramatic sentence, and in view of what happens, has a strong element of irony.
5 **a** This is much less formal than the second, and the narrator is incorporating a form of reported speech in the text.

6 **a** This again is much less formal, and made almost conversational by the use of *very*.
7 **a** This is a more idiomatic way of expressing the idea, and therefore more suitable in this context.
8 **a** This is more informal because of the use of *some* instead of *a*, and is also rather exaggerated. This use of hyperbole, which is common in speech, contrasts with the relatively flat alternative.

● *focus on style p170*

Irony. Another way of looking at the question of irony is to ask students which sentences in the story are presented as facts even though the person telling the story knows that they are not true. Bearing in mind that the central character was a con man, examples of this are:

Paragraph 2

K He was a Colonel in the SAS …
He was in the village to collect money that was being wired to one of the banks …

Paragraph 3

… he had become a Muslim, and as was the custom, had adopted a new Muslim name …
Gordon had opted for Ghadaffi…

● *writing task p170*

Set the composition in the class or for homework.

OVERVIEW 12

● *vocabulary p171*

K **1** A **2** C **3** D **4** C **5** A **6** C **7** D **8** A **9** D **10** A

● *blank-filling p171*

K
1 get used to living
2 out to be
3 of explaining
4 to being
5 no point in
6 being told
7 to having / rather than having
8 so as not
9 get used to
10 to say

● *rewriting p171*

K
1 He left the house without locking the front door.
2 It's not worth trying to get your money back.
3 He was sentenced to three years in prison / three years' imprisonment.
4 I am not to blame for this mix-up.
5 Thanks to the new equipment the work can be done more safely. / The work can be done more safely thanks to the new equipment.
6 What was the significance of his evidence?
7 If you send her away to boarding-school, it'll mean not seeing her for months on end.
8 You were a fool to turn down that job.
9 It came as no great surprise to hear that he had been stealing money from the company.
10 Peter was the first person to visit our new home. / The first person to visit our new home was Peter.

● *transformations p172*

K
1 Jane was conspicuous by her absence.
2 I didn't pay much attention to the man standing at the gate.
3 Soldiers are used to obeying orders.
4 He left without saying goodbye.
5 Do you mind if I smoke? / Do you mind my smoking?
6 I stopped seeing her (so much) / so much of her when she went to London.
7 The colonel was not on good terms with the doctor.
8 The three men each received a life sentence.
9 Try to keep a low profile / out of sight when you get there.
10 I can't help feeling that he shouldn't marry her.

UNIT 13

THAT'S ENTERTAINMENT

READING

Getting your Act Together

● *passages for comment* p173

Draw students' attention to the exam tip.

Notes (numbers **1–5** refer to extracts)

1 *swing* – jazz or dance music with an easy flowing rhythm

2 *double bill* – two films showing one after another for the same entrance fee
stab – attempt (colloquial)
line-up – an arrangement of people in a team; here, the two films

3 *nursed* – promoted or paid special attention to
transferred – moved to another theatre

4 *naïve* – artless or innocent, eg G. K. Chesterton's 'Father Brown', mentioned in Unit 12 Section 3
brisk – quick, lively
luxuriance – florid, richly ornate quality

5 *groovacious* – an invented word from 'groovy', meaning fashionable and exciting
shop window – display case
the margins – the 'outer edges' of music
in the pocket – to be in pocket means 'not to make a financial loss'

K Suggested answers

1 **a** the difference between classical music and jazz
b a classical musician (speaking)
c in an interview on TV or radio / in a music magazine / arts page of a newspaper

2 **a** two films showing one after the other at the same cinema
b a film critic (writing)
c a film review section of a newspaper / magazine

3 **a** two plays, which for various reasons were unsuccessful
b the playwright, or producer, of these plays (speaking)
c a theatre / play review section of a newspaper / magazine

4 **a** a musical, possibly an opera, operetta (one-act, short or light opera), and the conductor of the orchestra
b a music critic (writing)
c in the review section of a newspaper / magazine

5 **a** two interesting musical albums which represent good value
b a music critic (writing)
c in the review section of a magazine / newspaper

● *reading* p174

A Ask the students to look at the photograph accompanying the article on page 174 and to say what they think the article is about.

Notes

Walk the plank was a punishment given to prisoners of pirates at sea, ie walking to their death along a piece of wood into the sea below, with no hope of escape. It also refers to the 'gangway' for those boarding a ship, and here is inviting people to come on board and watch the show.

Caledonian Canal – a man-made waterway linking the east and west coasts of Scotland

the marina – a specially designed harbour with moorings for pleasure yachts

The Norfolk Broads – a flat area in the English county of Norfolk, in the east of England, famous for its waterways and popular for holidays in small boats

Bonfire Night – November 5th, when English people celebrate the failure of a plot to blow up the Houses of Parliament in 1605 by Guy Fawkes, who was later tortured and executed

B **Multiple-choice questions.**

K **1** D **2** D **3** C **4** B

C **Comprehension.**

K
1 coated in iron
2 to make every other ship look small
3 a show with fireworks
4 has been rather overshadowed
5 an extravagantly and profusely painted surface
6 the things that inspired them
7 a huge jump in aspirations / a much more ambitious concept
8 disperse like a fire out of control; used here it means 'to become known very rapidly'
9 they asked for sponsorship for every nautical mile they travelled, eg a certain amount of money would be paid by each sponsor for every mile travelled at sea
10 keep it on the water / stop it going bankrupt

● *vocabulary* p175

Expressions with *make*.

K
1 to make a name for yourself
2 to make the best of a bad job
3 to make amends
4 to make a move
5 to make a profit
6 to make a meal of something
7 to make believe
8 to make a mountain out of a molehill
9 to make a mess of

● *discussion p175*

PAIR WORK Allow four to five minutes for students to prepare their talks, then ask one or two pairs to read out their talks, with each student reading out half.

STRUCTURE

Formal Constraints

● *talking points p176*

Ask the students to look at the invitation on page 176. It is important to reply to a formal invitation like this in the third person.

a Acceptance.

K (Named person(s)) would like to thank / thank(s) (named person(s)) for his / her / their kind invitation to (named occasion) and have / take great pleasure in accepting.

b Refusal.

(Named person(s)) would like to thank / thank(s) (named person(s)) for his / her / their kind invitation to (occasion) but regret(s) that he / she / they will be unable to attend due to (reason, eg a prior engagement).

You would be expected to dress formally. For men, *black tie* means a dinner jacket and bow tie; *white tie* means more formal 'tails', ie a coat with tails and a top hat and bow tie. A morning coat is worn during the day, eg for garden parties and weddings, again with a top hat.

Ladies usually wear short or long evening dresses for the later evening, and short dresses or suits for the daytime or early evening.

● *cloze development p176*

Point out that there may be more than one suitable answer.

K
1 about / going
2 haven / point / landmark
3 mistaken / wrong
4 invited / asked
5 included
6 otherwise / normally / usually
7 until
8 advice
9 neighbour
10 occasions / events
11 suit / costume / outfit
12 will (possibly 'do / can')
13 inherited
14 kit
15 generations (possibly 'decades')
16 so
17 missing
18 effigy / image / model
19 concert
20 must

● *vocabulary p176*

A

K
1 dangerous / precarious / treacherous
2 simple
3 declined / turned down / refused
4 subordinate / inferior
5 commonplace / ordinary / mundane
6 pristine / in excellent condition
7 uncomfortably
8 took off

B

K
1 ordinary
2 took off
3 decline / turn down / refuse
4 dangerous / precarious / treacherous
5 inferior
6 simple

● *discussion p177*

K Suggested answers

1 He would have refused the invitation.
2 He felt it was below one's dignity to hire evening dress because it meant that you did not possess your own. You should give the impression that your family has always possessed clothing of this kind, ie always attended grand occasions.
3 He felt as if he was in a plaster cast or in a strait-jacket, like a waiter at tables, or a musical conductor, wearing the uniform of his profession.
4 She was incredulous / shocked / amused / surprised.

● *inversions p177*

K Inversions are usually used with negative adverbs, or words considered negative, like *seldom*, *scarcely*, *hardly*, *rarely*.

A

The inversion is used to emphasize two rather negative aspects of hiring the suit, and gives more weight to the writer's friend's comments. Contrast *You would not only spend £35 hiring it, but … .*

We normally use an inversion to form the interrogative. It is the verb in the main clause of a sentence that is inverted.

B

K
1 We need *do / does / did*.
   a do
   b does
   c did
2 These words suggest a negative or restricted meaning, eg *rarely* means 'not often'; *little* means 'not much'; *only then* means 'not before'.
3 You must add a *when* or *than* later in the same sentence.
   a when
   b than
4 Only when she set foot in the house did she realize that something was wrong.

C

K
1 Not only was he working all day but (also) all night (as well / too). **NB** Use either *also* or *as well / too*, not both!
2 Never had he stayed in such a dreadful hotel before.
3 Not only does she dance beautifully but she (also) sings sweetly (as well / too).
4 Never have I met such an infuriating person (before).

5 Not a drop did she spill.
6 Rarely do they spend any / much money on entertainment.
7 Little does she understand how much suffering she has caused.
8 No sooner had we finished putting up the tent than it started to rain.
9 Only by trial and error did they discover a cure for the disease.
10 Only when they saw the evidence for themselves did they understand what the fuss was about.

SUMMARY SKILLS

The Perks of the Job

● *talking points p178*

Ask students to look at the pictures on page 178.

A Allow two to three minutes for the picture discussion.

B **Expressing opinions.** GROUP WORK Allow three to four minutes for this activity. Encourage students to evaluate each item on the list in turn before making suggestions of their own.

● *comprehension p179*

A Ask students for their initial interpretation of the first paragraph before going on to Questions 1–4. Tell them not to worry at this stage if they do not understand what it is about.

K Suggested answers
1 It tells us that she was working in a publicity department.
2 *Key journos* means important / special journalists, and tells us that the event was an important publicity stunt designed to enhance the company's image, and that the *journos* were reporting it.
3 He finds it quite disgusting and so, he supposes, would most people.
4 He was pleased to have been considered an important journalist.

B

K *a dusty view.* What does this tell you about the writer's attitude to this kind of outing?
so-called freebie. What information does this give about the type of outing on offer?
I had confused high moral principle with envy. What does this convey about the writer's views prior to this event?
philosophical sea-change began to dawn on me. What does *sea-change* mean and what does it tell you about the writer's feelings?
skimmed through the skies. What impression does this give about the flight?
sparkled ... glittered. What are these verbs normally used to describe and how are they used effectively here?
threading their way down. What is the normal meaning of *thread* and what vision does it conjure up?

GROUP WORK When students have finished writing their own clues tell them to ask each other their questions, and discuss the suitability of the answers.

C

K Suggested answers
1 He had been impressed both by his surroundings and the hospitality, and he had changed his mind about the free trips, deciding that they were a good thing after all.
2 Heavenly suet refers to the date pudding (made with suet, a hard, white fat used to make dough), which the writer had just eaten.
3 A day's salmon fishing in Scotland.
4 Very little indeed.
5 A fishing expert.
6 Understand how to do it.
7 Then I became aware that the person who had thought up the trip understood very well indeed what fishermen, and journalists, needed.

● *summary p179*

K Points to include
1 He was flattered to be thought of as an important journalist.
2 He realized that his original objections to 'free' outings were founded on the fact that he had never been invited to one.
3 The company wanted to give journalists a free fishing trip in idyllic surroundings with excellent food, etc.
4 A malt whisky tasting suggests that this was probably the real point of the trip and the company was in fact a malt whisky producer.

Optional summary
Students could write a summary of 60 to 80 words describing the writer's day out and his feelings during the day.

Points to include
1 Journey to Scotland, enjoyed flying over beautiful countryside.
2 Excellent meal, with second helpings, in an attractive location.
3 Fly fishing for salmon, made difficult by strong wind and lack of experience, but he eventually began to master the art.
4 Malt whisky tasting, which he thoroughly enjoyed.

LISTENING AND SPEAKING

Glued to the Box

● *speaking p180*

A **Picture discussion: electronic wallpaper.** Ask students to look at the photographs on page 180, then ask them what they understand by the term *electronic wallpaper*. ANSWER It refers to the way that the television is often left on in a room almost out of habit, whether or not anyone is watching it.

PAIR WORK Student A can ask Questions **1–4**; student B can ask Questions **5–8**. After the questions, ask selected students to talk about the points their partner made.

B **Passages for comment.** This activity gives students the opportunity to revise skills required in the interview, by asking and answering questions on the passages for comment.

Remind students that they should always try to say whether a passage is formal or informal, spoken or written, who it is addressed to, who is speaking or writing, etc. They should also try to comment on the issues raised.

PAIR WORK Student A should prepare a set of interview questions on one of the three passages. Student B should prepare a set of interview questions on a different passage. When they are ready, students should ask each other the questions they have prepared.

Students may not be able to answer all the questions with certainty, so remind them of a few useful phrases of uncertainty, such as:
it might be …
it's hard to say categorically whether it is spoken or written …
it looks as though it might be …
I think it's probably from a newspaper because it says … .

Invite further phrases from the students and write them on the board.

Notes
After the activity, students may wish to know where the passages came from.

Passage A came from an editorial in *The Times* newspaper which is a serious 'quality' newspaper in the UK. This explains the formal tone of the passage. It raises the issue of television and justice, and whether it is a good thing for the legal system to be popularized by having real trials shown on television, as is sometimes done in America.

Passage B comes from the novel *Brave New World* by Aldous Huxley. It raises the issue of whether we are affected by what we see, and of whether people can be manipulated and brainwashed by television.

Passage C is taken from a popular newspaper; it is an unfavourable review of an episode in a popular soap opera. It could lead to a discussion of what students watch and why.

C **Discussion activity: moral issues and the media.** Explain to students that all of these situations are based on real events, but the names and exact locations have been changed.

GROUP WORK When the discussion is over, ask selected students for their reactions and decisions.

● *listening p181*

Ask students to look at the illustration on page 181 and to explain what is happening. Draw their attention to the exam tip.

A **Camcorder man.** The listening passage serves as a model for the communication activity that follows.

K **1** A **2** B **3** D **4** B **5** D

Tapescript
(**I** = Interviewer)

I In the past it has been the Sony Walkman and the PC, but the designer accessory of the moment is indisputably the camcorder. Here at the shrine of Camcorder Man, the electronics store Dixons, yet another camera is about to be bought. By the end of this year, an estimated three-quarters of a million will have been sold, an increase of nearly 50% on last year. This one costs nearly a thousand pounds, and if you believe the man selling it, it's worth every penny.

Salesman As I said, it comes with an eight times zoom, …

I Right.

Salesman … stereo sound, …

I Right.

Salesman … recording, as I said, wind, wind reduction, so you don't get the interference, a lot of people had that problem …

I Right. … A few feet away, June, a housewife from Cambridgeshire, has just paid out £700 for her camcorder. She feels she's keeping up with the Joneses.

June My next door neighbours took one on holiday when they went skiing and they had some very good results and they … you know, you could re-live your holiday or wherever you've been. And that was really the main reason.

I And what are you going to use it for?

June Er, I've got a very large dog which has a lot of photographs taken of him and that's probably why it will be useful.

I Watching a video of June's dog may not be most people's idea of compulsive viewing but then again most home movies weren't meant for public consumption. Occasionally though, something unexpected will be captured on film, in which case Camcorder Man is then in a position to fulfil his ultimate dream …

Presenter Ladies and gentlemen, it's Jeremy Beadle.

I The hugely popular *You've been Framed* TV series hosted by Jeremy Beadle consists of nothing but home movies. And the man with probably the most trying job in television is the show's executive producer. His team's just finished watching every second of five thousand domestic sagas sent in by hopeful film makers. The vast majority he says are, to put it mildly, uneventful. One film for instance featured ...

Livesey ... well, people, lying on the beach sunbathing. Um, and watching someone sunbathe for fifteen minutes, er, isn't ... is fairly mind-boggling, simply lying in the sun, turning over occasionally.

I But for every thousand boring tapes there are one or two bizarre ones.

Livesey Well, I think that probably the strangest tape we were sent was a whole ninety minute tape of a man decorating a room naked. We've not used the tape.

I Some who wield the single staring eye on their shoulders are aware of the jokes being cracked at their expense. But John Munroe says much of the humour's unfair. He maintains there's a difference between being a camcorder bore, or anorak, and a camcorder enthusiast like himself.

Munroe I don't sleep with my camcorder, I don't take it shopping with me, I don't, er, I was going to say I don't take it to work, but I have been known to bring it to work with me I'm afraid ... but , er, I'm not a camcorder anorak. You don't have to be to ... to have a good time with a camcorder.

Presenter That was a report by Jonathan Hales. The time is twenty-three minutes past eight. In the past few days we've had reports ...

B **Communication activity: radio broadcast.** This exercise should take no less than thirty minutes, so it is best to start it at the beginning of a lesson rather than trying to fit it into a fixed period towards the end. If you have additional time at the end of the lesson, you can move on to the composition or the overview sections.

Divide the class up into groups of three or four students. Allow them to read through the instructions in the Student's Book under the heading **Format**. If necessary, play the tape again so that students get a clear idea of the structure of the tape.

Write up these notes under the heading **Procedure** before asking students to complete the task.

Procedure

1 Select any topic that interests you. You might present a report on the exam you are about to take, your school, a local issue, something in the news, a fashion item, a travel report, horoscopes, a piece on the supernatural. Remember that you can use your imagination as much as you like, and your feature does not have to be factual or exact.

2 Allocate roles to the various members of the group. Discuss what points each of you will make in your interview extracts, and what points will be left for the presenter to summarize. The presenter should work out what to say in the introduction and at the end.

3 Make notes on what you will say in your extract. Try if possible not to write the whole interview out as this may make it lose some of its spontaneity. Run through the whole piece once or twice until you feel confident.

4 If you have access to a tape recorder, make a recording of your feature to play to the rest of the class. If not, each group should present their feature 'live' to the rest of the class. If there is time, each group should prepare a set of comprehension questions for other members of the class to complete.

One of the factors that will provide the motivation to do this task is the desire to give a good performance. Therefore the groups need to have an audience at the end, which should be the other students in the class. If the class is very small and only one group is feasible, the teacher should take on the role of the audience, and should not be involved in the production of the interview.

WRITING

Blended Description

• *introduction p182*

A Ask students to read the example of what is meant by a 'blended description'. Another question could be *In what ways has your character been affected by the place where you live?*

Explain that it is important at the planning stage to give adequate weight to all the elements in the question.

B **Outline planning.** Ask students to select the best outline for the composition. The second outline is the best, but the first outline would also be possible. The problem with the third approach is that it does not really answer the question and would be particularly difficult to write.

• *sample composition p182*

A Allow students to read through the composition and help with any vocabulary difficulties they may have.

B **Language study: illustrations and examples.** This is a very useful area of language both in the descriptive and in other kinds of composition.

1 such as / like
2 exemplifies
3 for example, for instance
4 the prime example
5 take
6 One such

Note
The picture shows the game of Aunt Sally, which is mentioned in **6**, being played.

● *writing task p183*

Set the writing task in class or as homework. Remind students again of the point made in Stage 5, which is that grammatical accuracy is very important. Ask them to rewrite any sections where they are unsure of their grammar.

OVERVIEW 13

● *vocabulary p184*

K **1** C **2** B **3** D **4** D **5** C **6** B **7** D **8** D **9** D **10** C

● *transformations p184*

K
1 Rarely do we see such a high standard of performance in an amateur production.
2 Never have I come across such a horrifying film.
3 Little did they suspect that the musical was going to be a runaway success.
4 No sooner had we started the performance than there was a loud explosion.
5 Only if you purchase a ticket for the show can you enter the competition to meet the cast.
6 Scarcely had I begun my solo when there was a noise of breaking glass off-stage.
7 Not only will you enhance your posture but you will (also) improve your acting ability (as well) on this course.
8 Hardly had we finished dinner when the thunderstorm broke.
9 Not only did he book tickets for the afternoon performance but he (also) booked for the evening performance (as well).
10 Not a tear did she shed when the story ended in tragedy.

● *blank-filling p185*

K
1 did he forget his keys / passport
2 did she realize (that)
3 had she sat down / got into the bath than
4 made a
5 survival
6 the added perk / benefit
7 to be thought
8 wrong / the matter with
9 to nothing
10 to the south lay

● *rewriting p185*

K
1 We wouldn't want to impose any restrictions on the freedom of the students.
2 The meaning of a 'freebie' suddenly dawned on me. / It suddenly dawned on me what the meaning of a 'freebie' was.
3 I did not want to visit Moscow without learning / having learned Russian (first).
4 I did not notice it was formal dress until it was too late.
or It was not until it was too late that I noticed it was formal dress.
or Not until it was too late did I notice it was formal dress.
5 Don't make a mountain out of a molehill.
6 It is / You will find it impossible to make amends for what you have done.
7 (It's) no wonder (that) they are always in trouble.
8 He has been unable to cope with the pressures of being in the public eye.
9 They failed to raise the necessary finance for the venture.
10 Scarcely had he bought the car when it broke down.

UNIT 14
The World in our Hands

READING

Day and Night

● *talking points p186*

Eco quiz. Point out that the Eco quiz is a general knowledge quiz, and students do not need to refer to the reading passage before they do it. When they are ready, refer them to the key on page 215.

● *reading p186*

A After they have chosen, refer them to the key on page 215.

Notes

Victorian – adjective referring to the reign of Queen Victoria (1837–1901).

County Hall – the centre of the local government.

Fossil fuels – coal, gas and oil.

The Plough – a constellation also known as Ursa Major which looks like a plough or saucepan.

the Observatory at Greenwich – a long established observatory near London; degrees of longitude are calculated from Greenwich, which has a longitude of 0.

B Comprehension.

K
1 *every nook and cranny* – every part of a place. Literally a *nook* is a corner and *cranny* is a crack in a wall or rock. The expression is used to underline the lack of privacy caused by the lights.
2 *semi-detached suburbia* – the outskirts of a city (ie the suburbs) consisting largely of semi detached houses. The word *suburbia* has negative overtones of being dull and uninteresting.
3 *haven* – literally means a harbour or a port. Here it means a safe place or refuge from all the light.
4 *would-be* – a *would-be intruder* is someone who wants to be or would like to be an intruder. It is commonly used to describe people who aspire to something without possessing the necessary qualities, as in a *would-be pop star*, a *would-be gentleman*.
5 *masterminded* – planned and controlled. The word implies a certain amount of impersonal control.
6 *Big Brother* – a totalitarian central authority. The phrase is from George Orwell's *1984*; in his futuristic novel, Orwell predicted the rise of a totalitarian state where everyone would be constantly watched via cameras by a central government (Big Brother). The writer is emphasizing the view that 'no longer do we feel cared for or in control'.
7 *the scourge of London* – the affliction or curse of London; literally a *scourge* was a whip used for chastising people for their sins.
8 *star-studded* – freely dotted with stars, in contrast to the uniformity of the *orange glow* of electric street lights.
9 *uniform orange glow* – a dull orange light from the streetlights that is always the same.
10 *dawn chorus* – birds singing together at daybreak.

C Multiple-choice questions.

K 1 C 2 C 3 A 4 D

● *vocabulary p187*

A Adjectives. Point out that in other contexts, the 'negative' adjectives might have more positive meanings.

K Positive adjectives connected with light = safe, civilized, mellow yellow
Negative adjectives connected with light = bright, penetrating, harsh, blazing, magnesium-lit, dreaded, uniform

B Allow students to use dictionaries if necessary to do this exercise.

K
1 Positive words connected with sound = mellifluous, catchy, harmonious
2 Negative words connected with sound = strident, cacophonous, shrill
3 Positive words connected with smell = fragrant, scented, aromatic
4 Negative words connected with smell = musty, acrid, fetid
5 Positive words connected with taste = palatable, tasty, delicious
6 Negative words connected with taste = insipid, tasteless, bland

Ask students to choose one word from each group and to write a sentence that contextualizes it. When they have finished, ask selected students to read out their sentences.

C Expressions. GROUP WORK Ask students to pool their knowledge and ideas. Check that they have correctly matched the expressions and the definitions as follows.

K 1 i 2 f 3 e 4 c 5 g 6 h 7 b 8 a 9 d

Ask students to complete the blank-filling exercise individually.

1 a dark horse
2 have come to light
3 makes light of
4 went out like a light
5 a shot in the dark
6 kept (them) in the dark
7 the light at the end of the tunnel
8 to see the light
9 the bright lights

Ask selected students for sentences to illustrate the meaning of the expressions.

STRUCTURE

Tomorrow's World

• *cloze development p188*

Write up the following questions on the board. Ask students to skim read the cloze passage for the answers.

What will the main effect of global warming be?
ANSWER A rise in sea levels.
Why has the full effect of global warming not yet taken place? ANSWER Because it takes a long time for the oceans to heat up.
Which areas in the developed world does the writer say will be affected? ANSWER East Anglia, the Netherlands, Miami.
What will the effect be on the developing countries? Why? ANSWER A dramatic increase in homelessness, because many people live on low-lying coastal land. A second effect will be famine as rainfall levels fall.

Refer students to the exam tip. Give them an example of a 'complete' sentence from the cloze passage, eg *Nobody knows (1) … what would happen in a warmer world, but we (2) … know some things.* Then ask students to fill in the blanks in the cloze.

K
1 quite, exactly, precisely
2 do
3 water
4 temperature
5 risen
6 just
7 so
8 means
9 up
10 use
11 working
12 what
13 be
14 at
15 located / situated
16 almost
17 swept
18 worse
19 according
20 worsen

• *tenses in future time clauses p188*

A Run through the examples with the students; ask if they can think of any other time words that follow this pattern. Examples are *as soon as*, *the moment*, *once*, *before*, *the minute*, etc.

Ask students to look at the use of the simple present tense and the present perfect.

K There is no significant difference in meaning between **1a** and **1b**. There is a difference between **2a** and **2b**. In the former, the speaker probably lives in London and is extending an invitation; in the latter, the speaker does not live in London, and may be asking for a report on what the city is like. The speaker expects the listener to go to London first before coming to see him / her.

B Ask students to choose one of four tenses, the present simple, present progressive, present perfect simple or present perfect progressive.

K
1 am
2 is leaving
3 have been swimming
4 have read
5 want
6 are waiting

• *the future p189*

A This is a revision section, as students should be generally aware of most ways of referring to the future; however, there may be certain areas which are not quite clear, and the exercise should help them locate any gaps in their knowledge.

Ask students to read through sentences **1–17**, and for each sentence choose the future form most appropriate to the context.

K
1 begins
2 will continue
3 is going to rain
4 am playing
5 am going to mend
6 'll take
7 won't start
8 was going to write
9 'll give
10 'll be
11 are not to fire
12 'll be sitting
13 was seeing
14 are to separate
15 will have finished
16 'll be going
17 will have been working

NB In sentence **2** CFC refers to chlorofluorocarbons, which are ozone depleting gases commonly found in some aerosol sprays, coolants and packaging materials.

B Make sure that the students fully understand the task here. Using sentences **1–10** of the exercise they have just completed, they must illustrate the ten grammar points being made.

K The sentences which illustrate these points are:
1 Present simple – timetables: Sentence 1
2 Present progressive – arrangements: Sentence 4
3 **a** Going to – decisions and intentions: Sentence 5
b Going to – predictions: Sentence 3
c Going to – 'future in the past': Sentence 8
4 Will – predictions: Sentence 2
The term 'temporal auxiliary' is used here because the word *will* is principally being used to indicate future time.
5 **a** Will – spontaneous decisions: Sentence 6
b Will – offers and requests : Sentence 9
c Will – deduction: Sentence 10
d Will – willingness: Sentence 7
The term 'modal auxiliary' is used here because the word *will* has a function other than expressing the future.

C Ask students to complete the remaining grammar notes with illustrations from sentences **11–17**.

K **6** **a** Future progressive – action in progress: Sentence 12
b Future progressive – matter of course: Sentence 16
The future progressive as used in **6b** emphasizes that the offer being made will not cause the speaker any inconvenience. Ask students to compare the following two sentences:
Give me the cheque – I'll go to the bank.
Give me the cheque – I'll be going to the bank.
In the first, the speaker may be making an offer to go out of his way to go to the bank; in the second it is clear that the speaker is already planning to go to the bank anyway.

7 **a** Infinitive – formal orders: Sentence 11
b Infinitive – plans and intentions: Sentence 14
8 Future perfect – completed actions: Sentence 15
9 Future perfect progressive – duration: Sentence 17
Remind students not to use the future progressive after *when*. For example, we would say *When Mr Merry has been working for us for 25 years, we'll have a party*. In this context *will have been working* would be wrong.
10 Past progressive – changed arrangements: Sentence 13
Point out to students that *was going to* can also be used for changed arrangements. So you could say either: *I was seeing her today, but we had to move it to Friday*, or: *I was going to see her today, but we had to move it to Friday*.
However, when we talk about changed plans / intentions, eg *I was going to paint the dining room, but I bought the wrong kind of paint*, *was going to* is the only possible choice.

● *context and future tenses p190*

K Acceptable ways of referring to the future in this paragraph are: *won't visit, won't be visiting, is not visiting*.

PAIR WORK Allow students five to ten minutes for this activity.

SUMMARY SKILLS

Where do we go from Here?

● *talking points p191*

Ask students to look at the picture accompanying the article on page 191. Allow three to four minutes for the picture discussion. If necessary, explain that the picture shows the Sphinx surrounded by scaffolding. The ancient monument was in urgent need of restoration when the photograph was taken in 1992.

Suggested prompts for further discussion:
- why it is vital to preserve our culture.
- other things we could more profitably do.
- should we repair ancient monuments, which are then different from the originals, and thus not true representations of what they must have been like?
- should the general public have access to ancient monuments and run the risk of destroying them even further?

● *reading p191*

K The best answer is **2** as the others are either too narrow in their application, or do not focus on the real point the article is making.

● *vocabulary p192*

K **1** g **2** c **3** j **4** a **5** i **6** e **7** b **8** h **9** f **10** d **11** l **12** k

Explain any words students may still not fully understand, or tell them to look up the words in a dictionary.

● *comprehension p192*

K Suggested answers
1 serious 'learned' articles on a particular subject
2 the absolute brutality / barbarousness of the gigantic form
3 hastened the occurrence of
4 strain on resources, etc. caused by too many people living in the area
5 no noticeable increase in the capacity of
6 lines drawn between the places mentioned would form a triangle, inside which the effects of pollution are severe enough to cause death
7 huge numbers of archaeologists arrive, enticed by ...
8 accounts of the dreadful effects mass tourism has on the environment
9 (survival may be) founded on a random choice or decision
10 an artistic or intellectual unrestricted discussion

● *summary p192*

K Points to include
1 the short- and long-term survival of Egypt's antiquities
2 too many inhabitants, pollution, too many tourists
3 changes of water patterns caused by the building of the Aswan High Dam
4 'salty' stone of monuments absorbing more extremely salty water from underneath
5 evaporation of water leaves salt deposits on the surface of monuments
6 leaking sewage from outdated sewage system increases amounts of underground water
7 encroaching human habitation increases airborne pollution
8 industrial emissions and traffic fumes produce unacceptable high levels of pollution
9 hordes of visitors to the area also contribute to pollution

Ask students to read out their headlines and decide which one is the most 'attention-seeking'.

Optional summary

Students could write a summary of between 60 and 80 words on people's attitudes towards Egyptian antiquities.

Points to include

1 the fascination they have held for travellers over the centuries
2 the universal familiarity we all feel towards them
3 people's reactions to seeing them in all their glory, eg shock, amazement
4 the opinion of those in the Middle East and the Western world that they represent everlasting life
5 the fear that they will soon exist no longer
6 the arguments about what can be done to preserve them
7 the realization that what happens to these antiquities could act as a model for the rest of the world.

LISTENING AND SPEAKING

A Tangled Web

● *listening 1 p192*

The park. One of the aims of this listening and speaking section is to lead to a discussion of some of the more complex issues related to the destruction of the rainforests. These issues are not black and white, which is why this section is called *A Tangled Web*. Different interest groups, all of whom have reasonable claims, are competing with each other. They all have very different aims.

The first listening passage looks at a proposed national park in the Amazon, and how it affects the government, the military, the local Indians and the gold miners.

Ask students to look at the map on page 192, so that they are clear what part of the world is under discussion.

K 1 F 2 T 3 T 4 F 5 F 6 F 7 T 8 F

Tapescript

(**S** = Speaker, **R** = Reporter)

S Good morning. It's good to see some familiar faces here as well as, er, some new ones. Perhaps for those of you who haven't been to one of our press briefings before, could I say just that here at Survival International we are doing our best to keep the press informed of the developments in North Brazil, and in particular the effects … how any developments will affect the Yanomami Indians, the indigenous population … The last time was sadly a rather more optimistic occasion than this one, and as those of you who were here will recall, we gave you the details of the proposed Yanomami park, and the idea was that land would be set aside and let to the local Indian population and would basically have the same protection as most National parks.

We have called this meeting because we are concerned now that there is a certain amount of backtracking going on and the whole concept of the park is under considerable threat from various pressure groups, and we want to make sure that they do not get their way.

At current estimates, there are about 7,500 Yanomami Indians in Roraima and Amazonas states in North Brazil, but the number is falling rapidly. The main threat comes from the gold miners, who have brought diseases like flu and measles which are fatal to the Indians, and their presence has brought other social problems such as alcoholism, and prostitution. FUNAI which is the Indian agency has had some success of ridding the Yanomami land of gold miners by closing down the miners' airstrips, but there are still far too many intruders in the area.

There is little support for the proposed park from local government. The governor of Roraima state, which will lose 45% of its territory, has actively assisted the gold miners, and the governor of Amazonas has complained that the park will create what he calls an 'enclave … where the Amazon's prime gold deposits are.'

The people opposing the park have resurrected the old but powerful paranoia, the internationalization of the Amazon. The fear is that the concern for the minorities and the environment is little more than a foreign plot. The suspicion is that foreign companies are angling for a separate Indian nation which they will then be able to dominate and exploit for its mineral wealth.

There are other threats to the park as well, even if it was actually created. The federal justice minister has suggested, rather cynically to my mind, that because so many of the Yanomami have been killed by disease, they don't need such a large area. There have been calls for mining to be allowed even if the park is created, and there has been a recent proposal, supported by the military, for the construction of a transfrontier highway which would cut through the heart of the park.

We believe that the attempts to block the creation of the park or to water down the protection it would offer need to be resisted; we need to encourage the government to carry out their proposals in full and to resist these pressures. The local Indians are not in a position to be able to ensure this themselves and need our help and as much publicity as you can give them. While the idea of a park may be important to us, for them it is literally a matter of life or death. Well, that briefly is what we wanted to bring to your attention. And now if any of you have any questions, I'd be happy to do my best to answer them.

R Mr Anderson, what if the Roraima state government agreed to implement these policies …

● *speaking p192*

A **Picture discussion.** PAIR WORK Ask students to discuss the photographs on page 193. Allow three to four minutes for this activity, then ask selected students for their comments.

B Ask students to read through the passage twice. When answering the questions, students should be encouraged to support their views by quoting the relevant parts of the text.

K
1 The speaker is probably a local politician.
2 The speaker might come from South America or any developing country where the environment is an important issue.
3 The countries being referred to are the industrialized countries in the Northern hemisphere; whereas the term *West* generally refers to Europe and the USA, *North* includes countries like Japan.
4 The tone is indignant, and the style is informal.
5 The main priorities of the North are to prevent developing countries from adding to pollution and the process of ecological collapse; however, the countries of the North are not prepared to pay for this.
6 The speaker's main priorities are economic growth and industrial expansion so that the country can eliminate malnutrition, disease and poverty.
7 No set answer.

C GROUP WORK Ask students to write down which character they have chosen, and check that students in any group have not chosen the same character.

When students are ready, they should read out their speech (in full or from notes) to the others, who must guess which character the student has chosen.

D **Discussion.** PAIR WORK Allow students five minutes to decide which factors are the most / least significant, then ask selected students for their ideas. Take this opportunity to check that students are familiar with the vocabulary connected with the environment, (CFCs, acid rain, global warming, etc) as this is a common discussion and composition subject.

● *listening 2 p194*

A lot of hot air. This listening passage presents an alternative view to the problems of the environment which students may find interesting. After checking the answers, ask students for their reaction to what they have heard.

K 1 T 2 F 3 F 4 T 5 F

Tapescript

(I = Interviewer, **DL** = David Lawson)

I Good morning and welcome to 'Green Issues'. Our studio guest today is David Lawson, someone who is well known for his scepticism about green issues, and whose recent TV documentary casting doubt on the theory of global warming caused something of a storm. Could you give us a brief outline of what your views are on the subject?

DL Well, this belief in global warming has become what you might call the conventional wisdom of our time … and as is the case with all these received ideas, I thought it would be worth taking a cold hard look at global warming and seeing what the facts really were.

I And so what did you find?

DL Very little, in a word, in the way of hard evidence, but a great deal in terms of rather dubious interpretations of statistics …

I Could you give us an example of that?

DL Yes, certainly … take temperatures as a case in point. Now there have been temperature measurements taken over this century which are generally supposed to show that temperatures are rising … Now, this thermometer record is beset with problems, partly because most of the weather stations are centred in the heavily populated areas of the North, but more importantly because most of them are also found in towns. And as anyone who lives in London will be aware, towns are hotter than the surrounding countryside because of the, er, so-called heat island effect …

I So you would say that the evidence is flawed?

DL The interpretation of the results is certainly flawed … and compounded with this is satellite data. There has been a ten-year study taken by satellites which obviously aren't affected by the heat island problem, and that shows no evidence at all of global warming over the decade.

I OK, but if there is no evidence of an increase in temperature, and I haven't been able to analyse your statistics, so I can't really comment on that, what about increases in sea-level?

DL It's much the same as with temperature change, and when you take a closer look, the evidence tells a different story. Most of the more reputable scientific predictions say there will be a rise of half a metre or so in the next 100 years. Now there is an underlying problem when you measure sea-level. Are you measuring the level of the sea or the level of the land?

I Does it make any difference?

DL Yes, if the land moves up the sea appears to fall and vice versa. If the sea-level is rising, you might expect it to rise everywhere, but this is not the case. Even within the British Isles, for purely geological reasons, the sea-level is rising in the Southeast and falling in the North of Scotland.

I You may have a point there, but what about carbon dioxide … would you deny that carbon dioxide emissions are rising?

DL No, that is certain. But what is less certain is what effect that will have. The whole business of quantifying the effects of carbon dioxide is immensely complex and relies on a computer model that may not be accurate. You only have to look at the problems they have with the weather forecast to see how difficult the process can be ... and interestingly, we are now beginning to hear a few voices suggesting that carbon dioxide may in fact not lead to a rise in temperature, because of a whole series of interactions that haven't yet been considered. And finally, as you know, plants react very well to increased levels of carbon dioxide and this may help to meet the growing food demands of an increasing population.

I Very well ... if temperatures and sea-levels are not rising and carbon dioxide is a good thing, how do you think we have been led to talk so seriously of catastrophe?

DL I think it's partly a question of scientific funding ... if you're a scientist you need to attract money to carry out research, and one way of getting attention is to predict a catastrophe ... and then everyone wants to jump on the bandwagon, and if you raise your voice in dissent you are ostracized. Politicians haven't been slow to see the advantages – after all, what could be less controversial than government action to save mother earth? And for the rest of us, perhaps it is just that in a world without ideals, we need a catastrophe to give us something to believe in.

WRITING

Putting your Case

● *introduction p194*

The argument composition. The plan that is outlined here, if it is understood fully, can be of considerable help to students who find it difficult to think of ideas to put in their compositions. Allow students to read through the introductory section.

Explain that the basic framework of the composition is to present the wrong ideas, dismiss them, and then present the right ones. The advantage of this approach is that students only need to produce about three central ideas to complete the composition.

Remind students that the kind of topics that can come up in the argument composition will tend to be the same as the topics in this book – the environment, family life, health, law and order, etc. They do not need to be experts on the subjects, but they need to have a few well-formulated opinions.

● *language focus p194*

Allow students to read through the selection of words and phrases that are useful in this kind of composition, and check that there are no problems with vocabulary.

Point out that in any given paragraph, there would be one or more phrases from each of the three sections here.

Ask students to suggest other words and phrases that are similar to the ones given here. Examples are:

K

A Introducing a false argument
There is a theory that ...
Some people feel that ...

B Demolishing a false argument
This is a contradiction in terms ...
On closer examination, this turns out to be untenable ...
The statistics on which this is based are unreliable ...

C Proposing a correct argument
One only has to look at ... to see that ...
Naturally ...
All the evidence points to the fact that ...

● *sample composition p195*

Allow students to read through the sample composition. Ask them to underline the set phrases mentioned in the language focus so they can see the framework of the composition more clearly. The phrases that are mentioned are:

It is often suggested ...
To a certain limited extent, there is some truth in this ...
However, the implication that ... is an over-simplification
It is clear that ...
There is also an idea implicit in the statement that ...
This argument has a certain superficial logic, but ...
The real situation ...
It is therefore quite wrong to suggest that ... ; on the contrary, ...

● *writing task p195*

Draw students' attention to the exam tip.

The writing task can be set for homework. If your students are likely to have difficulty with the title, allow some time in class to discuss the ideas mentioned in the brainstorming session.

OVERVIEW 14

● *vocabulary p196*

K **1** D **2** C **3** D **4** A **5** A **6** C **7** B **8** D **9** A **10** D **11** A **12** C **13** B **14** D **15** D

● *blank-filling p196*

K
1 will have been
2 that'll
3 or I'll
4 as I have read / finished
5 are not
6 no position
7 waste of time
8 'll give you a
9 goodness of her heart
10 an example to

● *rewriting p197*

K
1 Mass tourism is partly to blame for the problem.
Mass tourism has contributed to the problem.
2 He was kept in the dark about the company's new plans.
Details of the company's new plans were withheld from him.
3 Changes in the water table have done the monuments no good.
Changes in the water table have done a lot of damage to the monuments.
4 In all probability, there will be a rise in temperature in the next century.
There is a (reasonable) chance that there will be a rise in temperature in the next century.
5 Contrary to what it says on the label, / Despite what the label says, this product is not environmentally friendly.
6 You must resign yourself to / You must come to terms with the fact that she has left you.
7 According to the report the pyramids will deteriorate.
The report says (that) there will be further deterioration in (the condition of) the pyramids.

UNIT 15

The Media and the Message

READING

Windows on the World

● *talking points p198*

PAIR WORK If possible, take into the class real examples of serious broadsheet and popular tabloid newspapers and ask students to answer Question **1** in relation to these. If this is not possible, ask students to discuss the points in Question **1** in relation to the two newspapers in the picture.

Ask students to work through the points in Question **2**.

K Serious newspaper
stock-market prices
analysis of foreign news
law reports
arts review
an obituary

Popular tabloid
horoscopes
gossip column
a problem page
page 3 girls

Both
sports pages
TV schedules
crosswords (of varying degrees of difficulty)

Ask students to discuss Question **3** in groups.

● *register in the news p198*

K **1** The extracts come from the following papers.
popular – extracts B and D
serious – extracts A and C

2 The content varies in that the extracts from the serious papers are on more abstract subjects such as economics and sociology; the extracts from the popular papers are based on people, here focusing on the rich and famous (the Beatles), and a possible sex scandal.

3 In the extracts here, only one individual is named in the serious paper (Mr Ryder). The popular paper often uses nouns in front of an individual's name, eg *hubby* Paul, *ex-Beatle* Paul, *Bar owner* Wayne Lineker, *soccer ace* Gary, *beautiful schoolgirl* Zoe Davey.
The popular papers also give people's ages, eg Linda, 49, Paul, 50, Wayne Lineker, 29, Zoe, 15.

4 The extracts from the serious paper are written in neutral or formal language.
A feature of the extracts from the popular paper is that the language is very colloquial, eg *grabbed, hubby, slap-up, showbiz pals, rockers, hits, soccer ace, cuddled, absolutely crazy about.*
Another feature is the use of direct speech in two of the extracts. These quotations are often very short, eg 'I'll survive – I'm alive.' 'I'm no Bill Wyman.' (Bill Wyman is a member of *The Rolling Stones* who became the subject of intense tabloid interest when he married the teenager Mandy Smith).

● *reading p199*

A Ask students to skim read the extract to find the answer.

K Both serious and popular newspapers are biased.

The extract mentions a number of newspapers that would be familiar to British readers. It may be helpful to explain the differences between the newspapers very briefly. Below is a list giving a description of the papers and their political affiliation in very general terms.

Serious papers
The Times (Conservative)
The Guardian (Liberal / Labour)

Middle-market newspapers
Daily Express (Conservative)

Popular tabloids
Daily Mirror (Labour)
The Sun (Conservative)

Others
Socialist Worker (extreme left wing)

B

K **1** d **2** f **3** g **4** b **5** c **6** a **7** e

C Comprehension.

K **1** accept / acknowledge that there may be
2 the extreme left-wing; *loony* means 'lunatic' or 'mad', so this expression has negative overtones
3 hostilities towards and alliances with / similarities and differences in opinion
4 dominated and controlled by; *in the pockets of* often implies some financial connection as well. *Tories* refers to the Conservative Party.
5 photographs show things as they really are

D Multiple-choice questions.

K **1** C **2** C **3** C **4** B **5** D

● *vocabulary p200*

Ask students to look at the illustration on page 200 and to match it with one of the expressions.

PAIR WORK Ask students to do the matching exercise in pairs, so that they can pool their knowledge.

K **1** c **2** h **3** d **4** g **5** a **6** f **7** b **8** e

Allow students to complete the contextualized sentences individually, making any necessary changes.

1 have a vested interest
2 the gutter press
3 second thoughts
4 a few home truths
5 a raw deal
6 ivory towers
7 an entirely different kettle of fish
8 a far cry from

When students have written three contextualized sentences of their own, ask them to exchange the sentences with their partners to see if they can fill in the missing idiom. While they are doing the first part of this exercise, monitor the students to check that they are using the idioms appropriately.

STRUCTURE

Making Headlines

This is a revision section, and looks back at grammar points and idioms that have been used in the book up to now. If students find any part of this section difficult, it may indicate that they need to revise that particular area of grammar.

● *talking points p201*

Headline news. Allow students to look through the following authentic headlines and ask them to explain.

A what the headline is meant to refer to.
B what the secondary meaning is.

K MILK DRINKERS ARE TURNING TO POWDER
A milk powder is being used more and more by people who drink milk.
B people who drink milk are crumbling and turning into powder.

DRUNK GETS NINE MONTHS IN VIOLIN CASE
A a court case, which has involved a drunk and a violin, has resulted in the imprisonment of the drunk for nine months.
B a drunk has been sentenced to nine months' imprisonment inside a violin case.

TRAFFIC DEAD RISE SLOWLY
A the number of people who have been killed in car accidents is increasing slowly.
B the people who have been killed in car accidents are beginning to come back to life and get up slowly.

CARIBBEAN ISLANDS DRIFT TO LEFT
A the inhabitants of some Caribbean islands are adopting more left-wing policies.
B some Caribbean islands have broken loose from the ocean floor and are floating westwards.

IRAQI HEAD SEEKS ARMS
A an Iraqi leader is hoping to buy armaments.
B the disembodied head of an Iraqi is looking for some arms to attach to its body.

STOLEN PAINTING FOUND BY TREE
A a stolen painting has been found next to a tree.
B a tree has found a stolen painting.

GRANDMOTHER OF EIGHT MAKES HOLE IN ONE
A a grandmother, who has eight grandchildren, managed to complete a hole at a golf course with only one shot.
B a grandmother made a hole in one of her eight grandchildren.

POLICE DISCOVER CRACK IN AUSTRALIA
A police have discovered the drug 'crack' in Australia.
B police have discovered that Australia itself is broken, and there is a large crack in it.

MAN HELD OVER GIANT LA BRUSH FIRE
A a man has been arrested in connection with a large forest fire in Los Angeles.
B a man has been tied up and is being suspended over a large fire in Los Angeles.

THUGS EAT THEN ROB PROPRIETOR
A Some criminals ate a meal in a restaurant and then robbed the restaurant owner.
B some criminals ate a restaurant owner and then stole his money.

● *cloze development p201*

K

1	Gone	**11**	of
2	programs	**12**	for
3	past	**13**	rather
4	least	**14**	into
5	mean	**15**	open
6	said	**16**	where
7	have	**17**	pages / page
8	such	**18**	long
9	on	**19**	relation
10	to	**20**	hands

● *review of expressions p202*

A Tabloid talk.

K **1** B **2** A **3** A **4** B **5** D

B Draw students' attention to the cartoon on page 202, and ask them which idiom they think it illustrates, and what the idiom means. ANSWER an armchair critic (someone who expresses opinions about things he / she knows very little about).

Monitor what students are writing while they complete their sentences practising idioms. Check that the contexts they have thought of are appropriate.

C

K 1 He was so overcome with emotion that he was lost for words.
2 The police caught the burglar red-handed.
3 I always try to look on the bright side (of things).
4 After my divorce, she helped me pick up the pieces.
5 My brother's feeling a bit under the weather these days.
6 They managed to get to the airport in the nick of time.
7 I resent the way she looks down her nose at me.
8 The staff were upset that they had been kept in the dark about the company's plans.

● *grammar review p203*

A April Fool. Ask students whether newspapers in their own country have a tradition of printing joke stories on April 1st.

Ask students to find the mistakes in the April Fool story about the Channel Tunnel. Point out that this appeared before the tunnel was completed. The correct story should look as follows.

K Red-faced executives at Eurotunnel were trying **to make** light of a report that the two sides of the Channel Tunnel, which has been under construction for the last five years, **will not meet** in the middle. Not until the latest surveyor's report was published **did they realize** the terrible truth: the two ends will be approximately 300 metres apart when the digging is completed at the end of the year, **which** will cost an additional £20 million to put right. The error **is thought** to have stemmed from the fact that while English engineers have been doing calculations in feet and yards, the French have been **using** centimetres and metres. A Eurotunnel spokesman denied this **was** a serious matter and said: 'We never actually expected the two ends would meet up exactly. It **could** have been a lot worse, and we are absolutely **delighted** to have got so close. All we need to do is **put** in a few sharp corners and everything will be all right.'

B

K **1** on **2** for **3** to **4** of **5** Over / Through **6** up **7** about **8** in **9** to **10** to **11** up **12** in **13** to

C Transformations.

K 1 What really annoyed me was his refusal to listen to reason.
2 The company's recruitment policy has been under review for the last three months.
3 The comedian soon had everyone in the audience laughing.
4 He couldn't possibly have taken the money by mistake.
5 I wish I had never / hadn't started smoking.
6 He was absolutely thrilled / delighted to win / to have won / at winning the crossword competition.
7 The Prime Minister is thought to be considering raising taxes.
8 It wasn't until he was nearly 30 that he passed his driving test.
9 If the foundations hadn't been weak, the building wouldn't have collapsed.
10 We will have been married for ten years next Saturday.
11 He suggested that I should see a doctor.
12 I have no intention of discussing this matter any further.
13 Hardly had we started our walk when it began to rain.
14 Could you tell me when the last train to London leaves?

● *newspaper activity p204*

GROUP WORK If you have newspapers to hand, that would be useful, but if you do not, students can make up their own stories. Each group should write three short news stories. Two of these should be true, but allow students to change names and places if they cannot remember the precise details. One of them should be a completely fictitious April Fool's story.

When the groups have finished, ask them to read out the three stories to the rest of the class. The other students must try and guess which news story is the April Fool's story.

If some students have difficulty in thinking of suitable stories, give them the following possibilities.

April Fool Stories
Belgium is to be dissolved, and its territories allocated to France and the Netherlands.
The Eiffel Tower is to be dismantled and moved to Euro Disney.
To ease congestion in London, the government has decided to make the Underground free before 9 am in the morning.

Real stories
A man in India has started to type all the numbers from 1 to 1,000,000 in order to get into the Guinness Book of Records.
A man was refused social security payments on the grounds that he was dead. When he went to the office to complain, he was shown his death certificate to prove that he was no longer alive.
The European Commission has decreed that pork sausages can be made of chicken meat, as long as the percentage of chicken meat is less than 20%.

SUMMARY SKILLS

Getting your Message Across

● *talking points p204*

Ask students to look at the pictures on page 204 and identify their use. The objects are as follows:
Picture 1 – Howda chair
Picture 2 – humidifier
Picture 3 – knife sharpener
Picture 4 – pocket TV

Role-play. PAIR WORK Allow three to four minutes for this activity, then ask students to evaluate their powers of persuasion and determination in defending their standpoint.

● *summary 1 p204*

A Allow students a few seconds to skim read the paragraph before choosing an option in **B**.

B

K 2

● *comprehension 1 p205*

A Possible answers

K 1 C 2 B

B

K 1 never agreed with her/ been able to get on with her.
2 a huge amount of journalistic writing (a ream is 500 sheets of paper). Monica is an old-fashioned typewriter.

● *comprehension 2 p205*

Draw students' attention to the exam tip before they read the rest of the article which confirms the identity of Monica and the ironic tone of the passage.

K 1 **a** survived and developed a personality all of her own
b her secret little corners and places
c an old relic of the past which excites sympathy
2 their descriptions are so tedious and incomprehensible that they bore him 'to death'
3 **a** It is difficult to write well, and takes a long time.
b careless verbosity
c interrupting
4 He is playing on the word *processed* to emphasize that a word processor is not a substitute for creativity.
5 *Viruses* are disorders passed on from one computer program to another, like viruses in living things. RSI is a medical condition caused by using a word processor (repetitive strain injury).

● *summary 2 p206*

A Note on style. Read out the note to students and explain any references students may not understand, eg *train of thought, capture the essence, sequence events.*

B

K Points to include
1 His friends think he is mad.
2 They feel sorry for him because they think he is out-of-date.
3 They think they can win him over by extolling the virtues of their high-tech equipment.
4 He feels that they are incomprehensible and boring and doesn't bother to listen to them.
5 His relationship with Monica has been stormy.
6 He feels a loyalty towards and a bond with Monica because of all they have been through together.
7 As a journalist he needs an old and trusted friend as he spends many hours alone with only her to keep him company.
8 He feels new technology is too complicated and not worth bothering with.

Optional summary
A summary with a difference!

Ask students to write between 60 to 80 words from the point of view of one of the writer's friends. See if they can capture the same kind of 'amusing' tone and describe the writer as seen through the eyes of his friend.

Points to include
1 The journalist's 'insane' relationship with his battered old typewriter.
2 His 'ridiculous' belief that Monica is a real person.
3 His old-fashioned, out-dated ideas.
4 His refusal to adapt to modern technology.
5 The friend's attempts to inform the journalist of what he is missing.
6 The journalist's frustrating habit of 'switching off', ie not listening, when anyone tries to give him some useful or practical information.

LISTENING AND SPEAKING

Lack of Communication?

● *talking points p206*

PAIR WORK Encourage students to think of a) the immediate and b) the far-reaching consequences of these items malfunctioning.

K Suggested consequences
a stop watch – a watch with a mechanism for recording elapsed time
a can't time anything properly
b outcome of a race might be put in jeopardy

a tannoy system – a type of public address system
a announcements can't be heard
b in an emergency not possible to evacuate a building

a microchip – a small piece of semi-conductor (usually silicon) used to carry electronic circuits

a whole network of information could be lost or unobtainable if current switched off

b emergency systems could be rendered ineffective, eg ambulance systems

a black box – a flight recorder in an aircraft

a can't record what happens during the flight

b impossible to decide on the causes of an aircrash

a remote control device – means of controlling a machine or apparatus from a distance using signals transmitted from a radio or electronic device

a impossible to activate or deactivate, eg detonators to blow up something

b accidents could be prevented such as bombs going off, or caused because of unexpected delay

a nuclear power station – a place where nuclear fission produces energy

a system could develop a leak or explode, eg Five Mile Island, Chernobyl

b could result in widespread radioactive contamination causing deformities, cancer, death

an automatic sprinkler system – a device which releases water to extinguish fires

a water would not be released automatically or be released at the wrong time

b a building could burn down or extensive water damage could be caused

● *listening 1 p207*

A Play the tape once and allow two to three minutes for students to discuss their answers.

K
1 speakers: male service engineer / female customer
2 place: customer's home
3 the problem: fax machine won't work
4 cause of problem: cat has been sitting on it shedding fur
5 solution to the problem: protect the fax from the cat
6 misunderstanding about solution: don't fence in the cat, fence in the fax

B Sounds similar.

K
1 *fix* /fɪks/ – mend
flicks /flɪks/ – strikes or moves with a sudden movement or jerk
2 *fax* /fæks/ – copy produced by facsimile transmission
facts /fækts/ – true occurrences or details
3 *tiny* /taɪnɪ/ – very small or slight
tinny /tɪnɪ/ – of or like tin (metal)
4 *spots* /spɒts/ – marks / stains, singles out / recognizes
sports /spɔ:ts/ – games, wears / exhibits
5 *havoc* /hævək/ – widespread destruction or confusion
haddock /hædək/ – a marine fish
6 *shedding* /ʃedɪŋ/ – letting or causing to fall
shredding /ʃredɪŋ/ – tearing or cutting into pieces
7 *dirt* /dɜ:t/ – unclean matter
dearth /dɜ:θ/ – scarcity or lack
8 *word* /wɜ:d/ – meaningful part of speech
ward /wɔ:d/ – separate room in a hospital, young person under the protection of the court
9 *illegible* /ɪledʒəbl/ – not readable
ineligible /ɪnelɪdʒəbl/ – not eligible, undesirable
10 *screwed* /skru:d/ – twisted
skewed /skju:d/ – made oblique
11 *fence* /fens/ – barrier or railing
fends /fendz/ – looks after oneself, keeps away
12 *cages* /keɪdʒɪz/ – structures of bars or wires
gauges /geɪdʒɪz/ – standard measures, measures exactly

Point out to students that this is not an exhaustive list of the meanings of the words above. There are other meanings, which they can check in a dictionary.

Tapescript

(**M** = Male engineer, **F** = Female customer)

M Good morning. Called to fix the fax.
F Oh yes, come in. It's in the living-room over there.
M Hmm … what seems to be the trouble then?
F Well, look. Everything's covered in tiny black spots and criss-crosses – you see these fine strokes here …
M Ah ha! Where's the cat, then?
F Sorry?
M The cat. You've got one, haven't you?
F Well, yes, but …
M Happens all the time, madam. Cats are creating havoc on faxes. You're the third service call this morning and they've all been the same – damage caused by cats lying on the machine shedding fur and dirt.
F But surely a cat … ?
M Take my word for it. Nobody ever thinks about it until the faxes become messy, even illegible. Let me give you an example, I've just come from an open-plan office. Now this office has a resident 14-year-old cat that sits on the fax. Nothing comes through except in screwed-up bits and pieces unless someone's present to keep the cat away.
F Well, I must say I – I would never have thought …
M They're warm, you see. Cats like warmth – ironing boards that have just been used – that kind of thing …
F But what can I do? I don't want to get rid of my cat.
M If I were you, if you don't want to fence in the cat, fence in your fax.
F How do you mean?
M Get one of those aluminium cat-carrying cages.
F Oh, I couldn't put the cat in one of those …
M No, not the cat – the fax! That'll keep the animal far enough away so as not to do any damage.
F Oh! OK, right, right. Thanks very much for your advice.
M Right, that seems to be working fine now …
F Thanks again. Would you like a cup of tea?
M That's very kind of you. I wouldn't say no.

listening 2 p207

A

K **1** c **2** b **3** a

The correct attitude will depend on whether students think it is better to be assertive, aggressive or passive, but assertive would be the one recommended in a training session.

B

K Suggested skills feedback ratings

Areas for comment	**1**	**2**	**3**
Introducing themselves / department	C	A	A
Obtaining information / clarifying what the customer wanted	B	B	A
Calming the customer down	C	C	A
Repeating and recording information	C	C	A
Stating what will be done	C	A	A
Giving information to customer	C	C	A

GROUP WORK Allow two to three minutes for students to decide on ratings then compare their decisions with another group.

Tapescript

Conversation 1

(**R** = Receptionist, **C** = Customer)

R Morning

C Oh, good morning. Is that the Customer Service Department?

R Yes …

C I'm ringing to complain about the non-delivery of a washing machine …

R Oh, you're expecting a delivery, are you?

C Yes … I was. I waited in all morning and …

R So it was expected this morning, was it?

C Yes! Which is why I took the whole morning off. Have you any idea what might have happened?

R Well, no. Not really. You see the rota goes out with the driver in the morning, and unless I can page him, well ..

C So what are you going to do about it? I can't afford to take any more time off work.

R No … well, I'll have to have a word with supplies I suppose.

C Oh, for goodness' sake, let me give you my name and phone number and you can call me back. As soon as possible, please.

R Yes, all right, then …

Conversation 2

(**R** = Wilco Customer Service Department, **C** = Customer)

R Wilco Customer Service department.

C Oh, good afternoon. I'm ringing to make a complaint.

R A complaint. What kind of complaint?

C Well, it's about a bed I bought a couple of weeks ago for one of my children …

R Yes? What seems to be the trouble?

C Well, one of the castors – on the leg – has come off …

R I expect the children have been jumping off the end of the bed. It happens all the time.

C No, no. Nothing like that. In fact we've only just started to use the bed and the first time my son got into it the leg …

R And what exactly do you expect us to do about it?

C I was wondering if there was any kind of guarantee with the bed. It was obviously faulty and …

R I'll talk to the manager and we'll get back to you. Name and address?

C Right. It's …

Conversation 3

(**R** = Truckers' Customer Service department, **C** = Customer)

R Truckers' Customer Service. How can I help you?

C I'm ringing about a part for my tumble-drier. You ordered it for me a couple of weeks ago.

R Certainly, madam. But I believe we mentioned at the time that delivery could take up to four weeks.

C Yes, that's right but it's so difficult to manage without it.

R Of course, I quite understand. So you're checking on a part ordered when exactly?

C The beginning of the month for Mrs Wright, Acacia Avenue, North West 3.

R You wouldn't happen to have the part number by any chance?

C Oh dear … hmm … not with me … it might be on the slip …

R It would greatly assist us if you could provide the number of the part ordered.

C Oh, yes. Here it is … OZ241.

R OZ241. And what exactly is it?

C It's a rubber surround for the drum head.

R Fine. I'll get onto our suppliers right away and see if I can speed up delivery for you. I'll contact you as soon as I have any further information. Thank you for calling.

C Thank you.

R Not at all.

simulation p207

Allow four to five minutes for this activity. Lists will vary from one group to another but points could be based on the Listening 2 conversations. Encourage students to add some points of their own if possible. Allow time for feedback from each group after they have completed their list.

WRITING

Task-based Composition

● *introduction p208*

In preparing for the task-based composition students need to be made aware that the range of possible tasks is very wide. It is important to underline the fact that, whatever the task may be, students need to write in an appropriate style.

In this exercise, students are presented with short extracts in different styles and then have to write a number of paragraphs in specified styles.

Ask students to read through the three extracts and answer the questions that follow.

K 1 Extract **1** is from an advertisement for a computer company, and would be found in a magazine or in the company's publicity brochure. It is about the benefits of a particular model of computer.
Extract **2** is a transcript of spoken instructions explaining how to use the teletext facilities on a television to find out arrival times of aeroplanes coming into Heathrow Airport.
Extract **3** is an extract about tobacco from an encyclopedia.

2 Extract **1** is aimed at a potential customer; extract **3** is aimed at a general reader requiring factual information; extract **2** is aimed at a personal friend or member of the family.

3 Extract **3** is the most formal; extract **1** is less formal; and extract **2** is the$least formal.

4 Extract **1** uses the most descriptive adjectives including: *reliable*, *advanced*, *modular*, *lightning speed*, *fast*, *superior*, *ample*, *extended*, *perfect*, *professional*. This is because it is aiming to persuade people of the benefits of this particular machine.

5 Extract **1** is dominated by two sets of key vocabulary. There is the descriptive language above, and there is also a large measure of computer jargon, including the following terms: *modular design*, *expansions*, *MITAC MD 4033*, *Intel 33 MHZ 486DX microprocessor*, *system and cache memory*, *VGA graphics*, *1024x768*, *16 colours*, *desktop publishing*, *application*.
The key vocabulary in extract **2** is informal and conversational. It uses informal words such as: *TV*, *plane*, *bleeper* rather than the more formal equivalents of *television*, *aeroplane*, *remote control*.
The key vocabulary in extract **3** is scientific in that it includes terms such as: *narcotic*, *the Nicotiana family*, *volatile oil*, *alkaloid*, *cylindrical*. However, any specialist terms not known to a general reader are presented in inverted commas: 'shag', 'twist', 'pig-tail'.

6 Extract **1** uses one contraction, *there's*, as it is fairly informal.
Extract **2** uses contractions *I'll*, *I'm*, *doesn't*, in keeping with the informal tone.
Extract **3** does not use contractions.

7 Extract **1** uses the second personal singular, which is a feature of much publicity material. Many modern advertisements are aimed directly at the reader or potential customer and must answer the question 'What can this product do for me?'
Extract **2** makes extensive use of the second person singular because it is an extract from a set of instructions.
Extract **3** does not use the second person singular.

8 Extract **3** makes the most extensive use of the passive. The passive is often used in formal descriptions of a process.

9 Extract **2** is full of verbal padding or redundant language, and this is a feature of everyday speech. There are many examples of this, such as: *Incidentally*, *Well*, *OK*, *actually*, *Anyway*, *kind of*, *you know*, *Now*, *sort of*, *you see*, *basically*.

● *register shifts p208*

Ask students to complete the change from formal to informal instructions. Here is an example of how the finished task might look.

K It's very easy and quick to make an omelette. You just need two eggs, a little butter and water, a frying pan and somewhere to cook. Basically, you just break the eggs into a bowl and beat them, add a little water or milk and stir it. Then you melt the butter in the frying pan and pour the egg in. You cook it for a minute or so, and then fold it up and serve it.

● *writing task p209*

Ask students to look at the advertisement on page 209. Set the writing task in class or for homework. Point out to students that they should follow the style of the models to complete this task correctly.

OVERVIEW 15

• *vocabulary p210*

K **1** C **2** D **3** B **4** B **5** B **6** D **7** C **8** B **9** A **10** C

• *transformations p210*

K
1 Jane seems to have changed her mind about coming this evening.
2 No sooner had I got downstairs than the phone stopped ringing.
3 He has no intention of giving up work / retiring when he is 65.
4 He greatly regretted not seeing Audrey on her trip to London.
5 Despite the fact that he was disabled, he managed to sail / sailed round the world.
6 Had she known that he was married, she would not have agreed to go out to dinner with him.
7 He was allowed to leave after he had been questioned by the police. / He was released after questioning by the police.
8 The music teacher had the whole class singing in tune after a few weeks.
9 The singer had very little money (left) when he died, which surprised everybody.
10 It was only when they read about Peter in the paper that they found out / discovered who he really was.

• *blank-filling p211*

K
1 guess
2 a far
3 Contrary
4 hooks
5 more than anything
6 I didn't have
7 had we set out / left the house / started our walk when
8 had been me
9 far as I'm
10 the plane was / flight has been

• *rewriting p211*

K
1 I was lost for words.
2 The press seem to have got wind of the MP's indiscretions.
3 The arrived at the station in the nick of time.
4 He was having second thoughts about moving house. / He was beginning to have second thoughts about moving house.
5 I am fed up with all this violence on TV.
6 It's time we went home.
7 I enjoy being a big fish in a small pond.
8 I think you should try and look on the bright side (of things).
9 The sound is picked up by the microphone hand set.
10 The procedure is as follows.

UNIT TESTS

TEST

Unit 1

● *vocabulary*

Choose the word or phrase which best completes each sentence.

1 Don't be such a .... blanket – come and join the fun!
A rolling **B** stuffed
C nosy **D** wet

2 When he suddenly .... up the subject of genetic engineering, there was an embarrassed silence.
A took **B** brought
C showed **D** came

3 In southern Spain you can play golf on beautiful .... overlooking the sea.
A fields **B** pitches
C courses **D** courts

4 He had to retire from the match suffering from a .... ligament.
A torn **B** broken
C slipped **D** sprained

5 She was .... with the results of the photo finish, which proved that she had come second in the race.
A resentful **B** mistrustful
C sceptical **D** disappointed

6 The angry football fans .... their fists at the referee.
A pressed **B** gripped
C clenched **D** clasped

7 Children! It's time you .... away those toys!
A tidy **B** to tidy
C tidied **D** should tidy

8 My anti-sports tendencies were reinforced .... the years by reports of injured sports enthusiasts.
A in **B** for
C by **D** over

9 Don't let anything .... you from your training programme.
A defect **B** distract
C defer **D** disturb

10 Some doctors see their patients as a(n) .... into hospital efficiency.
A menace **B** intrusion
C obstacle **D** distraction

● *mini-cloze*

Fill each of the blank spaces with **one** *suitable word.*

For enthusiasts who are (**1**)............. on sport as (**2**)............. as music, a musical work-out will (**3**)............. them with the best of both worlds. Sportsmen and women can now (**4**)............. from the transfer of ballet and classical dance skills to sports (**5**)............. as skiing. Even those who (**6**)............. part in athletics are discovering that exercise to music helps their movements stay more (**7**)............. . Media exposure has (**8**)............. home the advantages of keep-fit activities like aerobics to a world-wide (**9**)............. . So what was (**10**)............. viewed with some scepticism is increasingly becoming a fact of life in the world of sport.

● *blank-filling*

Fill each of the blank spaces with a suitable word or phrase.

1 It's high time you .... yourself a proper job!

2 What do all sports .... common?

3 The pop star, ... single has just hit the top of the charts, is giving an open-air concert on Saturday night.

4 Some forms of genetic engineering are now .... of some public concern.

5 Some medical research is widely .... being beneficial.

● *rewriting*

Write a new sentence using the word given.

1 Participation in sports is compulsory for all students.
PART ....

2 He admits he's not one of the important members of the organization.
COG ....

3 In my opinion, classical music is far superior to jazz.
RATHER..

4 The final date of the games is still undecided, according to the committee.
ON ....

5 The increasing popularity of opera has been a great boon to the music industry.
FROM..

TEST

Unit 2

vocabulary

Choose the word which best completes each sentence.

1 To the .... , most of the concepts of higher mathematics are a complete mystery.
A people B layman
C commoner D community

2 The .... of the blast shattered windows in nearby buildings.
A wave B surge
C force D rush

3 I bumped into Janet quite .... chance when I was shopping in London.
A on B by
C with D at

4 It .... as a shock to realize that I was not alone in the room.
A came B appeared
C arrived D reached

5 The weather men say there is a .... chance of snow this weekend.
A one-one B two-two
C twenty-twenty D fifty-fifty

6 It is doubtful whether the momentum of the peace movement can be ....
A sustained B supplied
C supported D subverted

7 The doctors thought he had got over the worst, but his condition suddenly ....
A disintegrated B dissolved
C dismantled D deteriorated

8 Given the fact that his parents were aristocrats, it is .... that he should be the leader of the socialist party.
A sarcastic B ironic
C erratic D agnostic

9 He said he was dubious .... the chances of getting a pay rise.
A of B on
C to D about

10 Charles Babbage's 'difference engine' is widely regarded as the .... of the computer.
A ancestor B precursor
C antecedent D premonition

mini-cloze

Fill each of the blank spaces with **one** *suitable word.*

Although the numbers of elderly and disabled people are rising, the support provided by the state has not increased. (**1**).................... to a recent report by a leading charity, very (**2**).................... of them are in fact cared (**3**).................... in institutions, and the vast majority depend almost entirely (**4**).................... family or friends. This allows the elderly and disabled to (**5**).................... a much better quality of life than they might (**6**).................... have, and the fact that this army of workers is unpaid also (**7**).................... that the state is relieved of a considerable burden. However, it is (**8**).................... noting that there is a hidden cost to society on (**9**).................... of the fact that that these carers are prevented from (**10**)................ part in any economic activity outside the home.

transformations

Finish each of the following sentences in such a way that it means exactly the same as the sentence printed before it.

1 It was only because his wife helped him that he was able to finish the book.
Without ....

2 No one stands a better chance of winning the race than him.
He is the man most ....

3 I got to the bank only seconds before it closed.
I got to the bank just in ....

4 He was very gifted, but he never became a concert pianist.
Despite ....

5 The government have been reviewing their education policies recently.
The government's ....

rewriting

Write a new sentence using the word given.

1 You will have to share an office as a temporary measure.
BEING ....

2 He was too ill to work.
PREVENTED ....

3 Your attitude annoys me.
FIND ....

4 Most people took no notice of the stranger at the bar.
ATTENTION ....

5 Very few people can understand these new theories.
INCOMPREHENSIBLE ....

TEST

Unit 3

● *vocabulary*

Choose the word which best completes each sentence.

1 The death penalty was .... many years ago in this country.
A abstained B aborted
C abolished D absolved

2 Motorway traffic was .... after a lorry overturned and spilt its load over the northbound carriageway.
A diverged B digressed
C deflected D diverted

3 He .... that he had been involved in the decision not to attack the enemy position.
A declined B refused
C rejected D denied

4 As I was .... through the newspaper this morning, I came across a picture of an old army friend of mine.
A gazing B glancing
C staring D glimpsing

5 I could .... a note of panic in his voice.
A desist B detect
C detest D deter

6 .... the initial fears of the Commander-in-Chief, the campaign was a resounding success.
A Despite B Although
C Besides D Whereas

7 I won't .... those children making a noise in my house!
A allow B have
C let D permit

8 In all .... there will never be a third World War.
A odds B probability
C certainty D possibilities

9 We .... the plumbers to install an extra radiator in the living-room.
A had B made
C got D arranged

10 I think it's .... your luck to drive without wearing a seat-belt.
A risking B tempting
C pushing D proving

● *mini-cloze*

Fill each of the blank spaces with **one** *suitable word.*

The war affected different people in different ways. Some enlisted out of a sense of (**1**).................. to their country, others because they could not have done (**2**).................. its challenge. Volunteers were (**3**).................. to a rigorous routine which made some civilians (**4**).................. to commit themselves to a life of potential hardship. (**5**).................. the time they had joined up, however, it was too late to back out. Newcomers usually wore their (**6**).................. awkwardly but with pride, in (**7**) .... of their realization that their new-found status might be short-lived. Yet months after war had been (**8**).................. on the aggressor, and the initial elation had subsided, many began to (**9**).................. the fact that the fighting was intruding into their personal lives. They prayed for God to (**10**).................. them from untimely death.

● *blank-filling*

Fill each of the blank spaces with a suitable word or phrase.

1 As he .... backing, his company went into liquidation.

2 This crossword is so easy that I .... closed.

3 I .... rings stolen from the hotel bedroom.

4 It .... head to check on the departure times.

5 Whether you win or not is just the .... draw!

● *rewriting*

Write a new sentence using the word given.

1 I saw him disappear round the corner of the building.
GLIMPSE ....

2 Smoking damages your health.
GOOD..

3 I hope my behaviour didn't upset you.
OFFENCE..

4 He always makes everything look so difficult!
WEATHER ....

5 Thunder terrifies me!
DEATH..

TEST

Unit 4

vocabulary

Choose the word which best completes each sentence.

1 I never go in lifts because I am terrified of .... spaces.
  A contained B confined
  C constricted D compressed

2 It is .... impossible to tell the twins apart.
  A virtually B realistically
  C closely D extremely

3 I'm afraid I can't come over this afternoon because I'm tied .... at the office.
  A in B up
  C on D down

4 I thought you said that you were .... to be in Spain this weekend.
  A supposed B assumed
  C intended D planned

5 I am not a serious investor, but I like to .... in the stock market.
  A splash B splatter
  C paddle D dabble

6 The car skidded to a halt after .... its headlights smashed in the crash.
  A making B letting
  C having D doing

7 There were no lifeboats on the ship because it was .... to be unsinkable.
  A argued B claimed
  C believed D told

8 He said that the plane had already left and that I .... arrived an hour earlier.
  A should have B had to
  C must have D was supposed to

9 You have to be rich to send a child to a private school because the fees are ....
  A astrological B aeronautical
  C astronomical D atmospherical

10 The mysterious case of the missing millionaire has become the .... of considerable interest in the press over the last few weeks.
  A middle B target
  C pin-point D focus

mini-cloze

Fill each of the blank spaces with **one** *suitable word.*

We believe that we live in a rational and scientific age, but we do not. We have simply transferred our ancient beliefs (**1**)................... the paranormal to the scientific domain. In the Middle Ages, it was widely believed that the dead (**2**)................... be brought back to life. Such beliefs, however, are not limited (**3**)................... the Middle Ages. Nowadays (**4**)................... is science that is thought to be (**5**)................... to perform such a miracle, and even now there are people (**6**)................... kept deep-frozen in anticipation of the scientific developments that will resurrect them. Similarly, although we no longer (**7**)................... illness and madness as the work of witches and demons, we still attribute the inexplicable (**8**)................... paranormal phenomena such as UFOs or aliens from outer space. In all (**9**)..................., these ancient myths will endure and adapt because they meet a (**10**)................... for mystery that is a fundamental part of the human character.

blank-filling

Fill each of the blank spaces with a suitable word or phrase.

1 He was under suspicion because his account did not tie .... the other witnesses' reports.

2 I can't remember a thing about the accident, so I suppose I must .... asleep at the wheel.

3 In the end I .... give evidence in court as the suspect admitted she had started the fire.

4 The man being held by the police is thought .... for a number of break-ins in the area over the last few months.

5 He wouldn't have just gone away for the weekend without saying anything – he .... a note for you somewhere.

transformations

Finish each of the following sentences in such a way that it means exactly the same as the sentence printed before it.

1 Perhaps no one will ever know what happened that fateful night.
  What happened that fateful night ....

2 She is almost certain to turn down your proposal.
  I doubt...

3 No one stands a chance of beating Mansell in this year's championship.
  It's a foregone ....

4 If he had done his homework, his parents might have let him go to the party.
  If he had done his homework, he might...........

5 In the event, the extra insurance we took out wasn't necessary.
  In the event, we ....

TEST

Unit 5

vocabulary

Choose the word which best completes each sentence.

1 Try and .... on the bright side – the worst may never happen!
A see B look
C think D consider

2 It's distressing to see small children .... in the streets.
A pleading B imploring
C entreating D begging

3 Conversations you strike up with travelling acquaintances usually tend to be ....
A trivial B perverse
C insufficient D imperative

4 Being described by the Americans as a homemaker seems infinitely preferable to being referred to as a(n) .... housewife.
A only B lone
C mere D sole

5 After several hours on the road they became .... to the fact that they would never reach the hotel by nightfall.
A dejected B resigned
C depressed D disillusioned

6 The missing climber, who had not been seen or heard of for two days, appeared at the mountain hut .... and kicking.
A hale B safe
C alive D strong

7 I wish they .... change their minds so often!
A shouldn't B wouldn't
C mightn't D couldn't

8 Many of the jobs which have been created in this area can be directly .... to tourism.
A supported B dedicated
C attracted D attributed

9 Thousands of people use the .... of footpaths across these hills.
A grid B circuit
C network D channel

10 Surprisingly, the frontier guards seemed .... at our presence.
A unconcerned B uninterested
C unconscious D uncritical

mini-cloze

Fill each of the blank spaces with **one** *suitable word.*

I am a dedicated tourist, (**1**).................. with travel and I have always been (**2**).................. the opinion that travel really does (**3**).................. the mind. Although it could be argued that travellers (**4**).................. useless skills, they cannot fail to (**5**).................. at least the sights, sounds and smells of the places they visit. Years ago, many explorers regarded their exploits not as an (**6**).................. to be endured, but as exciting adventures, which they had willingly (**7**).................. to go on. Despite great hardship on these journeys, there was no shortage of young people eager to join (**8**).................. to the remotest places on earth. In those days it (**9**).................. great courage to penetrate the unknown, often with no proper equipment and supplies (**10**).................. out long before the mission had been completed.

blank-filling

Fill each of the blank spaces with a suitable word or phrase.

1 If only you .... bring the cheque book, we could have taken some money out of the bank!

2 The Victorian lived at a time when travel .... improve the spirit.

3 I regret .... abroad to work when I had the opportunity!

4 We regret .... that flight AZ123 has been delayed as a result of a strike by baggage handlers.

5 There .... to learning a language than studying grammar.

rewriting

Write a new sentence using the word given.

1 You needn't feel so superior – you are no better than they are!
NOSE ....

2 We have nearly reached the deadline for this job!
SHORT ....

3 Any personal involvement on the part of the Prime Minister in this scandal would be disastrous.
CAUGHT ....

4 Our little son is really looking forward to going to Disneyworld.
THOUGHT ....

5 They were married last year.
MAN ....

TEST

Unit 6

vocabulary

Choose the word which best completes each sentence.

1 I like current affairs programmes that aren't afraid to tackle .... subjects.
A concurrent B controversial
C consecutive D contradictory

2 The man known as Bonnie Prince Charlie claimed that he was the .... heir to the throne.
A due B correct
C authentic D rightful

3 It always .... me as odd that he should go off to work so late in the day.
A struck B hit
C knocked D smacked

4 He said that if I looked back far enough in my family tree, I would see that I was .... related to Charles Darwin.
A previously B tenuously
C slightly D distantly

5 In a five-hour operation, surgeons managed to sew the boy's .... hand back on.
A cut B severed
C crushed D grazed

6 The delay to the flight was brought .... by bad weather.
A up B in
C down D about

7 The effectiveness of Escher's work relies .... his use of perspective.
A on B in
C by D of

8 I thought the way you behaved was .... outrageous.
A quite B very
C extremely D exceptionally

9 She was .... disappointed when she learned that she had not got the job.
A gravely B fully
C highly D bitterly

10 Although he hadn't spoken French for many years, he picked it .... again after a few weeks.
A on B up
C over D through

mini-cloze

Fill each of the blank spaces with **one** *suitable word.*

Talk to an auctioneer and you will soon discover that there is a market for almost anything. Naturally the (**1**).................... we tend to hear about are those where they sell famous works of (**2**).................... by Picasso, Monet and (**3**).................... on, and where each lot is (**4**).................... millions of pounds. But (**5**).................... most people do not realize is how varied the auction market is, and that auctioneers would be very rare if they relied exclusively (**6**).................... the sale of great masterpieces. An auctioneer will trade (**7**).................... almost anything, from a tractor seat (**8**).................... a phone card, as long as he or she believes that it can (**9**)...................., and sometimes it only takes a change in fashion to (**10**).................... an item that was previously worthless suddenly very valuable.

blank-filling

Fill each of the blank spaces with a suitable word or phrase.

1 You'd better take an umbrella – it looks as .... to rain.

2 There's no need to go over the story again – I am fully .... has happened.

3 His broken leg is in plaster and so at the moment he can't walk .... of crutches.

4 My lawyer seems to spend most of his time playing golf instead .... after my interests.

5 I've only met Mary once, but she strikes .... rather nice.

transformations

Finish each of the sentences in such a way that it means exactly the same as the sentence printed before it.

1 He stormed out of the room after he had handed in his resignetion.
Having..

2 My brother seemed to have been involved in a fight.
My brother looked ....

3 Traditional crafts have died out except in remote rural areas.
It is only in..

4 I found some of the things he said absolutely appalling.
I was..

5 The two paintings look identical to me.
I can ....

TEST

Unit 7

● *vocabulary*

Choose the word which best completes each sentence.

1 He was in his late fifties, with staring eyes and a .... hairline.
A straggling B receding
C bushy D curly

2 Leadville was .... out when the silver boom collapsed in 1893.
A phased B wiped
C knocked D eased

3 The Tabors' fortune was .... at more than $100 million.
A guessed B judged
C imagined D estimated

4 The Tabors lived a life thought to be .... even by their contemporaries.
A extortionate B exorbitant
C extravagant D extraneous

5 Companies have to consider the age of the population when they are .... new staff.
A recruiting B enrolling
C enlisting D raising

6 The rather humid climate in no way .... from the beauty of the place.
A protracts B subtracts
C attracts D detracts

7 She was .... out of 115 applicants for the position of Managing Director.
A short-changed B short-listed
C short-sighted D short-handed

8 The murdered man is thought to .... known the identity of his killer.
A be B being
C having D have

9 Although he seemed convincing, I was somewhat suspicious .... his over-confident manner.
A of B with
C by D for

10 On my birthday my son presented me with a beautiful .... of violets.
A pack B pile
C bundle D bunch

● *mini-cloze*

Fill each of the blank spaces with **one** *suitable word.*

When companies realized there was going to be a sharp fall (**1**).................... the number of school leavers entering the labour market, they had to think of new ways to attract recruits. One leading department store gave its shop staff a 26% pay (**2**).................... to persuade them not to move on to other jobs. A do-it-yourself chain opened a store staffed only by what is known (**3**).................... 'mature' workers – people aged 50 and over, many of whom had retired from previous careers. Over the (**4**).................... few years, however, the mood of employers has changed. With unemployment (**5**).................... sharply, they feel (**6**).................... inclined to spend money (**7**).................... retaining staff. A high-street bank is said (**8**).................... have planned to set up 300 crèches, thus (**9**).................... it easier for women to return to work. But recently it emerged that the bank will open (**10**).................... more crèches after the end of this year.

● *transformations*

Finish each of the sentences in such a way that it means exactly the same as the sentence printed before it.

1 They believe that the manager absconded with the company's pension fund money.
The manager..

2 They thought the terrorists had been hiding from the police in an abandoned caravan.
The terrorists..

3 The fund-raisers have not officially decided where to send the proceeds of the concert.
No..

4 They say the government is bringing in a new tax on property.
The government..

5 They secretly declared independence two days ago.
A secret..

● *rewriting*

Write a new sentence using the word given.

1 I'm afraid we can't do anything about it.
HELPED..

2 You've been deceived by them.
RIDE..

3 It didn't take us long to finish doing the accounts.
SHORT..

4 Statistically, fewer babies are being born.
ACCORDING..

5 Interest rates have fallen sharply recently.
DECLINE..

TEST

Unit 8

● *vocabulary*

Choose the word which best completes each sentence.

1 The politician refused to be drawn into answering .... questions.
A imaginary B speculative
C antithetical D hypothetical

2 During the lecture, the student took down .... quantities of notes.
A copious B voluminous
C extended D detailed

3 Archaeology is one of the most interesting scientific ....
A divisions B disciplines
C matters D compartments

4 They sent a sample of the pottery they had found to the laboratory so that a date could be .... on it.
A put B placed
C set D fixed

5 Fitting together the thousands of fragments of the broken vase was a long and .... task.
A minute B careful
C painstaking D minuscule

6 The American Indians are suing the government for the return of their .... lands.
A antique B inherited
C ancestral D hereditary

7 I find it difficult sometimes to .... between green and red.
A disseminate B discriminate
C classify D categorize

8 At first, very few people believed Darwin's theory of evolution because it did not seem at all ....
A plausible B creditable
C feasible D discernible

9 The police have not had time to complete their investigations, but they have concluded .... that the explosion was caused by a bomb.
A temporally B tenuously
C tentatively D terminally

10 The politician rehearsed his speech again and again until he was sure that he was word ....
A precise B exact
C accurate D perfect

● *mini-cloze*

Fill each of the blank spaces with **one** *suitable word.*

In many countries there are traditionalists who try to hold back the development of language on the basis of correctness or purity. (**1**).................... they are university professors or members of the public, they all have a perception (**2**).................... language that does not tie (**3**).................... with the facts. The English language, marvellous as it is (**4**).................... a means of communication, developed (**5**).................... its present form (**6**).................... constantly changing and adapting to new circumstances. It is a mongrel tongue, and (**7**).................... is because of this impurity, rather than (**8**).................... it, that it has survived so well. (**9**).................... the traditionalists sometimes fail to realize is that they are fighting a losing battle, because no (**10**)................ how vociferously they complain, the language will continue to develop and change.

● *blank-filling*

Fill each of the blank spaces with a suitable word or phrase.

1 The economic situation is serious, and it looks .... improve for at least a few more months.

2 .... lines, I got the distinct impression that her apparent cheerfulness was only a front.

3 .... of his nervousness, rather than despite it, that he did so well in the race.

4 She is always prepared to forgive him, no .... badly he behaves.

5 Most European languages are believed .... evolved from a protolanguage from the Middle East.

● *transformations*

Finish each of the sentences in such a way that it means exactly the same as the sentence printed before it.

1 It is possible that some of the students saw the exam paper last week.
The exam paper may ....

2 It was because he was driving so fast that he skidded off the road.
If ....

3 Some linguists believe all the world's languages to be related.
According ....

4 When she accepted the job, the au pair girl assumed that she would be free every weekend.
When she accepted the job, the au pair girl took ....
....

5 I have little confidence that he will be able to do the job.
I have serious ....

TEST

Unit 9

vocabulary

Choose the word or phrase which best completes each sentence.

1 Open plains are .... of the geography of Kenya.
A distinctive B characteristic
C separate D specific

2 He gave a dramatic .... of his adventures in the heart of Africa.
A tale B legend
C saga D account

3 Crops are often completely destroyed by .... of locusts.
A bands B troupes
C swarms D flocks

4 The storm played .... the cross-channel ferry crossings.
A down B havoc with
C cat and mouse with D along with

5 He says he doesn't like his new school because he feels like a .... out of water there.
A boat B duck
C fish D swimmer

6 If the phone ...., she would rush to answer it.
A rings B had rung
C has rung D rang

7 If you have finished your homework, you .... check through it carefully.
A would B should
C will D were to

8 Many people are campaigning for the .... of whale hunting.
A annihilation B extinction
C abolition D extermination

9 I was very .... not to pass on the message about the holiday being cancelled.
A elicited B enticed
C cajoled D tempted

10 Some animals are on the .... of becoming extinct.
A edge B verge
C tip D side

mini-cloze

Fill each of the blank spaces with **one** *suitable word.*

You probably know the (**1**).................... . Four turtles were accidentally dropped into an American sewer. They mutated and emerged (**2**).................... the Teenage Mutant Turtles. But (**3**).................... of the real creatures behind these super heroes? The international trade in turtles is nothing (**4**).................... However, sales (**5**).................... because of the craze for turtle products. But (**6**).................... toys, animals need special care. As sales became more popular, so (**7**).................... the number of unwanted pets. On the other hand, many species of turtle are endangered. The Aquatic box turtle is found in Mexico. Its survival is (**8**).................... by the destruction of its habitat. The wetlands where the turtle is found are (**9**).................... drained to make way for human (**10**).................... .

rewriting

Write a new sentence using the word given.

1 Just pretend to agree with his suggestion.
ALONG ....

2 We have more important things to do at the moment.
FISH ....

3 There is a risk that the black rhino will become extinct.
THREATENED..

4 No one is allowed to smoke in the laboratory.
BANNED ....

5 The protection of the animal world is pointless unless we take steps to protect our planet as well.
WORTH ....

transformations

Finish each of the following sentences in such a way that it means exactly the same as the sentence printed before it.

1 Fancy forgetting the free tickets – now we'll have to pay to get in.
If you ....

2 In an emergency ring 999 for an ambulance.
Should you..

3 Imagine winning a million pounds – I'd be over the moon!
If I were ....

4 You'll have to be patient with your pet if you want to house-train it.
Unless ....

5 You'll be able to learn something if you don't misbehave in class.
Provided ....

TEST

Unit 10

● vocabulary

Choose the word which best completes each sentence.

1 They invited me to dinner and provided a wonderful meal .... for a king.
A apt **B** suited
C appropriate **D** fit

2 I've got a dark .... on my leg where I got hit by the squash ball.
A graze **B** bruise
C sprain **D** gash

3 At the height of his fame, the pop star returned to his native town .... a hero.
A like **B** as
C on **D** in

4 Car theft .... accounts for more than half of all recorded crime in this country.
A alone **B** individually
C solely **D** uniquely

5 The TV station, in .... to massive popular demand, decided not to discontinue the soap opera.
A reaction **B** reply
C answer **D** response

6 I never wanted to upset you; ringing you up in the middle of the night was only meant to be a bit of .... fun.
A practical **B** harmless
C light **D** gentle

7 When the diverted flight landed, the airline staff simply abandoned the passengers and left them all .... and dry at the wrong airport.
A safe **B** down
C high **D** warm

8 When one looks at the statistics, it is clear that the traditional nuclear family is something of a ....
A story **B** legend
C myth **D** fabrication

9 The private detective who had been hired to .... down the missing man finally found him in France.
A track **B** follow
C chase **D** catch

10 His delight at getting the job was .... by the realization that it would involve long hours commuting every day.
A dimmed **B** tempered
C modified **D** moistened

● mini-cloze

*Fill each of the blank spaces with **one** suitable word.*

The institution of marriage is found in almost every society, and its prevalence suggests that it must meet certain needs. The most fundamental of these is security, as the nuclear (**1**)................... provides a shelter for the weaker members of (**2**)..................., such (**3**)................... infants or ageing relatives. However the (**4**)................... is that the institution of marriage is now (**5**)................... decline, and this indicates that we no (**6**)................... feel the need for the protection that a family can offer. Many people feel that as (**7**)................... as the state is prepared to (**8**)................... responsibility for them, there is little need to enter into an unsuitable marriage. However, it remains to be seen (**9**)................... marriage will continue to (**10**)................... in popularity or whether this trend will turn out to have been nothing more than a temporary phase.

● blank filling

Fill each of the blank spaces with a suitable word or phrase.

1 What on .... doing? You're in a terrible mess!

2 She was nervous about going to France because she .... abroad before.

3 I told my sister I didn't think she was old .... married – after all, she's only seventeen.

4 If you rush into a new business, you have little .... success.

5 It would be a false .... back spending on education.

● rewriting

Write a new sentence using the word given.

1 They have discovered some interesting new information.
LIGHT ....

2 I haven't used the phone for several days.
SINCE..

3 The man claimed to be completely innocent.
ANYTHING ....

4 As my problems got worse, I stopped speaking to people.
LONGER ....

5 Were you at all worried about moving to London?
MISGIVINGS ....

TEST

Unit 11

vocabulary

Choose the word or phrase which best completes each sentence.

1 My brother was always picking .... me when we were children.
A up **B** out
C at **D** on

2 The opposition leaders .... the government for not taking action sooner.
A warned **B** criticized
C threatened **D** urged

3 When the stock market crashed, the traders were .... to beggary.
A collapsed **B** reduced
C ruined **D** inclined

4 The multi-millionaire had .... huge sums of money in the new venture and was devastated when it proved to be unsuccessful.
A traded **B** dealt
C dabbled **D** invested

5 It was our fault – we allowed the matter to .... on far too long.
A stay **B** pull
C drag **D** extend

6 As the .... owner of the property, I would be able to sign the application for credit.
A sole **B** lone
C solitary **D** lonely

7 My grandmother was partial .... a glass of sherry before dinner.
A for **B** of
C to **D** with

8 As the price of tulips ebbed and ...., many people grew rich.
A floundered **B** fluctuated
C fell **D** flowed

9 She has a .... for tidying up her room.
A madness **B** desire
C mania **D** craziness

10 By .... trading it was possible for many speculators to make a fortune on the stock exchange.
A judicious **B** judicial
C judgemental **D** judge like

mini-cloze

Fill each of the blank spaces with **one** *suitable word.*

One day I was walking over the Mill's suspension bridge, (**1**)................... my sample volumes and (**2**)................... bitterly about the weight of world knowledge. One middle-class kid had already won a trip to Mexico for his efforts. I (**3**)................... was in my third week of no-sales. Our sales manager had (**4**)................... me of going home and sleeping every afternoon. My spirits had long since (**5**)................... in. I finally admitted what I had known (**6**)................... along: I just couldn't go on with the same old memorized (**7**)................... . I threw my whole (**8**)................... in the river. Out volumes shot: cat through graph. All human learning (**9**)................... soggy and ruined on the rocks below. I was greatly comforted by the thought that I (**10**)................... never again have to try and persuade anyone to buy 'Knowledge'.

transformations

Finish each of the following sentences in such a way that it means the same as the sentence printed before it.

1 'Why don't you take tomorrow off?' suggested my boss.
My boss suggested ....

2 'I did not leave the phone off the hook yesterday,' protested John.
John denied ....

3 'Brian, did you borrow the dictionary last week?' enquired the teacher.
The teacher asked Brian ....

4 'I wish I didn't have to get up at five o'clock tomorrow morning,' said Pat.
Pat complained ....

5 'I must tell you the news here and now,' said my daughter.
My daughter insisted ....

blank-filling

Fill each of the blank spaces with a suitable word or phrase.

1 If the company ....
..... even this year, we shall be more than satisfied.

2 What's the ....
.... sending me a catalogue without a price list?

3 The company fell .... to a common problem of success: not concentrating on customer service.

4 The student proudly ....
.... passed every single exam with top grades.

5 The bus conductor politely asked the passenger if
....
.... putting his dirty shoes on the seat opposite.

TEST

Unit 12

vocabulary

Choose the word which best completes each sentence.

1 I .... to think what your mother will say when she finds out you have broken her favourite vase.
A regret B daren't
C dread D dislike

2 The charity felt that they had to help the old man, who had no visible .... of support.
A resources B means
C methods D ways

3 The police believed what I told them because it was .... with other reports they had heard.
A tallied B tied
C connected D consistent

4 You'll love staying with Mr Willing because he is such a .... host.
A ingenuous B genial
C ingenious D genuine

5 Nearly everyone was at the village meeting, but the Planning Officer from the council was .... by his absence.
A conspicuous B remarkable
C significant D noticeable

6 When his daughter returned after midnight for the third time, Henry decided to .... down the law and refused to allow her out at all.
A set B put
C hand D lay

7 As the evening wore ...., everyone at the party became more relaxed.
A on B away
C along D down

8 Why don't we go to the canteen and discuss what is worrying you .... a cup of coffee.
A on B over
C above D onto

9 I was .... alarmed to see how much money I had been spending.
A somewhat B something
C somewhere D someone

10 It was only when I got to the office that I realized I had left my briefcase ....
A back B away
C behind D down

mini-cloze

Fill each of the blank spaces with **one** *suitable word.*

Whatever may be said about the causes of crime, one can be certain of one thing. Crime levels, particularly among the young, are far higher than they (**1**).................... to be even a decade ago, and the tabloids are continually claiming that society seems to be falling (**2**).................... . The government's current policies are not working well (**3**).................... and clearly (**4**).................... re-evaluating. The government should (**5**).................... at this problem from two points of view. If crime (**6**).................... to fall they must deal with its social causes, as well as take steps to (**7**).................... social conditions, even if this means (**8**).................... more money. They must also develop new means of (**9**).................... with young offenders, which may entaml the (**10**).................... up of new institutions.

blank-filling

Fill each of the blank spaces with a suitable word or phrase.

1 English drivers find it takes some time to get .... on the right in France.

2 When my grandmother was young, she used .... her summer holidays in India.

3 In his lifetime he was one of the world's richest men, and is believed .... his fortune by arms dealing.

4 I didn't let him in because he didn't have an identity card; for .... knew, he might have been a burglar.

5 I am surprised and rather disappointed that he left .... goodbye.

rewriting

Write a new sentence using the word given.

1 He received a five-year sentence for his part in the robbery.
SENTENCED ....

2 Unfortunately I will not be able to come to the wedding.
REGRET ....

3 I think you ought to have your coat dry-cleaned.
NEEDS ....

4 The houses that were very close to the blast were badly damaged.
IMMEDIATE ....

5 With hindsight, we should have been more careful.
RETROSPECT ....

TEST
Unit 13

● *vocabulary*

Choose the word which best completes each sentence.

1 The show has only recently .... from the Warehouse Theatre to the Playhouse.
A transmitted B transposed
C transferred D transpired

2 The titanic form of the monument seems to .... any other in the vicinity.
A belittle B dwarf
C diminish D shrink

3 There is a constant .... of visitors to this important historic site.
A current B tide
C river D stream

4 The company finds itself in considerable financial difficulties and the shareholders have been considering various means of keeping it ....
A abreast B aloft
C afloat D aboard

5 This painting has been in the family for over a(n) ....
A generation B epoch
C era D age

6 From a distance the jacket looked new but a closer inspection revealed that it was .... at the edges.
A fraught B frustrated
C frayed D fringed

7 The audience did not seem very .... about the sudden changes to the advertised programme.
A sarcastic B sympathetic
C enthusiastic D respectful

8 .... the concert had begun did we realize what a splendid show it was going to be.
A No sooner B Only after
C Hardly D Scarcely

9 The film starts in half an hour – we really must be making ....
A up for B a move
C mess D believe

10 I wish we'd never bought him a TV – all he ever does it sit .... to the box!
A fixed B stuck
C glued D sealed

● *mini-cloze*

Fill each of the blank spaces with **one** *suitable word.*

Last week I was lucky enough to be invited to share a box at the opera. The invitation **(1)**.................... my husband, and I eagerly **(2)**.................... . It was not **(3)**.................... it was too late that I remembered how he detests going to the opera, or attending any **(4)**.................... where he has to 'dress up'. Not only **(5)** .... he hate having to wear formal clothes, but he also resents the fact that he has to spend money hiring them. By sheer good fortune we managed to **(6)**.................... him out in a suit belonging to my brother. We were **(7)**.................... to leave, when he noticed that the jacket was **(8)**.................... a button. I quickly found a spare one and **(9)**.................... it on. My husband was muttering under his breath that he felt like a wax **(10)**...................., like a penguin in a parade, and it was with some misgivings that we eventually set off fifteen minutes late.

● *transformations*

Finish each of the sentences in such a way that it means exactly the same as the sentence printed before it.

1 The plane had only just landed when the storm broke.
No sooner..

2 The only way you can hope to succeed is by trial and error.
Only ....

3 They did not realize that the film had been nominated for an Oscar.
Little..

4 I set foot in the house and at the same moment the fire alarm went off.
Scarcely ....

5 He bought a suit and some shoes as well.
Not only ....

● *rewriting*

Write a new sentence using the word given.

1 Soon the whole town had heard the news about the bank robbery.
WILDFIRE ....

2 His reputation as a Shakespearian actor has been established.
NAME ....

3 I am not a solitary person, I'm sociable.
RATHER..

4 Ill health resulted in his inability to do the job.
COPE ....

5 You must set the burglar alarm before you leave the building.
WITHOUT ....

TEST

Unit 14

• *vocabulary*

Choose the word which best completes each sentence.

1 I decided not to wait for her any longer because it had .... eleven o'clock, and I had to get back home.
   A had **B** gone
   C been **D** done

2 The Space Centre lost sight of the satellite, which was blotted .... by the light of the sun.
   A out **B** away
   C down **D** up

3 Miss Prism remained something of a dark .... in the village where she lived, and nobody knew anything about her past.
   A sheep **B** horse
   C cat **D** fox

4 It was .... when her cheque bounced that I realized that she had no money at all.
   A merely **B** simply
   C only **D** just

5 In the hot summers, the water levels in the reservoirs fall because of ....
   A condensation **B** evaporation
   C distillation **D** precipitation

6 The electorate will not easily forgive the government for failing to fulfil its ....
   A promises **B** vows
   C aspirations **D** offers

7 Although he stood to gain nothing at all, he helped us out of the .... of his heart.
   A benevolence **B** generosity
   C charity **D** goodness

8 There is no .... difference between the levels of atmospheric pollution in France and Germany.
   A sensible **B** gradable
   C comprehensible **D** appreciable

9 The chain of events that led to the First World War was set in .... by the assassination of Archduke Ferdinand at Sarajevo in 1914.
   A progress **B** train
   C momentum **D** development

10 If you're going into the kitchen, could you just .... the outside light off for me?
   A stop **B** pop
   C lop **D** top

• *mini-cloze*

Fill each of the blank spaces with **one** *suitable word.*

One of the main problems facing the environmental movement is that it may become a victim of its own success. It is now generally accepted that issues **(1)**.................... as global warming need to be dealt with seriously, and that the Scandinavian forests are being destroyed **(2)**.................... to the effects of **(3)**.................... rain. Views **(4)**.................... these have now become an accepted part of the political scene, and consumers are constantly bombarded with green or **(5)**.................... friendly products. However, this does not mean that environmental groups can now afford to relax. On the **(6)**...................., the green movement must consider how the momentum will **(7)**.................... sustained when the current enthusiasm **(8)**.................... passed. The environment must not be **(9)**.................... to fade from people's minds, because the process of ecological collapse has already been **(10)**.................... in train, and so far very little has been done to reverse it.

• *blank-filling*

Fill each of the blank spaces with a suitable word or phrase.

1 I had to send my dog away to be properly trained because he just wouldn't .... told.

2 He wasn't at all angry when the car was stolen; ...., he seemed delighted to have got rid of it.

3 I've just had a lovely thought – this time next week, we .... lunch on a beach in Barbados.

4 The computer he bought was expensive but it doesn't work – it was a complete .... money.

5 You won't be able to collect the car from the garage on Friday because I don't think they .... by then.

• *transformations*

Finish each of the sentences in such a way that it means exactly the same as the sentence printed before it.

1 Burglars are only deterred by an efficient alarm system.
   The only deterrent.................................

2 A recent report has found a strong link between ozone depletion and CFCs.
   According ....

3 It's pointless to try and make him change his mind.
   It's a waste.......................................

4 The population of the UK has not expanded appreciably in the last decade.
   There has been no................................

5 In the summer, there are thousands more tourists than locals.
   In the summer, the locals are vastly................

TEST

Unit 15

● *vocabulary*

Choose the word which best completes each sentence.

1 When addressing his constituents, the Member of Parliament pointed out a few .... truths, which he knew would cause resentment.
A ivory **B** home
C raw **D** second

2 The trouble with armchair .... is that they very rarely have any creative ideas themselves.
A parkers **B** blankets
C potatoes **D** critics

3 The news conference was brought .... an abrupt halt by protestors demonstrating against the corruption of local officials.
A at **B** to
C for **D** in

4 The misunderstanding is thought to have .... from an ambiguous article which appeared in yesterday's newspapers.
A stirred **B** steered
C strayed **D** stemmed

5 The newspaper is well-known for being .... against trades unions.
A biased **B** skewed
C twisted **D** distorted

6 When asked if she had ever been in trouble with the police before, she replied in the ....
A aggressive **B** assertive
C affirmative **D** abrasive

7 The new weekly magazine is aimed .... those with an interest in the world of finance.
A for **B** to
C at **D** with

8 Before being offered the job, the applicants had to .... a series of extremely exacting interviews.
A underact **B** undergo
C underplay **D** underlie

9 As you are non-resident in this country, I am afraid that you are .... to vote.
A inequitable **B** illegible
C illegal **D** ineligible

10 News items are .... to a stringent process of selection.
A determined **B** subject
C reliant **D** dependent

● *mini-cloze*

Fill each of the blank spaces with **one** *suitable word.*

New technology has made a tremendous impact on modern life and communications. For example, (**1**).................... are the days when newspapers were full of misprints and spelling errors. These are now virtually things of the (**2**).................... . Whilst it cannot always bc (**3**).................... that the content of some newspapers has improved, and it may be true that the moral standards of others are open to (**4**)...................., no one would deny that the papers themselves are more visually (**5**).................... than they ever were before. Nevertheless, if you opt (**6**).................... a paper which has its origin in the more dubious gutter (**7**)...................., it is unlikely that you can expect to find accuracy, for (**8**).................... is usually blended with fiction and seems to be of little import, as (**9**).................... as the paper wins the major battles of the circulation (**10**).................... .

● *transformations*

Finish each of the sentences in such a way that it means exactly the same as the sentence printed before it.

1 We regret not carrying out a more thorough investigation into the matter.
We wish ....

2 I was shaken by the pictures I saw in the newspaper.
What...

3 It appears that the money was earned by 'insider-dealing' on the Stock Exchange.
The money is ....

4 I hardly had time to step inside the office before the phone started ringing.
No sooner..

5 You didn't tell me you were coming – I have already arranged to go out.
If ....

● *rewriting*

Write a new sentence using the word given.

1 Not a word came out of her mouth.
LOST ....

2 You can't compare tabloids with quality newspapers.
FISH ....

3 A lot of fuss has been made about nothing.
TEACUP...

4 Your attitude will have to change if you want to succeed.
LEAF ....

5 He gets very annoyed when you criticize him!
BULL ....

KEY

Test Unit 1

● *vocabulary*

1 D 2 B 3 C 4 A 5 D 6 C 7 C 8 D 9 B 10 B

● *mini-cloze*

1 keen / hooked 2 well / much 3 provide 4 benefit 5 such 6 take 7 fluid / supple / flexible 8 brought 9 audience 10 once / long

● *blank-filling*

1 got / found 2 have in 3 whose 4 a matter / the focus 5 regarded as / thought of as

● *rewriting*

1 All students must / are obliged to take part in sports.
2 He admits he is ('s) (just) a small cog in a big wheel.
3 I would ('d) much rather have / listen to classical music than jazz.
4 The committee has / have not yet made a decision about / on / regarding the final date of the games.
5 The music industry has greatly benefited from the increasing popularity of opera.

Test Unit 2

● *vocabulary*

1 B 2 C 3 B 4 A 5 D 6 A 7 D 8 B 9 D 10 B

● *mini-cloze*

1 According 2 few 3 for 4 on 5 have / enjoy 6 otherwise 7 means 8 worth 9 account 10 taking

● *transformations*

1 Without his wife's help he would not have been able / would have been unable to finish the book.
2 He is the man most likely to win the race.
3 I got to the bank just in the nick of time.
4 Despite being / the fact that he was very gifted, he never became a concert pianist.
5 The government's education policies have been under review recently.

● *rewriting*

1 You will have to share an office for the time being.
2 His illness prevented him from working.
3 I find your attitude annoying.
4 Most people paid no attention to the stranger at the bar.
5 Most people find these new theories incomprehensible.

Test Unit 3

● *vocabulary*

1 C 2 D 3 D 4 B 5 B 6 A 7 B 8 B 9 C 10 C

● *mini-cloze*

1 duty 2 without 3 subjected 4 reluctant / unwilling / loath 5 By 6 uniform(s) 7 spite 8 declared 9 resent / deplore 10 preserve / save / keep / deliver / protect

● *blank-filling*

1 failed / was unable to get any financial 2 can / could do it with my eyes 3 had my 4 never entered my 5 luck of the

● *rewriting*

1 I caught a glimpse of him disappearing round the corner of the building.
2 Smoking is no good for your health / does your health no good.
3 I hope you didn't take offence at my behaviour.
4 He always makes heavy weather of everything.
5 I'm scared / frightened to death of thunder!

Test Unit 4

● *vocabulary*

1 B 2 A 3 B 4 A 5 D 6 C 7 C 8 A 9 C 10 D

● *mini-cloze*

1 from 2 could 3 to 4 it 5 able 6 being 7 interpret / see 8 to 9 probability 10 need

● *blank-filling*

1 in with 2 have fallen 3 didn't need to 4 to be responsible / to have been responsible 5 must have left

● *transformations*

1 What happened that fateful night may / will possibly never be known.
2 I doubt (very much) whether she will agree to / accept your proposal.
3 It's a foregone conclusion that Mansell will win this year's championship.

4 If he had done his homework, he might have been allowed to go to the party.
5 In the event, we needn't have taken out the extra insurance.

Test Unit 5

● *vocabulary*

1 B **2** D **3** A **4** C **5** B **6** C **7** B **8** D **9** C **10** A

● *mini-cloze*

1 obsessed **2** of **3** broaden / improve **4** acquire / develop **5** experience / enjoy **6** ordeal **7** volunteered / chosen **8** expeditions **9** took / required **10** running

● *blank-filling*

1 had remembered to / hadn't forgotten to **2** really did / was thought to **3** not going / not having gone **4** to inform you **5** is more to

● *rewriting*

1 You needn't look down your nose at them – you are no better.
2 We are running short of time / Time is running short before the deadline for this job.
3 If the Prime Minister got caught up in / were to get caught up in this scandal, it would be a disaster.
4 Our little son is really excited at the thought of going to Disneyworld.
5 They became man and wife last year.

Test Unit 6

● *vocabulary*

1 B **2** D **3** A **4** D **5** B **6** D **7** A **8** A **9** D **10** B

● *mini-cloze*

1 auctions **2** art **3** so **4** worth **5** what **6** on **7** in **8** to **9** sell **10** make

● *blank-filling*

1 if it is going **2** aware of what **3** without the aid / help **4** of looking **5** me as (being)

● *transformations*

1 Having handed in his resignation, he stormed out of the room.
2 My brother looked as if he had been involved in a fight.
3 It is only in remote rural areas that traditional crafts have survived / not died out.
4 I was absolutely appalled by some of the things he said.
5 I can see no difference between the two paintings.

Test Unit 7

● *vocabulary*

1 B **2** B **3** D **4** C **5** A **6** D **7** B **8** D **9** A **10** D

● *mini-cloze*

1 in **2** rise / increase **3** as **4** past / last **5** rising **6** less **7** on **8** to **9** making **10** no

● *transformations*

1 The manager is believed to have absconded with the company's pension fund money.
2 The terrorists were thought to have been hiding from the police in an abandoned caravan.
3 No official decision has been made about where to send the proceeds of the concert.
4 The government is said to be bringing in a new tax on property.
5 A secret declaration of independence was made two days ago.

● *rewriting*

1 I'm afraid it can't be helped.
2 You have been taken / They have taken you for a ride.
3 We made short work of finishing the accounts.
4 According to statistics, fewer babies are being born.
5 There has been a sharp decline in interest rates recently.

Test Unit 8

● *vocabulary*

1 D **2** A **3** B **4** A **5** C **6** C **7** B **8** A **9** C **10** D

● *mini-cloze*

1 Whether **2** of **3** in **4** as **5** into **6** through / by **7** it **8** despite **9** What **10** matter

● *blank-filling*

1 unlikely to **2** Reading between the **3** It was because **4** matter how **5** to have

● *transformations*

1 The exam paper may have been seen by some of the students last week.
2 If he hadn't been driving so fast he wouldn't have skidded off the road.
3 According to some linguists, all the world's languages are related.

4 When she accepted the job, the au pair girl took it as read / for granted that she would be free every weekend.
5 I have serious doubts about his ability to do the job.

Test Unit 9

● *vocabulary*

1 B 2 D 3 C 4 B 5 C 6 D 7 B 8 C 9 D 10 B

● *mini-cloze*

1 legend / story 2 as 3 what 4 new 5 increased 6 unlike 7 did 8 threatened 9 being 10 settlement / habitation / development

● *rewriting*

1 Just (pretend to) play / go along with his suggestion.
2 At the moment we have other fish to fry.
3 The black rhino is threatened with extinction.
4 Smoking in the laboratory is banned.
5 It is ('s) not worth protecting the animal world unless we take steps to protect our planet as well.

● *transformations*

1 If you hadn't forgotten / had remembered the free tickets, we wouldn't have to pay to get in (now).
2 Should you require / need an ambulance, ring 999.
3 If I were to win a million pounds, I'd be over the moon.
4 Unless you are patient with your pet, you will never / won't be able to house-train it.
5 Provided you behave / stop misbehaving in class, you will ('ll) be able to learn something.

Test Unit 10

● *vocabulary*

1 D 2 B 3 B 4 A 5 D 6 B 7 C 8 C 9 A 10 B

● *mini-cloze*

1 family 2 society 3 as 4 fact 5 in 6 longer 7 long 8 take 9 whether 10 decrease / decline / fall

● *blank-filling*

1 earth have you been 2 had never been 3 enough to get 4 chance of 5 economy to cut

● *rewriting*

1 Some interesting new information has come to light.
2 It is ('s) several days since I used the phone.
3 The man said / claimed he hadn't done anything.
4 As my problems got worse, I no longer spoke to people.
5 Did you have any misgivings about moving to London?

Test unit 11

● *vocabulary*

1 D 2 B 3 B 4 D 5 C 6 A 7 C 8 D 9 C 10 A

● *mini-cloze*

1 lugging / carrying 2 complaining 3 myself 4 accused 5 caved 6 all 7 routine 8 kit 9 lay 10 would

● *transformations*

1 My boss suggested that I (should) take / that I took / my taking the next / following day off.
2 John denied that he had left / leaving / having left the phone off the hook the day before / previous day.
3 The teacher asked Brian if he had borrowed the dictionary the week before / the previous week.
4 Pat complained about having to get up at five o'clock the next / following morning.
5 My daughter insisted on telling me the news there and then.

● *blank-filling*

1 breaks 2 point / use / good of 3 victim 4 said / announced / told me that (s)he had 5 he would mind not

Test Unit 12

● *vocabulary*

1 C 2 B 3 D 4 B 5 A 6 D 7 A 8 B 9 A 10 C

● *mini-cloze*

1 used 2 apart 3 enough 4 require / need 5 look 6 is 7 improve / change 8 spending / providing 9 dealing 10 setting

blank-filling

1 used to driving 2 to spend 3 to have made / built up 4 all I 5 without saying

● *rewriting*

1 He was sentenced to five years / years' imprisonment for his part in the robbery.
2 I regret to say that I will not be able / be unable to come to the wedding.
3 I think your coat needs dry-cleaning.
4 The houses in the immediate vicinity of the blast were badly damaged.
5 In retrospect, we should have been more careful.

Test Unit 13

● *vocabulary*

1 C **2** B **3** D **4** C **5** A **6** C **7** C **8** B **9** B **10** C

● *mini-cloze*

1 included **2** accepted **3** until **4** occasion / function **5** does **6** kit **7** about / ready **8** missing **9** sewed **10** image / effigy

● *transformations*

1 No sooner had the plane landed than the storm broke.
2 Only by trial and error can you hope to succeed.
3 Little did they realize that the film had been nominated for an Oscar.
4 Scarcely had I set foot in the house when the fire-alarm went off.
5 Not only did he buy a suit but he bought some shoes as well.

● *rewriting*

1 The news about the bank robbery spread through the whole town like wildfire.
2 He has made his name as a Shakespearian actor.
3 I'm a sociable rather than a solitary person. / Rather than being a solitary person, I'm sociable.
4 He was unable to cope with the job because of ill health.
5 You must not leave the building without setting the burglar-alarm.

Test Unit 14

● *vocabulary*

1 B **2** A **3** B **4** C **5** B **6** A **7** D **8** D **9** B **10** B

● *mini-cloze*

1 such **2** due / thanks **3** acid **4** like **5** environmentally **6** contrary **7** be **8** has **9** allowed / permitted **10** set

● *blank-filling*

1 do as he was **2** on the contrary / in fact / to tell the truth **3** will be having **4** waste of **5** will have finished (it)

● *transformations*

1 The only deterrent to burglars is an efficient alarm system.
2 According to a recent report, there is a strong link / a strong link has been found between ozone depletion and CFCs.
3 It's a waste of time trying to make him change his mind.
4 There has been no appreciable expansion of the population of the UK in the last decade.
5 In the summer, the locals are vastly outnumbered by the tourists.

Test Unit 15

● *vocabulary*

1 B **2** D **3** B **4** D **5** A **6** C **7** C **8** B **9** D **10** B

● *mini-cloze*

1 gone **2** past **3** said **4** question / interpretation **5** attractive / appealing / stimulating etc. **6** for **7** press **8** fact **9** long **10** war

● *transformations*

1 We wish we had carried out a more thorough investigation into the matter.
2 What shook me was / were the pictures I saw in the newspaper.
3 The money is thought / said to have been earned by 'insider -dealing' on the Stock Exchange.
4 No sooner had I stepped inside the office than the phone started ringing.
5 If you had told me you were coming, I wouldn't have arranged to go out.

● *rewriting*

1 She was lost for words. (possibly 'She had lost her tongue.')
2 Tabloids are a different kettle of fish from quality newspapers.
3 This / It has ('s) been a storm in a teacup.
4 You will ('ll) have to turn over a new leaf if you want to succeed.
5 Criticizing him is like a red rag to a bull. / Criticism is like a red rag to a bull to him.

PROGRESS TESTS

PROGRESS TEST 1 (1½ hours)

reading

Read the following passage and choose the best way of finishing each of the sentences below.

Ismene Brown takes a teddy-bear to work with her. She is a sub-editor for a newspaper, and the teddy comes in handy as a preventative measure against repetitive strain injury (RSI). The term describes a variety of musculo-skeletal disorders of the hand, wrist, arm, elbow, shoulder and neck, caused by frequent, identical movements. On advice from her physiotherapist, Ismene puts the teddy under her right wrist and it allows the blood to flow more freely throughout her arm. RSI is causing acute problems for many journalists who use new technology. *The Financial Times* suffered an epidemic when thirty-five of the paper's journalists were confirmed by the company doctor as suffering from RSI. There were eighteen to twenty cases in the serious category, and a further thirty to forty people who experienced tolerable pains from time to time, according to a National Union of Journalists officer at the newspaper. 'Serious means they've been off work for many months, with no signs of improvement and no way of even doing other things with their limbs'.

One production editor describes the symptoms of RSI: 'At first, I had a numb feeling in my fingertips, with pins and needles, cold hands, tingling and a general feeling that I wasn't all right. Then it got increasingly worse, with more acute pain throughout my wrist'.

The newspaper used a complex American computer system that caused nearly 100 cases of RSI on the *Los Angeles Times*. Not much hand movement is required to make all the necessary keyboard strokes. Sub-editors and writers may keep their hands in the same positions for long periods, preventing a regular blood flow.

The Financial Times switched off screens for fifteen minutes at 3 pm and 5 pm, when journalists were forced to take breaks. This apparently helped, but with constant deadline pressures some argued that it could serve to exacerbate the problem, and more frequent, but shorter breaks might be more effective.

The term RSI originates from Australia where, in 1985–6, the country's white collar workers experienced a national outbreak of the syndrome. Since then, though, it has subsided, giving rise to two different theories – that the medical profession started ignoring it, so it went away, or that people gradually found ways of coping with it.

1 RSI is caused by a movement which is both
  A jerky and sporadic.
  B unchanging and recurrent.
  C mechanical and varied.
  D awkward and irregular.

2 Why does Ismene take a teddy bear to work?
  A To keep her company when work becomes repetitive.
  B To protect her from the glare of her computer screen.
  C To prevent injury to her arm while she is working.
  D To tuck under her arm for support while working.

3 Serious cases of RSI are defined as
  A necessitating a long period of absence from work.
  B the inability to perform other functions at work.
  C experiencing bearable pain on a constant basis.
  D the inability to enjoy the work which they are doing.

4 What caused the cases of RSI on the *Los Angeles Times*?
  A An out-of-date computer system.
  B A lack of adequate training in the use of equipment.
  C A sophisticated computer system necessitating little physical input.
  D An over-complicated computer system requiring frequent repetitive movement.

5 Although journalists on *The Financial Times* took two short breaks,
  A this had no effect whatsoever on performance.
  B the number of breaks was considered to be over-generous.
  C most people were convinced it made the problem worse.
  D this did not completely resolve the problem.

6 According to the writer, it appears that since 1985 RSI
  A has increased dramatically.
  B has spread to the medical profession.
  C is no longer so widespread.
  D is undergoing intense medical research.

comprehension and summary

Read the following passage, then answer the questions which follow it.

William Wordsworth wrote that the Lake District was 'a sort of national property, in which every man has a right and interest who has an eye to perceive and a heart to enjoy'. Visitors are still welcome but too many visitors can cause long-term damage. That is one of the dilemmas of the planners who run the park: how far is it in danger of becoming a victim of its own success?

In 1988, 13.9 million tourist nights were spent there. This makes the Lake District one of the country's busiest holiday destinations. But the landscape is not 'natural' in the true sense of the word. It bears the imprint of centuries of human activity. As people have settled in the area, grassy fields and stone walls have replaced the old, deciduous forests, with roadways spreading across the valley floors. On the fells, grazing sheep helped clear slopes to make way for the grass, heather and bracken which grow there today.

From Roman times until the nineteenth century, thc arca was quarried and mined. The process has left scars on the landscape in the form of disused mine shafts and buildings and piles of rock. But as the area continues to encourage visitors, people have become aware of the fragility of the landscape and of the need to protect it. There are now conflicts between those who see tourism as creating wealth and employment, and those who argue that large numbers of visitors damage the environment. Farmers are therefore concerned about steady streams of people crossing their land, gates left open, fences and walls damaged, the risk of injury to livestock caused by litter left in fields, and of dogs worrying sheep, particularly at lambing times.

Environmentalists argue that support systems, introduced by the Government and the European Community to stabilize the price of lamb, are encouraging farmers to overstock the fell lands with sheep. They claim that the number of sheep grazing on the land leads to the erosion of slopes. In some parts of the Lake District farmers are replacing stone walls and hedges with wire fencing. This enables them to use larger machinery. But environmentalists argue that this makes the landscape less attractive to look at.

Planning restrictions, for example on the height of new buildings, or on the destruction of stone walls to create larger fields, have been introduced to preserve the traditional landscape. However, some farmers feel that these prevent them from introducing modern farming techniques. Other farmers have been able to take advantage of the tourist industry. They have opened up their land to a variety of activities including fishing, pony-trekking and shooting, and provide camping facilities or bed and breakfast accommodation. Some have also managed to obtain planning permission to convert disused farm buildings into holiday cottages. During the summer months the Lake District villages are swamped by visitors. In winter, they are quiet and isolated. Outside the tourist season there are few jobs for local people and public transport is limited. The need for work and the high cost of local housing has forced many people to leave the villages for the bigger towns.

(a) Explain what Wordsworth means by 'who has an eye to perceive and a heart to enjoy' (line 3)

....

(b) What does the writer mean by 'becoming a victim of its own success' (line 7)?

....

(c) Explain what the 'imprint of centuries of human activity' refers to (line 12)?

....

(d) What is a 'deciduous' forest (line 14)?

....

(e) Why does the writer use the word 'scars' (line 19)?

....

(f) Explain the meaning of the word 'worrying' as it is used in line 31.

....

(g) What is the knock-on effect of the support systems introduced by the Government and the European Community?

....

(h) According to environmentalists, what makes the landscape less attractive to look at?

....

(i) Outline the farmers' objections to planning restrictions.

....

(j) How do the lives of local people differ from summer to winter?

....

(k) In a paragraph of 60 to 80 words summarize the differing points of view presented in this passage, both in favour of and against tourism in the Lake District.

● *transformations*

Finish each of the sentences in such a way that it means exactly the same as the sentence printed before it.

1 The football team have won all their matches this season, and their manager is a famous Spanish footballer.
The football team,..............................

2 I think you should buy a new pair of shoes and get rid of those trainers.
It's high time..............................

3 You certainly can't play your music after midnight.
I won't have you ....

4 I'm sorry I didn't study harder at school.
If only ....

5 He is always forgetting to take his keys with him.
I wish..............................

6 You can't call yourself a real traveller just because you have made one trip abroad.
Making one trip abroad ....

7 If he hadn't needed the money, he wouldn't have asked me for it.
He must..............................

8 What a pity you didn't come to the meeting because it was most interesting.
You should ....

9 It was wrong of me to tell him about the secret files.
I regret..............................

10 We got the travel agency to send a list of holidays within our price range.
We had ....

● *interview*

Note Interviews can take place with individual students, pairs of students, or groups of three. The respective amounts of time to be allowed are as follows. Activity **A** should take five, seven or ten minutes; Activity **B** should take two, three or three minutes; Activity **C** should take five, eight or twelve minutes.

A Photographs and discussion.

(Refer students to the photographs on page 212 of the Student's Book.)

1 Describe one or compare two of the photographs. Where do you think the picture was taken?

2 How do you think the people in the picture are feeling?

3 Discuss one or more of the following topics
- the price of fame
- the necessity of knowing the truth
- the importance of preserving our natural world.

B Passages. Read **one** of the following passages to yourself then comment on
- the style of the passage (eg spoken or written / formal or informal)
- where it might come from or where you might see it (eg a set of instructions / an advertisement / a speech)
- what it is about.

1 First, remove the camera body-cap and lens rear-cap by turning them counterclockwise. Then align the red dot on the lens with the Lens Mounting Index on the Mount of the camera body, gripping the lens barrel firmly, and turn the lens clockwise until it locks with a click. Using a lens cap of snap-on type, attach or remove it from the lens by pressing the two side-tabs.

2 Picture yourself sailing away from crowds, not taking them with you. We have found that with a maximum of 100 passengers a tangible sense of camaraderie is created, when like-minded people come together to explore the wonders of ancient civilizations, nature and culture. On board you will find no formal entertainment programme, just a first-class expedition ship operated for the benefit of real travellers.

3 A new enhanced picture of the bank robbers was broadcast on TV last night, showing a much clearer image of the men involved. The computer-enhanced picture, produced by photographic experts at police headquarters using evidence from a security camera, showed the two men entering the bank and brandishing pistols. There was an overwhelming response from the public, who jammed telephone lines to the TV studio and police headquarters.

C Communicative activities. Choose one of the following activities.

1 Simulation
You are part of a team choosing a series of photographs to represent a city in your country which is making a bid to stage the next Olympic Games. Decide on six photographs you would include in the brochure setting out the advantages of the city you have chosen.

2 Rank-ordering
What do you consider to be the greatest threat to the world today? Arrange the following starting with what you consider to be the most serious.
- Famine
- The break-up of the family unit
- Invasion from outer space
- A third World War
- Global warming
- Disease
- Unemployment

PROGRESS TEST 2 (1½ hours)

● *vocabulary*

Choose the word or phrase which best completes each sentence.

1 Sailors often have colourful images of butterflies or anchors .... on their arms or backs.
A etched **B** inscribed
C inlaid **D** tattooed

2 Thomas Mann's *Dr Faustus* is a long, complex .... rewarding novel to read.
A yet **B** while
C since **D** however

3 It is astonishing that so many young people complete their education .... learning to read properly.
A unless **B** except
C apart from **D** without

4 In their new production of *Hamlet*, the theatre company have done .... with props and scenery, and the play is performed on an empty stage.
A down **B** without
C away **D** out

5 I am .... worried about how we are going to cope with eight house guests next weekend.
A rather **B** utterly
C absolutely **D** totally

6 We were all terrified of the headmaster, who had .... eyebrows and a long moustache.
A shabby **B** bullish
C bushy **D** curly

7 All they found was a .... farmhouse and an abandoned tractor.
A desperate **B** destitute
C desecrated **D** desolate

8 The TV game show host was sorry they didn't win the holiday, and gave them a clock and T-shirt as a .... prize.
A consolation **B** condolence
C compassion **D** compensation

9 In our country, the President is usually elected for a five-year .... in office.
A term **B** passage
C duration **D** length

10 You cannot use an Irish bank note to buy things in English shops because it is not legal ....
A payment **B** currency
C money **D** tender

11 I did not mean to offend her, but she took my comments .... and now will not talk to me.
A amiss **B** awry
C apart **D** aside

12 No .... how hard I practise, I never seem to get any better at tennis.
A bother **B** worry
C matter **D** effect

13 I've never been one to .... words so I'm prepared to say that your report was diabolical.
A mix **B** mince
C mind **D** make

14 .... to the negative reports one often reads in the press, the standards of education are improving all the time.
A Opposed **B** Contrary
C Adverse **D** According

15 When I noticed the .... stare he was giving me, I realized he hadn't understood a word I was saying.
A blank **B** empty
C void **D** open

16 Her allergy to fish is so severe that the .... sight of it makes her feel sick.
A simple **B** easy
C plain **D** mere

17 I'm afraid that these bad reports of your son's school work are .... too true.
A some **B** all
C each **D** every

18 As the end of term approached, he longed to break free from the .... of life in a boarding school.
A constraints **B** shackles
C strings **D** ties

19 Let's not decide yet where to stop on the journey – we'll just play it by .... and see how we feel.
A lip **B** eye
C ear **D** hand

20 I was worried about how my daughter would fit in to her new school, but she took to it like a .... to water.
A swan **B** fish
C duck **D** raindrop

21 .... you need any more information, please call me on 081–221–9912.
A As long as **B** Provided
C Should **D** Had

22 .... the barrier at the side of the road, the car would have crashed into the valley below.
A But for **B** Apart from
C Except **D** Unless

23 He had to cancel his weekend away because of .... of work at the office.
A stress **B** load
C tension **D** pressure

24 After the pop festival, the field was .... with empty beer cans.
A soiled **B** scattered
C dirtied **D** littered

25 My husband doesn't treat me with as much consideration as he used to; I rather feel that he takes me for ....
A given **B** accepted
C supplied **D** granted

 PHOTOCOPIABLE

● *reading*

Read the following passage and choose the best answer to the questions below.

Now that I come to think about it, it seems to me to be quite on the cards that, had my Aunt Evelyn employed an unpretentious groom-gardener (who would really have suited her original requirements far better than jaunty young Dixon) I should never have earned the right to call myself a fox-hunting man. Dixon's predecessor was a stolid old coachman who disliked riding. One of my earliest recollections is the advent of Dixon, who lost no time in persuading my aunt to pension off her pair of worn-out carriage horses, which he replaced by two comparatively juvenile animals "warranted quiet to ride or drive". Dixon dearly loved to do a deal, and my aunt was amenable to his influence. She even went so far as to sanction the purchase of a side-saddle, and although a timid and incompetent horsewoman, she came to the conclusion that riding was good for her health.

Two or three times a week, then, on fine days, shepherded by the dignified and respectful groom, she was to be seen ambling along the lanes in a badly cut brown habit. She never attended a meet of the hounds however, for we lived in an unhunted part of the country, and the nearest meet was more than eight miles away.

So far as I was concerned, for several years "the hounds" remained a remote and mysteriously important rumour, continually talked about by Dixon, who never ceased to regret the remoteness of their activities. Foxes were few in our part of the country, and the farmers made no secret of shooting them. In fact ours was a thoroughly unsporting neighbourhood. There wasn't so much as a pack of beagles in the district.

My first appearance in the hunting-field was preceded by more than three years of unobtrusive preparation. Strictly speaking, I suppose that my sporting career started even earlier than that. Beginning then with the moment when Dixon inwardly decided to increase my aunt's establishment by the acquisition of a confidential child's pony, I pass to his first recorded utterance on this, to me, important subject.

I must have been less than nine years old at the time, but I distinctly remember how, one bright spring morning when I was watching him assist my aunt into the saddle at her front door, he bent down to adjust a strap, and having done this to his final satisfaction made the following remark: "We'll soon have to be looking out for a pony for Master George, 'm."

His tone of voice was cheerful but conclusive. My aunt, who had, as usual, got her reins in a tangle, probably showed symptoms of demurring. She was at all times liable to be fussy about everything I did or wanted to do. As a child I was nervous and unenterprising, but in this case her opposition may have prejudiced me in favour of the pony. Had she insisted on my learning to ride I should most likely have felt scared and resentful.

As it was, I was full of tremulous elation when, one afternoon a few weeks later, Dixon appeared proudly parading a very small black pony with a flowing mane and tail. My aunt, realizing that it was about to become her property, admired the pony very much and wondered whether it went well in harness. But since it was already wearing a saddle, I soon found myself on its back, my aunt's agitated objections were rapidly overruled, and my equestrianism became an established fact. Grasping the pommel of the saddle with both hands, I was carried down the drive as far as the gate; the pony's movements were cautious and demure: on the return journey Dixon asked me whether I didn't think him a little beauty, but I was speechless with excitement and could only nod my assent. Even my aunt began to feel quite proud of me when I relinquished my apprehensive hold on the saddle and, for the first time in my life, gathered up the reins. Dixon greeted this gesture with a glance of approval, at the same time placing a supporting hand on my shoulder.

"Stick your knees in, sir," he said, adding, "I can see you'll make a rider all right."

He had never called me "sir" before, and my heart warmed towards him as I straightened my back and inwardly resolved to do him credit.

1 Dixon was a groom-gardener who
- **A** had aspirations above his station.
- **B** had originally applied for a post elsewhere.
- **C** exerted little influence on the writer's aunt.
- **D** was more than willing to work hard.

2 When it came to horse riding, the writer's aunt
- **A** was reluctant to ride a horse side-saddle.
- **B** regretted the fact that she could not travel further afield.
- **C** had a habit of galloping along the country lanes.
- **D** became convinced she could derive some benefit from taking exercise.

3 How did the people mentioned in the passage feel about 'the hounds'?
- **A** The writer's aunt had an aversion to them.
- **B** The writer doubted that they even existed.
- **C** Dixon wished they would not pass so close to where he lived.
- **D** The local farmers were more than happy to kill them on sight.

4 How did the writer obtain his first pony?
- **A** His aunt had insisted that he learned to ride one.
- **B** He had implored his aunt to allow him to have one.
- **C** His aunt had acquired one from a childhood friend.
- **D** Dixon had decided that he should have one.

5 The writer felt that his newly-acquired pony
- **A** would be an extremely difficult creature to ride.
- **B** would mean his giving up some of his other hobbies and interests.
- **C** had raised his status in the eyes of those around him.
- **D** had involved his aunt in a lot of unnecessary worry and expense.

● *transformations*

Finish each of the sentences in such a way that it means exactly the same as the sentence printed before it.

1 They will not announce the decision formally.
No formal...

2 They believe that the robbers got into the bank through the roof.
The robbers...

3 Karajan was the first person to recognize her extraordinary musical gift.
It ....

4 Its lack of irregular verbs makes Esperanto a unique language.
Unlike ....

5 Thanks to Laura's support I was able to finish the project.
Had it...

6 It was his over-confidence that led to his defeat in the Wimbledon final.
If ....

7 They have been living in Germany for five years now.
It ....

8 I have never been to Paris before.
This is ....

● *blank-filling*

Fill each of the blank spaces with a suitable word or phrase.

1 Keep a sense of proportion and don't make a .... molehill.

2 If we were .... the job, when would you be able to start?

3 He somehow managed to get down the mountain, in .... that he had a broken ankle.

4 Had it .... his insistence on filming the scene again, we would have finished on time.

5 Despite all the warnings, a lot of people are .... ride by unscrupulous timeshare salesmen.

6 You must have moved your hand when you took this photograph, because everything is out ....

● *rewriting*

Write a new sentence using the word given.

1 Leave us your address so that any post can be sent on to you.
FORWARD...

2 Could you help me with these cases as they're very heavy.
LEND ....

3 This interpretation is as valid as that one.
EQUALLY ....

4 Assembling the furniture is extremely easy.
PLAY ....

5 He modestly understated his part in the rescue.
DOWN ....

6 I feel that I don't fit in with the people in the new office.
FISH ....

7 The authorities in Kenya claim to have eliminated poaching.
ACCORDING...

8 I would like to receive a copy of your latest annual report.
GRATEFUL ....

 PHOTOCOPIABLE

● *interview*

Note For approximate timing of these activities, please see beginning of Progress Test 1 interview.

A Photographs and discussion.

(Refer students to the photographs on page 213 of the Student's Book.)

1 Describe one or compare two of the photographs.

2 What aspects of entertainment do the pictures show? How might the people be feeling?

3 Discuss
- the reasons for art being 'great' or not
- differences between reading and other ways of obtaining information
- how we define 'entertainment'.

B Passages. Read **one** of the following passages to yourself then comment on
- the style of the passage (eg spoken or written / formal or informal)
- where it might come from or where you might see it (eg a set of instructions / an advertisement / a speech)
- what it is about.

1 Sir Arthur Conan Doyle's greatest achievement was his creation of Sherlock Holmes, who soon attained international status and constantly decoyed his creator from work that he preferred. At one time Conan Doyle killed him but was obliged by public protest to restore him to life. Holmes was a rival who had so many of the characteristics and experiences of Doyle that he even turned one of the creator's friends, Dr Watson, into one of the most famous characters of fiction.

2 Now you can enjoy the ultimate recording of Beethoven's complete symphonies at an unbeatable price. When you accept this superb offer, you'll also get a free monthly full-colour illustrated magazine. From each magazine, our classical music editor will make a top recommendation as the ideal way to build up your classical library. Your only obligation is to buy a minimum of three regular priced recordings per year for the first two years of membership.

3 'Ladies and gentlemen, today's in-flight feature film will be *Look Who's Talking Too*. Sound familiar? But fly Euro Business Class or Economy and you get a choice of up to six feature films. In First Class you can also choose from a library of thirty movies. In addition to the films there are four video channels of the best in sport, comedy, current affairs, children's viewing and various language programmes.

C Communicative activities. Choose one of the following activities.

1 Decide which of the following statements you agree with and explain why.

'Art is a waste of time.'
'Art is the essence of life.'

You might consider the following
- life without art
- art as the expressions of man's spirit and inner feelings
- the failure of some great artists to be recognized until after they were dead
- the incomprehensibility of some modern art
- the importance of ancient art
- the ridiculous prices paid for some works of art.

2 Decide which of the following statements best sums up your attitude to soap operas and explain why. (**NB** 'soap operas' are radio or TV programmes like *Dallas*, *Neighbours*)

'I'm hooked on soap opera – never miss one!'
'What a load of rubbish – can't see why anyone should waste their time watching it!'

You might consider
- why people watch soap operas on a regular basis
- what kind of people watch soap operas
- why some soap operas succeed / fail
- where the title 'soap opera' came from
- how some people actually believe that the soap opera is reality.

PROGRESS TEST 3 (3 hours)

● vocabulary

Choose the word or phrase which best completes each sentence.

1 It is hard to find a vaccine for influenza because there are so many different .... of the disease.
A species **B** branches
C strains **D** divisions

2 He lost all of his money in a speculative business venture and was .... to beggary.
A demeaned **B** compelled
C reduced **D** converted

3 After a fiasco at the start, the result of the horse race was declared null and ....
A void **B** cancelled
C over **D** barred

4 At the height of the property boom, even the smallest houses .... vast sums of money.
A got at **B** went for
C made out **D** came on

5 They have just .... their engagement in the papers, and they are getting married next December.
A detailed **B** announced
C claimed **D** conceded

6 The company will reimburse you for any expenses you .... on your business trip to Europe.
A create **B** lose
C make **D** incur

7 We like our students to participate .... in the school's social programme.
A actively **B** basically
C comprehensively **D** dynamically

8 When I was young, everyone in the family .... gather together at home for Christmas.
A were used to **B** used
C would **D** use

9 The latest crisis was brought .... by the mishandling of the economy.
A over **B** in
C down **D** about

10 When the police insisted that he should move on, the tired old tramp .... off reluctantly across the muddy field.
A skipped **B** trudged
C tore **D** hopped

11 I suppose I've always loved music because I grew .... composers like Bach and Beethoven.
A up to **B** on at
C in with **D** up on

12 He was depressed towards the end of his life, because although he had been quite successful, he never felt that he had really .... it.
A made **B** reached
C climbed **D** arrived

13 Gorbachev was the last leader of the .... Soviet Union.
A previous **B** earlier
C anterior **D** former

14 I think that successfully bringing up four children on your own has been no .... achievement.
A pale **B** mean
C slim **D** poor

15 I am fully prepared for my interview and am confident I can answer any question they may care to .... me.
A throw at **B** slide to
C drop on **D** roll to

16 I am sure she will make a good nanny, but her experience of dealing with very young children is rather ....
A delineated **B** curtailed
C restricted **D** limited

17 His enthusiasm at starting his own company has been .... somewhat by the amount of red tape he has to deal with.
A doused **B** dampened
C moistened **D** sprinkled

18 .... from the occasional late night party, our neighbours are very quiet.
A Apart **B** But
C Except **D** As

19 No sooner had the refugees been evacuated from the town .... the shelling started again.
A when **B** then
C than **D** as

20 If you've had an upset stomach, it's better to stick to .... foods like milk, eggs and potatoes.
A mild **B** insipid
C tasteless **D** bland

21 For many young people, driving cars at high speed seems to .... a rather fatal fascination.
A contain **B** comprise
C weave **D** hold

22 On the news there was some dramatic .... of the earthquake that had been captured by an amateur cameraman.
A shooting **B** scenery
C clipping **D** footage

23 I have a .... interest in getting you to join the club because I get paid for every member I recruit.
A hidden **B** vested
C ulterior **D** financial

24 Most popular magazines have a(n) .... page where letters about difficulties with relationships are answered.
A agony **B** advice
C personal **D** problem

25 It took the panel of judges a long time to agree .... which book should win the prize.
A to **B** by
C on **D** with

transformations

Finish each of the sentences in such a way that it means exactly the same as the sentence printed before it.

1 'Why don't you buy a new coat?' Mary said to her brother.
Mary suggested ....

2 He said that he had been a long way from the scene of the crime at the time.
He denied ....

3 He said he was sorry that he had not written to me.
He apologized ....

4 I was very surprised to hear that I had won the competition.
It came ....

5 I am determined to refuse his offer.
I have no ....

6 If you complained to the manager it would just be a waste of time.
There's no ....

7 You have little realization of how much I have sacrificed for you.
Little ....

8 All the students rushed to the notice board as soon as the exam results were put up.
No sooner ....

blank-filling

Fill each of the blank spaces with a suitable word or phrase.

1 That's the house I ....
.... live in when I was a child.

2 The scandal involving the directors was the last straw, and the company ....
.... wall.

3 The headmaster ....
.... punish everyone in the school unless the person who broke the window owned up.

4 He has had servants all his life, so is not used
.... up after himself.

5 I am outraged! Never before ....
.... spoken to like this.

6 I feel that, ...
extent, he is responsible for his own problems.

rewriting

Write a new sentence using the word given.

1 'Have you ever been to America?' the officer asked me.
WHETHER ....

2 This car only cost me five hundred pounds.
PICKED ....

3 Someone paid five thousand pounds for the painting.
WENT ....

4 We have made neither a profit nor a loss this year.
EVEN ....

5 She wasn't keen on leaving after dark.
RELUCTANT ....

6 She is not to blame for the accident.
FAULT ....

7 He is becoming quite famous as an interviewer.
NAME ....

8 I feel I am not being treated fairly.
RAW ....

composition

Note Two hours is allowed for this section.

Write **two only** *of the following composition exercises. Your answers must follow exactly the instructions given.*

1 Describe the job that would be best suited to your personality. (About 350 words)

2 'Military service should not be compulsory.' Discuss. (About 350 words)

3 Write a composition with the title 'The Premonition'. (about 350 words)

4 *The Conservatory* is a new restaurant in town. Write a report for a local newspaper about it, based on your own meal and the following comments from other diners. (About 300 words)

'First class prices, but hardly first class service.'

'They've obviously spared no expense on the decor.'

'Quite the best French restaurant I've ever been to – the fish was marvellous.'

'Stick to the house wines – the others are exorbitant.'

'The salmon in cream sauce was perfect, but the beef wasn't all that special or innovative.'

'It's a pleasure just to sit here and look around, which is probably just as well as I had to wait ages for my starter.'

● *interview*

Note For approximate timing of these activities, please see beginning of Progress Test 1 interview.

A Photographs and discussion.

(Refer students to the photographs on page 214 of the Student's Book.)

1 Describe one or compare two of the photographs.

2 Where might these pictures have been taken? How do the photographs capture the past and present?

3 Discuss
- the reasons for the nostalgia we often feel for the past
- the possibilities of combining the old with the new
- the importance of preserving our history.

B Passages. Read **one** of the following passages to yourself then comment on
- the style of the passage (eg spoken or written / formal or informal)
- where it might come from or where you might see it (eg a set of instructions / an advertisement / a speech)
- what it is about.

1 But as the years passed, as I collected wife, house, child, monuments from that journey bubbled up to buoy me through dark times: the nostril-singeing cold of an Andean night, the break-bone crush of a white-water rapid, the smoky musk of an Indian hut. Flexing against such memories, my soul renewed itself. I came to believe that at times risk is the price you pay to reach a place that can blast your spirit clean.

2 Even at the end of the eighteenth century, vast areas of the earth were still a garden of Eden for animal life. Man's intrusion upon these paradises was a tragic innovation. The craze for furs explains why the sailing ship, The Lion, carrying the Ambassador Macartney to China, discovered five terribly dirty inhabitants on Amsterdam Island in 1793. Boats from Boston had set the men ashore to organize a gigantic slaughter.

3 Just starting out with a personal computer? You've probably already learned that the PC speaks a different language from us. This book takes you step-by-step through the world of MS-DSK and PC-DSK . You'll find clear explanations and plenty of 'hands on' examples here of using DSK. Learn the information you'll need to become more comfortable working with your PC in a very short time. Soon you'll be speaking DSK almost as well as your computer.

C Communicative activities. Choose one of the following activities.

1 'The more things change, the more they remain the same.'

Comment on the quotation saying whether you agree or disagree with what it is saying. You could consider the quotation in the light of the following
- political philosophies
- treatment / cures for diseases
- working conditions
- bringing up / being a member of a family
- educational theories
- historical balance of power.

2 Decide which of the following statements you find it easier to identify with and explain why.

'I don't know what the younger generation is coming to! We never did that kind of thing in my day.'
'My parents are so old fashioned – they think our generation should behave exactly as theirs did.'
You might consider
- why people hold these points of view
- whether different generations will ever agree
- whether we need to be different to make progress.

KEY

Progress Test 1

reading

1 B **2** C **3** A **4** C **5** D **6** C

comprehension and summary

(a) Everybody who is able and willing to visit the Lake District and capable of appreciating / capable of an emotional response to its beauty.
(b) The area has suffered by becoming too popular, as greater numbers of visitors cause greater damage to the environment.
(c) Evidence on the land of human presence, how man has influenced the landscape over the years.
(d) A forest of trees which shed their leaves annually.
(e) 'Scars' are marks left on a person caused through injury. They are ugly to look at and suggest (previous) pain. The countryside has suffered in the same way.
(f) 'Worrying' refers to the dogs chasing after, frightening or harming the sheep.
(g) Farmers increase the number of sheep they own which leads to erosion of the soil / slopes.
(h) Wire fencing that / which replaces old stone walls.
(i) The planning restrictions stop them from using modern farming techniques and limit the height of buildings.
(j) Winter is not the tourist season, so the locals find themselves without jobs and with limited public transport.
(k) Points to include:
In favour of
- everyone should have the right to enjoy beautiful countryside
- jobs are created and money is brought into the area
- farmers benefit financially from tourist activities on their land
- farmers can turn abandoned buildings into tourist accommodation
- public transport is improved.

Against
- visitors damage the environment
- litter can harm animals
- visiting dogs can disturb the sheep.

transformations

1 The football team, whose manager is a famous Spanish footballer, have won all their matches this season.
2 It's high time you bought a new pair of shoes and got rid of those trainers.
3 I won't have you playing your music after midnight.
4 If only I had ('d) studied harder at school.
5 I wish he would ('d) remember to take his keys with him.
6 Making one trip abroad doesn't make you a traveller.
7 He must have needed the money, otherwise he wouldn't have asked me for it.
8 You should have come to the meeting as it was most interesting.
9 I regret telling him / having told him about the secret files.
10 We had the travel agency send a list of holidays within our price range.

Progress Test 2

vocabulary

1 D **2** A **3** D **4** C **5** A **6** C **7** D **8** A **9** A **10** D **11** A **12** C **13** B **14** B **15** A **16** D **17** B **18** A **19** C **20** C **21** C **22** A **23** D **24** D **25** D

reading

1 A **2** D **3** B **4** D **5** C

transformations

1 No formal announcement of the decision will be made.
2 The robbers are believed to have got into the bank through the roof.
3 It was Karajan who first recognized her extraordinary musical gift.
4 Unlike other languages, Esperanto has no irregular verbs.
5 Had it not been for Laura's support, I would not have been able to finish the project.
6 If he hadn't been (so) over-confident, he wouldn't have been beaten in the Wimbledon final.
7 It is five years since they moved to / went to live in Germany.
8 This is the first time I have been to Paris.

blank-filling

1 mountain out of a **2** to offer you **3** spite of the fact **4** not been for **5** taken for a **6** of focus

rewriting

1 Leave us your address so that we can forward any post to you.
2 Could you lend me a hand with these cases – they're very heavy?
3 Both (of these) interpretations are equally valid.
4 Assembling the furniture is child's play.
5 He (modestly) played down his part in the rescue.
6 I feel like a fish out of water in the new office.
7 According to the authorities in Kenya, poaching has been eliminated.
8 I would be grateful if you could send me a copy of your latest annual report.

Progress Test 3

● *vocabulary*

1 C **2** C **3** A **4** B **5** B **6** D **7** A **8** C
9 D **10** B **11** D **12** A **13** D **14** B **15** A
16 D **17** B **18** A **19** C **20** D **21** D **22** D
23 B **24** D **25** C

● *transformations*

1 Mary suggested to her brother that he should buy / buy / bought a new coat.
2 He denied having been / being near / at / on the scene at the time of the crime.
3 He apologized for not writing / having written to me.
4 It came as a great surprise to me to hear that I had won the competition.
5 I have no intention of accepting his offer.
6 There's no point (in) complaining to the manager.
7 Little do you realize how much I have sacrificed for you.
8 No sooner had the exam results been put up than all the students rushed to the notice board.

● *blank-filling*

1 used to **2** went to the **3** threatened to
4 to tidying / clearing / cleaning **5** have I been
6 to some / a certain

● *rewriting*

1 The officer asked me whether I had been to America.
2 I picked this car up for only five hundred pounds.
3 The painting went for five thousand pounds.
4 We have broken even this year.
5 She was reluctant to leave after dark.
6 The accident was not (n't) her fault.
7 He is making (quite) a name for himself as an interviewer.
8 I feel I am getting / being given a raw deal.

Oxford University Press
Walton Street, Oxford OX2 6DP

Oxford New York
Athens Auckland Bangkok Bombay
Calcutta Cape Town Dar es Salaam Delhi
Florence Hong Kong Istanbul Karachi
Kuala Lumpur Madras Madrid Melbourne
Mexico City Nairobi Paris Singapore
Taipei Tokyo Toronto

and associated companies in
Berlin Ibadan

OXFORD and OXFORD ENGLISH are trade marks of Oxford University Press

ISBN 0 19 432824 4

First published 1984
Fourth impression 1996

Printed in Hong Kong

Acknowledgements

The authors and publisher are grateful to the following for permission to use extracts from copyright material:

Actionaid: adaptation of leaflet about sponsoring a child; **Angus Finney**: extract from 'Chancing your arm' published in *The Listener*, 31.8.89; **Faber & Faber Ltd**, and **The K. S. Giniger Company**, New York City: extract from Siegfried Sassoon: *Memoirs of a Fox-Hunting Man*, 1971; **The Guardian**: extract from article by Richard Whitehouse 'Not so green and pleasant land', and adapted extract from article by Judy Williams, 'Hidden Clues to Crime,' both © The Guardian; **The Observer Ltd**: adaptation of Travel Guide by Willy Newlands, 'Safari Holidays', *The Observer Magazine*, © The Observer; **The Oxford Story/Heritage Projects**: commentaries, © The Oxford Story exhibition; **Serious Productions Ltd** and **Dove Audio**: adapted extract from Douglas Adams: *A Hitch Hiker's Guide to the Galaxy*, Pan Books, 1979, (audio version produced and distributed by Dove Audio); **University of Cambridge Local Examinations Syndicate**: marking information from CPE Papers 2 and 5, June 1993, ©UCLES.

Although every effort has been made to contact copyright holders, if notified, the publisher will be pleased to rectify any errors or omissions at the earliest opportunity.

The authors would like to thank the following people for their useful comments on the manuscript:

Paul Carne, Mary Geaney, Goodith White, Annie Watson.